The Way to the Salt Marsh

Books by John Hay

A Private History

The Run

Nature's Year

A Sense of Nature (with Arlene Strong)

The Great Beach

The Atlantic Shore (with Peter Farb)

Sandy Shore

In Defense of Nature

The Primal Alliance: Earth and Ocean

Spirit of Survival: A Natural and Personal History of Terns

The Undiscovered Country

The Immortal Wilderness

The Bird of Light

A Beginner's Faith in Things Unseen

In the Company of Light

The Way

to the Salt Marsh

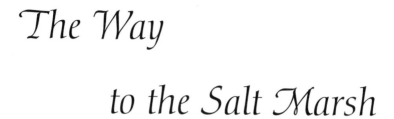

A John Hay Reader

EDITED AND WITH AN INTRODUCTION

BY CHRISTOPHER MERRILL

University Press of New England

HANOVER AND LONDON

University Press of New England, Hanover, NH 03755

© 1998 by University Press of New England

All rights reserved

Printed in the United States of America

5 4 3 2 1

CIP data appear at the end of the book

ACKNOWLEDGMENTS:

An earlier version of the introduction appeared in *Orion* and is reprinted by permission.

From *A Private History* by John Hay. Copyright © 1947 by John Hay. Reprinted by permission of the author.

From *The Run* by John Hay. Copyright © 1959, 1979 by John Hay. Reprinted by permission of Beacon Press, Boston.

From *Nature's Year* by John Hay. Copyright © 1961 by John Hay. Reprinted by permission of the author.

From *The Great Beach* by John Hay. Copyright © 1980 John Hay. Reprinted by permission of W. W. Norton & Company, Inc.

From *In Defense of Nature* by John Hay. Copyright © 1969 by John Hay. Reprinted by permission of the author.

From *The Undiscovered Country* by John Hay. Copyright © 1981 by John Hay. Reprinted by permission of W. W. Norton & Company, Inc.

From *Natural Architecture* by John Hay. Copyright 1984 by John Hay. Reprinted by permission of the author.

From *The Immortal Wilderness* by John Hay. Copyright © 1987 by John Hay. Reprinted by permission of W. W. Norton & Company, Inc.

From *The Bird of Light* by John Hay. Copyright © 1991 by John Hay. Reprinted by permission of W. W. Norton & Company, Inc.

From *A Beginner's Faith in Things Unseen*, by John Hay. Copyright © 1995 by John Hay. Reprinted by permission of Beacon Press, Boston.

From *In the Company of Light* by John Hay. Copyright © 1998 by John Hay. Reprinted by permission of Beacon Press, Boston.

"The John Burroughs Medal Address" originally appeared in *The Congressional Record*, volume 110, number 96, 14 May 1964, pages 10535–36.

"Music by the Waters" and "Comb Jelly" originally appeared in *The Massachusetts Review*, volume 21, number 2 (Summer 1980).

❧ Contents ❧

INTRODUCTION   vii

❧ from *The Run* (1959)   1

The Drive to Be   3
The Power of Fragility   8
Going Out   13

❧ from *Nature's Year* (1961)   17

A Wild Home Land   19
Colors of the Season   25
An Old Place, an Old Man   31
Deeper News   37

❧ from *The Great Beach* (1964)   41

An Unimagined Frontier   43
Who Owns the Beach?   52

❧ from *The Congressional Record*   63

John Burroughs Medal Address   65

❧ from *In Defense of Nature* (1969)   69

A Dependable Endurance   71
The Eye of the Heart   84

❧ from *The Undiscovered Country* (1981)   95

The New World   97
Homing   102
The Prodigal Style   114
Listening   125

❧ from *The Immortal Wilderness* (1987)   133

The White Pelican   135
Open to the Sun   146
Sacred Places   153

❧ *Natural Architecture*: Poems   165

❧ from *The Bird of Light* (1991)   171

Migrants in Winter   173
Ritual   184
The Speech of Terns   196

❧ from *A Beginner's Faith in
Things Unseen* (1995)   203

Stranded   205
A Faire Bay   216
Fire in the Plants   227

❧ from *In the Company of Light* (1998)   239

The Way to the Salt Marsh   241
Life in Space   248

❧ Introduction ☙

"You have to stand still and listen for a while," said John Hay. It was a clear, crisp winter afternoon, and he was gazing at an estuary near his home. The morning clouds had given way to sunshine, the snowfall from the night before had melted, and the trees in the marsh offered some protection from the wind whipping across the water. This salt marsh—a recent discovery for the writer—bordered on an abandoned cranberry bog; cattails lined the levee where we stopped to look for signs of river otters. Their numbers, Hay was sad to report, had dwindled lately.

It was the kind of observation born of close association with a place, one of the earmarks of Hay's work. He is the nature writer's writer, an elegant stylist and illustrator of the Emersonian notion that "the world is emblematic." The American Transcendentalists are indeed his literary ancestors; his fifteen books may be read as a fulfillment of Emerson's injunction "to establish an original relation with the universe," in this case to that portion of it known as Cape Cod. Hay and his wife, Kristi, have lived there for more than a half century, on a plot of land the locals call Dry Hill—sixty acres of pitch pine and oak within walking distance of Cape Cod Bay.

"The earth is composed of communities, all interlocked," he was saying, "and we can't decide which is dispensable, because none is. Because we invented electricity, despite thunderstorms, we think we're the supreme generators, so we limit ourselves enormously." He shook his head. "Nature *is* civilization, and what we've done to the earth in this century has reduced not only nature's ability to express itself—the disappearing otters, for example—but also our ability to express ourselves."

He pointed at a smooth trail leading from the lip of the levee down into the water. "Everything looks as though it has a potential story. How many miles does a male otter travel with all these slides it makes around the water? They've taken huge territories. Or if you go for a walk on the beach, you can be aware of the birds flying by not just because of their names but also for their stories."

His story begins in Ipswich, Massachusetts, where he was born in 1915. Raised in New York City (his father worked as an archaeologist for the Museum of Natural History), Hay traces his interest in nature to vacations at his grandfather's summer house in New Hampshire. "First enchantments outlive all the later judgements we make about the world," he writes. And the spell of summer days along the shore of Lake Sunapee hangs over all his work. "What I am really doing," he writes, "is trying to keep open to the unexpected. Who knows what miracles may lie in wait?"

Upon graduation from Harvard in 1938, Hay took a job as the Washington correspondent for the Charleston, South Carolina, *News and Courier*, following in the footsteps of his illustrious grandfather and namesake, John Milton Hay, a journalist who became Lincoln's private secretary and later served as secretary of state under Presidents McKinley and Theodore Roosevelt. But the cub reporter's career was cut short by the outbreak of the Second World War, during which he worked on *Yank* magazine. Hay's grandfather was a man of letters—he wrote a ten-volume history of Lincoln—and this was the calling he obeyed after his discharge from the army. He and his new wife settled in Brewster, Massachusetts, where he began an informal literary apprenticeship with his neighbor, the poet and novelist Conrad Aiken.

Hay's first book, a collection of poems titled *A Private History*, appeared in 1947, and what may strike readers of his subsequent prose writings is his continuing allegiance to poetic cadences and patterns of imagery. Joseph Brodsky described a certain fiction writer's work as "essentially a poetic operation." The same applies to Hay's essays. It was in *The Run*, a meditation on alewives, published in 1959, that he discovered his true subject—the mysteries of nature. The alewives' migration from the ocean to the Cape's freshwater ponds alerted Hay to all that was "unused" in him, orienting him to the world around him, inspiring him to further exploration as a naturalist and a writer. "The alewife is another of the amplifications and extensions of life," he suggests. The totality of life is what he seeks. Marrying natural facts to personal experience in a distinctive lyrical style, *The Run* established Hay as one of the leading voices of the environmental writing movement spawned by Aldo Leopold and Rachel Carson.

If, as Emerson believed, "nature is a discipline" that instructs and governs, Hay learned its lessons well. He became what Thoreau might call "the scribe of all nature" in his next book, *Nature's Year* (1961), a chronicle of the seasons on the Cape, where "both calm and calamity are in the cards." After writing the text for a book of photographs by Arlene Strong (*A Sense of Nature*, 1962), he published *The Great Beach* (1964), a celebration of the Cape's outer beach, in the tradition of Henry Beston's *The Outermost House*. Here is a landscape "full of a wide motion" to revel in, a world of wind and waves, of shipwrecks and shorebirds. From the top of a fragile cliff he observes how "the open plains of the Atlantic roam with a wilderness light, and you are back with one of those high places on the continent that still offer you original space, the right scale and proportion for life on earth." For his discovery of that "original space" he was awarded the John Burroughs Medal.

A more strident tone entered his work with the publication in 1969 of *In Defense of Nature*, perhaps as an outgrowth of his educational work and growing activism. He helped to found the Cape Cod Museum of Natural History, which he served as president, board member, and senior fellow; and for fifteen years he taught environmental studies at Dartmouth College. The survival of many salt marshes on Cape Cod was due in no small measure to his tireless efforts on the Brewster Conservation Committee. For his is a grand effort at connection: he abhors the sacrifice of natural complexity in the name of progress, for what he finds in nature corresponds to unexplored reaches of his own soul—gifts to share with readers, museumgoers, students, and sojourners.

"We tend to size things according to a much narrower point of view than they warrant," he told me in this salt marsh. "We coexist with a complexity we don't address. If you feel stuck with what you've got"—his voice rose—"you have to enlarge your universe. And if you can't get other people to lead you, you have to lead yourself out into new discoveries."

This, then, is the theme of the essays collected in *The Undiscovered Country* (1981), which charts his search for our place in nature. And his "education in dimensions" takes on even greater urgency in *The Immortal Wilderness* (1987), where he travels farther afield only to realize that "in common things are greater extensions of ourselves than we ever conceived of. We may think that as a race we travel beyond all limits, but we have hardly started out in life"—a crucial recognition for mankind, which is accustomed to imposing its will on the so-called lesser orders.

"We put the whole animal kingdom down as being lower than ourselves," he said, "but their travels are flexible and they have minds which work according to rhythmic consistencies and recurrences of the earth. That's about as deep as you can get. And it's all we have to reckon by."

He thought of the terns, the subject of *Spirit of Survival* (1974) and *The Bird of Light* (1991). "I began to see them as a community in and of themselves," he said. "And the community has different ways of expressing themselves. These are vibrant, strong, graceful, energetic, enthusiastic birds. They're excitable, they're easily agitated, they can't stand being shut up, and at the same time they travel half around the world. That's a tremendous accomplishment. So I tried to put together a picture of this community—vibrant and lively and full of dimension."

His method combines a naturalist's field notes, carefully recorded in small spiral notepads, journalistic discipline (he spends most mornings in a study a short walk from his house), and poetic insight. In a poem he described a wood frog as "a pulse of earth on earth," a pulse he detects in every part of nature. And he is fond of quoting Thomas Traherne, the seventeenth-century writer: "You never enjoy the world aright, till the Sea floweth in your veins"—a lesson mastered in *The Run* and relearned again and again. "Exaltation takes practice," he reminds himself and his readers.

"What's more complex than a body of water?" he said, gesturing toward the bay. "Tides roll in from the outer world, retreat, rise up, go back. People refer to the monotony of the tides but that's what holds everything together. What I picked up from studying English literature was the language of rhythmic expression, and when I saw this in the alewives I was very excited. It meant my expression could join them and their behavior, if I didn't think I was superior to them."

In *Spirit of Place*, Frederick Turner recounts a journey with Hay to Mount Katahdin. Turner wanted to make contact with the aboriginal spirit of *The Maine Woods*, Thoreau's classic encounter with what he called "the unhandselled globe," and he wisely chose Thoreau's truest heir to lead him up the mountain. The night before their climb, Hay gave Tuner a look of "fierce astonishment"— an apt description of his bearing toward the world, I decided in the salt marsh.

"We must be awakened to what's outside us," he insisted, "by participating with other forms of life, other rhythms, other communities not our own. We have so many unused qualities."

And this attitude may help to explain how, in his ninth decade, he finds compensations even in his failing eyesight—the theme of his latest books, *A Beginner's Faith in Things Unseen* (1995) and *In the Company of Light* (1998). Though he must now use a projection machine and magnifying glass to read and write, he is ever more aware of his surroundings. When he gave up his driver's license, he realized how much of the world he had missed driving by it. With his slower walking pace and circumscribed world (in Brewster he rarely ventures beyond the four-mile radius he walks around his house) come new discoveries—interstices and details he never noticed before. "One day last September," he said with a smile, "I smelled grapes in the thickets which otherwise I would have passed by. So I poked in around the bushes, just like a fox, and when I found a cluster of grapes I was refreshed."

His work offers the same invigorating discoveries. "When I felt it was important to know what a salt marsh was composed of, I began to learn its distinctions," Hay writes in the concluding essay of *A Beginner's Faith in Things Unseen*, a piece that journeys from intimations of mortality in the New Hampshire woods to a vision of sunrise over the Gulf of California. A talent for experiencing "amplitude and awe" is what he believes he found in childhood, and this is illustrated in his reflections on a marsh not unlike the one we were walking through:

> Every species there was expressing itself in terms of the tidal, rhythmic character of its surroundings. The colors of the salt-tolerant grasses changed with the season, from wide patches of blue-green or yellowish-green that looked like the shadows made by traveling clouds, to fall colors of tawny gold.
>
> A society interested only in quick results has little time to spend on the rhythmic responses in a salt marsh or a wood that might be its salvation.

The Way to the Salt Marsh offers an abridged course in nature's distinctions and dimensions. I hope these selections will prompt readers to search out the whole of John Hay's impressive body of work and take the measure of the man who was walking now along the levee, deeper into the marsh, until he saw what he thought were brants flying low across the water. He stared into the distance long after he had identified the birds and watched them vanish, making time for salvation.

from

The Run

(1959)

The Drive to Be

*T*HE FISHING OPERATION NEAR THE OLD GRIST
mill was in full swing after the twenty-third of April. The
Salvadore crew was hauling in their net with the aid of a
winch. It was loaded with fish, enough to fill four or five barrels.
The victims were flipping and flashing with a whirring violence, a
high sound going up in the gray morning air, a beautiful iridescence in their white-silver sides. The whole dripping net was
heavy and alive with their shivering, thrashing, and dying. Heads
butted through the mesh and gills caught, in their frantic, vibrating despair . . . and all for lobster bait, worth six dollars a barrel.

The early colonists spoke of alewives coming up their streams
in "incredible" numbers, and so it still looks, though Stony Brook,
for one, is narrow in its upper reaches, and when the fish are
forced into it they are crowded beyond all proportion. The inland
stream, with its fresh-water grasses, insects, and small fish is suddenly host to a large and almost foreign form of life, except that
they are both closely joined to the sea.

On the whole, it had been a rainy month. The brook below the

seining pool was roaring and foaming down. Such was the teeming crowd of alewives trying to swim up through the ladder,
through the violently heavy flow, that there was a constant falling
back, a silver slapping and flapping over the concrete rims of the
pools. Farther down, where the waste stream tumbled over a
small mountain of rocks, too high for the fish to jump (their limit,
on a vertical leap, seems to be not much over two feet), there was
a scene to force the heart. Always a certain number of fish, divid-
ing from those that swam the main stream toward the ladder,
would attempt the impossible at this place. Ordinarily, when an
alewife meets obstacles in its advance upcurrent it will quickly go
forward into it, then leap in short dashes over rocks and the lip of
fishways. I had seen them go up without apparent rest where the
stream falls down the inclined ladder at the pond outlet above.
They were dancing and flipping up those waters, which were
rushing and bubbling down, like kites in a fast wind.

Yet here, for all their instinctive valiance, was the unsurmount-
able. Now, as they had done for thousands of years, they tried and
failed. White tons of water smashed down over the rocks, but
time and time again one fish after another made a quick dash into
it and almost flew, hanging with vibrant velocity in the torrent
until it was flung back. Many were exhausted and found their way
back to the main stream, circling and swimming slowly, and a
large number were smashed against the rocks to turn belly up
and die, eaten later by young eels, or gulls and herons, as they
were taken downstream by the current. Some were wedged in
the rocks and could be seen there for days as the water gradually
tore them apart until they were nothing but white shreds of skin.

A wooden bridge crosses over Stony Brook at this point. A
neighbor of mine, a mother of children, was standing there
watching when I came up, and I heard her say, "Terrible!" I guessed
that she knew what she saw, besides death and defeat. It was the
drive to be, a common and terrible sending out, to which men are
also bound in helplessness.

We are astonished by this fantastic drive. "What is the point?
What makes them take these suicidal chances? Why?" It is as if we

were trying to get back, or down, to an explanation in ourselves that we had lost sight of. But somewhere in us, through this feverish, undecided world, we still know.

Are they stupid? There is no measure in the world of nature more excellent than a fish. It may be comparatively low in the evolutionary scale of complexity, but no animal is more finely made, or better suited to its own medium. All the same, the unvaried blindness their action seemed to show would sometimes strike me as hard as did their ability in the water.

Stony Brook was black with them. There was no open patch of stream bed to be seen. And with the excessive crowding, the general procession, so steadily insistent on its own time, was hurried up to some extent. Their motion became almost ponderous and tense, while individual fish leaped like dolphins, pewter- and gold-sided, over and through the dark herd. Others circled in and out or kept pace with the rest, staring ahead.

They had a synchronized momentum of their own. If I dropped a stone in the middle of them, they would separate at that point and then close in to fill the gap. There could be no nullifying or breaking their united persistence. Their onwardness, their desperate dashing against the rocks, had its own logic—a logic which had nothing to do with hope, reason, or choosing another alternative. No way out, in other words. I have heard it described as: "Slavery to the reproductive urge," although scientists acquainted with the complex, far-reaching, and powerful nature of reproduction might balk at the closed quality of "slavery" in this context and the sluggish connotations of "urge." To many onlookers, all the same, these alewives seem more dumb than sheep. If you were to press your own sympathy hard enough, you might feel a terrible lack of variety in them, or, paradoxically enough, of daring. The lidless-eyed and plunging multitude seems brutally driven, without a chance. This is "togetherness" with a terrible vengeance.

Perhaps there is another element here, with which we might have some connection as fellow animals. At the risk of making one of those vaguely anthropomorphic assumptions against which the scientists have warned us, I would guess that the self-motivation in this onward mass of fish might be compared to those human crowds that take action under stress, independently of the individuals who make them up. Suddenly a crowd, hitherto a random combination of people, assumes a frightening rhythm and purpose of its own. It seems to be governed by tides or sources of action which go back infinitely farther in the history of life than the immediate goals of its anger or exultation.

I have explained nothing. I can only say that when I first saw these fish I was moved in spite of myself. Instinct is no more blind than wonder. To have the human attributes of mind and spirit and the race's ability to control its own environment does not give me the wit to beat the infinitely various will of life at its own game. All I could wish for would be to join it.

I walked on down the banks of Stony Brook, past the Herring Run area with its neat paths, bridges, and fish ladders, my shoes squashing in the mud. The stream turns a slight angle at this point, gets broader and shallower and begins to run through the little valley that ends in tidal marshes and the Bay. The alewives, for a hundred yards at least, were running up against the downward currents, massed almost stationary, not in ranks, but ordered mutuality, with a long waving like water grasses or kelp, and curving, twisting, swirling like their medium the water as they moved very gradually ahead. There was no indiscriminate rushing ahead. It was done to measure; but it seemed to me that through their unalterable persistence I saw the heaving of crowds of all kinds, of buffalo, cattle, sheep, or men. I had seen as much motion in crowds pouring out of a subway entrance or massing through a square. History was in their coming on, without its shouts and cheers. They could not speak for themselves; but who knew how deep the silence went?

Ahead of them there was a net; behind, down the broader reaches of the brook, the greedy herring gulls dropped down into the water after them, or stood along the bank in apparently glutted satisfaction, while others screamed and sailed overhead. In spite of their slow gliders' grace and local lethargy compared with swift sea birds like the terns, gulls travel the rims of the world. They had always made me think of far-distance, voyages unending. Many of them had congregated on a bald hill that overlooks the run and were standing like white sentries under the shafts of the northern sky beyond. From far off they sometimes suggest rows of military crosses, and I have heard them compared to a field of flowers. Soldiers, flowers, graves . . . all these they might suggest on the heights of fate, by their pure bold greed and unmatched design. They stood on a wide stage.

The Power of Fragility

*J*THINK ONE OF THE GREATEST CHALLENGES IS TO watch each bounded living thing with care for its particularity, as far as we can go, to find out we can go no farther. Flower, fish or leaf, child or man—they take none of our suggestions as to rules. Each has a strong language that we never quite learn. No matter how many times I try to describe the alewife by the uses of human speech, or classify its habits, its intrinsic perfection resists me. It is *something else*. It goes on defying my own inquiring sense of mystery.

The beauty of a little alewife held between the fingers, struggling out of water, dying, by human arbitrary reach, becomes the subject of thought and language, creative protestation in themselves. But the two-inch creature makes a mightier protest than my conscious sight of it . . . wild, fragile, vibrant, shivering with a quickness that will die out in a matter of seconds. It is a marvelously knit animal, compact, flexible, shining, with its tiny meshed scales that interlock the light, iridescent silver like the adults, green, yellow, purple, receiving earth and sky. And the eyes, wholly black, interminably deep. By a chance scoop of my hand it is out in the long killing air, the little vibrancy out with the bird-gray clouds, a leashed arrow straining for the stars, that have their running too in the circle of immensity.

Fragile they are, and powerful, a wonderful work of which so many are made as to afford them death as well as life. Let us say, arbitrarily, that 150,000 female alewives lay their eggs in the ponds above Stony Brook each year. After the pond suckers take their share and the remaining eggs hatch out, then the young alewives run the gantlet of their first few days and weeks of life. The toll taken would seem incredible if it were not also natural and expected. From billions the young are reduced to millions.

If a run is to keep up over the years, there has to be an annual survival, or "escapement," of somewhere between 3 and 7 percent. Say a hundred million hatched, out of the original nine billion eggs. Five percent of that, or five million, have to reach salt water in order to assure a normal spawning migration in three or four years' time. From that figure, of course, you subtract the alewife mortality during their years of growth in the sea. I claim nothing for my calculations, but, rough as they are, they may help to indicate how much potential goes into the end result.

It is not only the alewives that are provided for by these great numbers, but the predators which hunt them. The alewives are only part of a great complex of need. Sometimes I have watched the fry as they swam out across the Brewster flats on an ebb tide, running in shallow water from the mouth of Paine's Creek. In September, before they have migrated south, crowds of terns, along with the resident herring gulls and ring-billed gulls, would be hovering over the water and diving or flocking in as the alewives appeared. I watched the constant, sinewy beat of their wings as they held against a west wind. The sky was swept way up with long cirrus clouds. The young alewives were running into death and beyond it, in a windy world that teemed with risk and creation.

A friend of mine, who worked in the vicinity some years ago, watched the tiny fish coming down above the old mill one autumn day. He saw some night herons standing in the lip of the dam gobbling the "poor little devils" up as they went over. He was amazed at their stomach capacity. Then he noticed that at the rocky falls where the pool ended above the water wheel and sein-ing pool only a few were dropping over as compared to the thou-sands coming in from the pond, and the toll the quawks took did not account for it. Somehow, somewhere, in this short stretch of water, they were disappearing into a gulf, or, more properly, a maw. It didn't seem right. It made him angry, although: "You can't get mad at nature because that's the way it is." He got a hook and line, baited it, threw it into the pool; and in two hours he had fished out seventy-six eels.

These slithering, hoselike creatures are still there in season waiting to prey on the fish. It does not take long as a rule to see one coming up at the edge of the bank, though I have never seen them in any great quantity, because they usually lie hidden in the muddy bottom. Sometimes you can see a small group of eels of varying sizes in one of the resting pools of the fishway below the road, where the little alewives as they go down must almost fall into their mouths. With broad-ribboned tails on one end of their long-finned bodies and pointed snouts on the other, they weave and flip over, arch and float in the water. Partly because of the nar-row space, and their tendency to stay or be caught in the turbu-lent pools, many of the little fish cannot avoid being eaten. They have only the safety of numbers.

Having developed a certain affection for the race by this time, I must say I had feelings of pity for these little ones; helplessly tossed in and out of death. They *are* fragile, like the young of other animals. They will not last more than about three-quarters of a minute out of water. But they are not ones to know or care whether I think of them or not. They are parts of a great ordered hunger, and a vast provision for things. They are both victims and executioners, the feeders and the fed upon, in the intercommuni-cation of every single plant and animal in the natural world. There is nothing for affection in that order perhaps, unless we conceive of it in terms of love as well as annihilation.

I have followed them out and seen where their consistent motion, their automatic reaction to the waters they swim in, has brought them to grief. It serves for survival and also for disaster. When the young alewives get out to salt water on an ebb tide, they are not able to calculate how long it will last, or so we presume, and whether they should move out soon or stay behind. The result is that many are left stranded and wildly skittering in the rivulets that thread the sandy flats at extreme low tide. From the time the outgoing waters of Paine's Creek begin to get low, they are also subject to attack by crowds of herons and gulls—but supposing they survive that and still have a chance in a matter of an hour or an hour and a half to reach deeper water? It is very often the case that because of their habit of heading back against the current they delay too long and lose their chance of escape. They are caught high and dry on the sand or in water so shallow that they are unable to move on, and so are easy prey for the birds. I have followed them through low water and seen them turn back, just as they had a chance to follow one waning current to join another and so out to safety; but when I use the word safety I have to remind myself that the flow goes where it will.

Now it is possible that you might interpret this behavior as a reluctance to leave the inland waters. They have a drive in them to go to salt water eventually, but they may be in no hurry. In some areas they stay in estuaries or tributaries for a long time. Unless the eventualities of force, predators, rushing falls, or roaring tides, act suddenly upon them, the alewives move with the stream—fluid, deliberate, step by step, reach after reach. The alliance of fish and water is a subtle and constantly changing one. There was no area from the ponds to the sea where it was possible for me to watch the alewives, adult or young, without being conscious of a constant diversity of action. From the still, deep waters of the pond, to tumbling falls and fish ladders, down the running brook, with its own turns, tensions, eddies, rushes, and retreats, to the tidal estuary, I was aware of the life of water, its pulse and the pulse of the fish that adjusted to it.

Without knowing the exact relationship of the fingerling ale-

wives to their change in environment—fresh, brackish, and salt—
as they approached the bay, I could see in general what their motion was. It might be true to say that they were carried "passively"
until they became a part of the sea water, gradually getting adjusted to changes in salinity and temperature. It certainly took so
long a time that it occurred to me that their "parent stream" might
become very familiar to their senses. One day I watched them in
the channel at Paine's Creek near its mouth at low water, on an
outgoing tide. With a kind of fluttering flight the little schools
would run back up under the outgoing current. They would
hover, then suddenly run, slip, coil, or fly back loosely and errati-
cally to re-form and hold again. This went on hour after hour, and
when the tide rose and became deeper, overspreading the mouth
of the creek, they were still in the channel, with the added look of
schooling marine animals with hurrying heads and vibrant bodies, their silver sides flashing in the light. How long it took them to
be taken up completely in the salt-water environment I could not
say. When and if they finally reach Cape Cod Bay they probably
school in fairly shallow areas where the water is warmest, inviting
bass or bluefish of course to "come and get it."

In this area at least, their adjustment to new waters and new
food is not a sudden one. Their behavior seems to show it and be
ready for it, with the gradual moving up and back, the holding, the
running and waiting. Whether or not it is the kind of unconscious,
obedient motion that leaves them no leeway, leaves them dead
and unadjusted on the sand flats at low tide, surely they accumu-
late experience, a water wisdom of a kind. They practice the great
relationship of body and place. They are made for these flashing
waters and rolling tides.

Going Out

THE FIRST ALEWIFE I SAW IN EARLY SPRING WAS wild and new to me, feeling its way upcurrent alone, cautiously, as if testing out an old trail. Down Stony Brook there were long patterns in the water dappled like fish scales. In the sky above there were cloud tosses and wind turns during a break toward spring that the fish itself exemplified. Later on the fry in the apparently indiscriminate times they moved out and headed for salt water seemed to be pulled as if by moon tides and turning earth. The course I followed was full of natural complexity. Forms and patterns were endlessly coordinate and suggestive, but with the mystery of their making, the universal power, at once ordered, vast, fluid, out of reach.

The alewife migration taught me how to start. Had we been two and a half miles up from salt water to the farthest pond, then back again, or was it three thousand? I had learned that measurement was indefinite.

I still knew next to nothing about their lives in salt water. And what was ahead on land? I could expect them to follow certain rules of behavior. They would come back year after year unless the run was so consistently overfished that the population dwindled. I knew where to look for them now, and had some acquaintance with laws of supply and demand, plus the effects of management or the lack of it. Perhaps alewives could be expected in general to do what they had done before. But those laws that lead all migrants on have more in store for us than we can anticipate. The variations I had found in action and circumstance, following those fish, variations like the changes of air and water, leaves, grass and ground, intermoving light and shadow, were unexpected and perpetual. If the alewives ever proved that anything was static, it could only have been in me. There is no personifying the unknown fish. I am not acquainted with it yet; but now we are on a run together.

The alewife is another of the amplifications and extensions of life. In the flip of its body, its communicable "Let's go," it offers to be followed. So that race with its recoil and approach, approach and recoil, circling in consonance with the forces of the earth has the lesson of migration in ourselves. When I watched them coming in on their old, persistent track and felt so much in my own senses of that exploring, through the growing and falling off of leaves, the wind charging and easing off, the bright waters, I knew there was an infinite sum in me of the unused. What *is* migration? Is it to "pass from one place to another"—just that? And its causes may be the need for food or to reproduce in season; but surely the term comprises a great deal more.

Whether the migration of animals seems random, or with definite intent, it leads across the earth. All the studies made of individual species result in new directions to be explored, new unknowns about the actions of other lives, and the ways they follow. The mystery about the travels of birds, eels, monarch butterflies, or alewives is not only a matter of routes or seasonal behavior. It has to do with an internal response to this spinning globe and its unendingly creative energies. As a result of a respectful regard for other animals we may find that we are being led onto traveled ways that were once invisible to us, and in their deep alliance with natural forces we find a new depth in ourselves. This is the common ground for all living things, where migration has in it the blood of contact, the winds and waters of communication.

On that July week when I first saw the young alewives coming down through the outlet, the roads of Cape Cod were roaring and humming with cars. The tourist season had suddenly come to its height. The population of the Cape had jumped from sixty thousand to two hundred thousand or more. There were new demands, new pressures in the air. This was the yearly coming on of an immense, expanding world, a migratory phenomenon in itself. Voices and prices were rising. Man's abundance vied with the natural summer.

It was a hot day, though it had started out cool in the early morning, with drifts of fog along the shore and patches of it through the inland hollows. I had followed the alewife fry down from the Herring Run to the shore road. They had become increasingly hard to find; but when I reached the slow waters of the channel at Paine's Creek I could see multitudes of them heading in the direction of the Bay. Farther on where the water ran out through the sands on the ebb tide there were groups of them moving with it like little clouds.

There were a few people walking on the flats in the distance where herring gulls were yelping and an occasional tern gave a light, harsh cry. An old panting setter dog lunged aimlessly across the sands, then splashed through the shallow waters of the creek at its outlet. On the beach a family crowd of bathers were listening to a portable radio that noised out the baseball scores. Some of them got up and saw to their children, or fell, sat down, or dove into the water at the edge of the sands. They sounded low, then high, like the gulls—"Stop it!" "Come on!" "Here, bunny" "Come back here!" "Jump in"—full of alarm, solicitude, friendliness, irritation, communality.

Back in the channel where the tiny fish, progeny of *Alosa pseudoharengus*, were swimming on in the brown water, a couple of growing, gawky children, a boy and a girl, half round, half lean, were pushing each other down, floundering and thrashing, while they laughed and threatened each other, completely oblivious of the great migration a few yards away. Or can anything be oblivious? I felt that I had come to the middle of things.

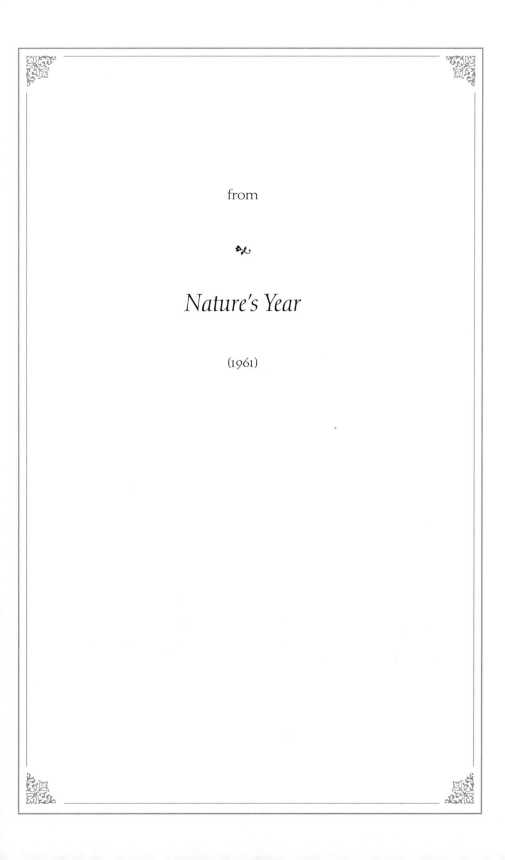

from

Nature's Year

(1961)

A Wild Home Land

WHAT I WANTED TO DO WAS FOLLOW THE YEAR around, recognizing that hours, days, months, or years are as elusive as unseen atoms (even though, universal law being consistent, we deduce their behavior with some success). I am not sure where July left off and August began. Summer flies away from me, like an unknown bird.

Out into August then, while there is time. When I step into it as if into something new, I sense thousands and thousands of roving lives, taking their opportunities where and when they can. The day is hot and shining. The oak leaves, no longer fresh and young, but spotted with growths, chewed by insects, frayed and scarred, are still tough, deeply green, harnessing the sun, under a stir and slide of air. Two big red-tailed hawks sail high overhead screaming constantly. A blue jay screams, in a fair likeness. The hawks wheel lower down along the trees, inside the horizon. Then two little tree sparrows flit by. Insects drone, stir, and buzz. There is a drag-ging, rattling sound of leaves as a box turtle moves slowly along. A cicada chorus rises like a sudden breeze from the southeast and then subsides. Two black and white warblers go through the cover of the woods in a quick butterfly flight together. The "Tock! Tock!" of a chipmunk sounds behind a brush pile, almost like the end notes of a whippoorwill's song.

I feel a balance in space between them all: the roamers, hawks, or gulls, in the sky's great allowance; the spider swinging on a thread and making its own web of a world; colorful, elusive warblers through the trees; the chipmunk on its chosen ground. These sounds, synonymous with motion, seem to hold them in mutual alliance, round in a lightness of air that is strict and easy in its coming and release, like the cicadas; but there is an intensity here that makes my heart beat faster.

A jay jumps down to a branch, cocks its crested head, with those black eyes full of readiness, and brays. The spider wraps up a captured moth with rapid skill. A robber fly waits on a leaf with throbbing abdomen and a look of contained vitality. It is not to be known. I see the brown, glazed wings folded back in the sunlight, and two black, sky-light eyes on top of its head. It seems preternaturally lean. It stays there for ten minutes and I watch it closely, almost suspended with it in my attention. A robber fly is a tough predator, but to call it cold, indifferent to pain, careless of life, darkness personified? Our terms are useless. I do not know. Then my attention is cut, as it abruptly darts off, swinging in an arc, perhaps to catch a housefly a hundred feet away.

In the buzz, the running light, the stir of summer, I feel as if each motion, each event had its own pressing concern. This homeland, no longer graced with the name of wilderness, is full of wild, unparalleled desire.

Everyone knows that the month of August is loaded with insects, although they come under the heading of "bugs," a menace to human society. Their fibrous trills are incessant in the grass. Their high, shrill sounds announce the heated air. Those two species that we hate more than most, just for their familiarity, the flies and mosquitoes, drone around us. In the heat of noon our senses are a little clouded. We may be mumbling something about "the will of life be done," and it is being done . . . in great part by the insects. The summer rage to take and to share in taking is carried out in minute detail from the tiniest mite in the soil to the dragonfly.

Manifest energy, using its short summer span, fills our surroundings with its wealth of insects. It has not been long since I was taught the modicum of knowledge needed to name a few of them, to start in on a fraction of the 680,000 species that fill the earth; but it was enough to add to my sight. I had never realized that such foreign and incredible variety existed so close to me.

A yellow jacket tugs furiously at a dead cricket on the road, like a hungry dog with raw meat. Delicate aphids waver on flower stalks. A big striped cicada killer roams through the oaks. Other wasps sip juice or nibble carrion. Dragonflies dart across both land and water on their tangential licks of speed. The cabbage butterflies flutter and alight with pale, yellow wings held together like one thin sail against the sunlight. Over and under, in and out, flying, crawling, suspended in plants and in the growth of plants, seizing their time, waiting, indefinitely if need be, held in chrysalis or egg, emerging, feeding, adding to death and life in death . . . what are these strangers?

There are wasps as red as rubies; flies of a more scintillating, vibrant green than emeralds; and shiny bronze or golden beetles which are the envy of human art. If color is life, to make the human eyes ring and the body respond, they have it, and they also lack it. Some are so diaphanous as to belong only to the sunlit air, and some are so dark, as though part of unseen depths, that all color is only a dance, springing away.

We use up constant, frustrated energy keeping them in check. Their dry throbbing annoys us. They eat our crops, transmit disease, and drive us away from our pleasures: although in the bold stare of nature they are effective employees. We might, slapping a mosquito, recognize their necessity as pollinators, earth movers, or food, respect the role they play in decomposition and growth . . . then we must turn around and invent new poisons. Insects are redoubtable enemies. We are never quite sure which of us is in the ascendancy, just as we are never sure of what they are.

Still we can look and marvel at their complex detail: these wings like lace or spun glass; wings cut short and wide or thin as a hair; wings with the pattern of flowers, or veins of a leaf; bodies round and narrow, oval or oblong; strange truncated abdomens; huge, compound eyes; legs impossibly thin and long, or unbelievable in number and still coordinated; heads like alligators; bodies like sticks; false eyes; false horns; repulsive, intangible, unreal.

Here seems to be automatic, nerve-end response in unreflecting zeros, whose lives pass with their deaths, but still, on this earth crust they are affiliated with everything. That which may frighten or startle a bird, like the eye spots on a moth's wing, is related to a bird. Animals are adapted to their environments and the medium in which they live and act; but so many tricks and curiosities are embodied in the insects, so many far-fetched connections of shape and motion, as to leave all particular environments behind.

In their variety they are in balance with our imagination. Don't they show as many bursts, tricks, starts, halts, and fires, as much somnolence and surprise in their color, shape, and action as we desire in the exercise of our consciousness? Nature is unbiased in its attention, concentrating equal power on all forms of its expression. When we begin to conceive of nature in terms of creative process—continually evolving, fantastically complex, immensely resourceful—then we recognize our counterparts wherever the sunlight strikes across the air. We share in a communication.

Last month I noticed a group of small butterflies on the mauve flower of a milkweed. They were, as I found out, hairstreak butterflies, with a dusky, grayish-lavender coloration, and little orange patches on the lower edge of their wings. When the wings are folded, their hind tips have tails resembling antennae, which may have the effect of a protective device to confuse a predator. After I frightened them off, they returned in a little while to rest on the very same flower. Their color was not the same as a milkweed's but in tone and value it was close enough so as to hide them from view at a fairly short distance. The flower and the animal were united in a sensitive embodiment of contrast.

A few days later I noticed that the flower was gradually paling. Then, on the twenty-fifth of July, the last blossoms dropped off, and the butterflies were gone. An obvious affinity, and a mystery at the same time, of two forms of life in a unique response to nature's web of motion.

It took me a long time to become aware of just how much these affiliations and responses made up the life of earth, how much of an elaboration they amounted to. In the past also, when I saw a robin hop across the lawn, a frog jump into the water, or a tree swallow glide through the air, I reacted with pleasure or disregard—by chance, in other words—without realizing just how big a role chance played in their appearance. In the same sense the obvious upheavals of a season—drought, or heavy rains—meant little to me beyond their immediate, local effect. After a while I began to be aware of all the circumstances that must surround me. One dull day I realized their unlimited context, and thought how slow and agonizing my own changes were in comparison.

Expected things happen. But the variations are just as compelling as the stable order from which they come. This June, for example, was cold and wet, and the rains continued into the summer months. The hatching of insects was delayed and the development of some plants and grasses. Many fledgling tree swallows were found dead in their nests, a disaster which seems to have been caused directly by the weather. Aquatic insects are a favorite food of the tree swallows, but in cold, wet weather these insects tend to remain in immature stages and do not develop into flying adults. (Swallows chase after their food in flight.) And, in fact, when insects are few, the tree swallows seem to be discouraged from looking for them. If such conditions keep up, they may leave a nesting area to look for food elsewhere.

Our local run of alewives, those inland herring that migrate from salt water every spring to spawn in freshwater ponds, seemed to be a little later than usual; and the young, hatched from the eggs they left behind them, started down to salt water past schedule in July. If the ponds are colder in temperature than is normal, it probably affects the young alewives' size and chance of survival. They grow larger and healthier in warm-water ponds because they are started sooner and have a richer supply of food. A smaller, slightly weaker fish is more easily caught by a predator.

Because this spring was somewhat off the average mark (and in a sense there is no average), many of the relationships between plants and animals dependent on it were altered. Some of the effects, in animal population or health, might be felt for a long time to come.

Although ice, fire, storms, hurricanes, unusually wet or dry seasons, and now the hand of man, may alter the local earth almost beyond recognition and bring its inhabitants to disaster, natural occurrence has an indomitable will. Its changes outlast all others. Uncounted lives are sent ahead, balanced always, but with relationships through time and space that are never exactly the same. A leaf drops earlier. Frogs start to shed their skins, or migrate locally at a time that depends on new climatic conditions. Why have I seen so few mole runs this year? Last year there were comparatively few Baltimore orioles. This year in orange pride they were leaf calling and diving everywhere. I have seen very few phoebes in our vicinity of late, and scarcely any bluebirds. There may be more mosquitoes this summer and fewer grasshoppers than usual. I can inquire, for each species, and find out what I want to know, if there is logic, and cause and effect to its behavior; but all are related in a realm that is wider than I ever imagined.

Colors of the Season

*T*HERE IS YELLOW AND PEACH PINK ON THE LEAVES of the red maples, and some of the oaks begin to show signs of changing, but the most colorful plants are the mushrooms. The wet weather has been providential for them, and they have come up in some areas where I cannot remember having seen them before. They thrust mysteriously but stubbornly through the grass in a wide semicircle of white moons. They parade up the side of trees, and across the wood floor their cups or parasols stand comfortably grounded in dead leaves or decaying wood. (We see only the flower of the mushroom protruding above the ground, while underneath lies the complex mat of fine fibers from which they blossom, the mycelium.)

For such pulpy, soft, almost immaterial-looking plants, mushrooms show a strange power to lift, which is caused, in reality, by hydraulic pressure within them, amounting to as much as six or eight pounds per square inch. They come up through an inch or two of concrete, or through the asphalt surface of a road. They move the heavy bark of old logs aside. One of them puts up a scaly dome under the edge of a pump house eave that almost touches the ground, as if it intended to lift the roof off.

When we think of fungi, we have a justifiable association with rot and decay, mildew and mold. They lack chlorophyll, that famous green substance by which other plants are able to absorb the energy of the sunlight and through it convert carbon dioxide and water into food. The mushrooms, like other fungi, get their food directly from organic matter, rich soil, rotting wood, or leaf mold. They reproduce by billions of tiny spores, each of which, or rather, the comparatively few that catch, are started in such a matrix. In a sense they are procreative flowers of the darkness, annuals which the earth puts forth in its own teeming right, regardless of the gay slaves of the sunlight. But they are colorful. They wear the earth's sulfurs, umbers, and ochers, its iron rusts, light greens, grays, and whites, as well as some startling rose-reds and vermilions.

I find a small one in the wet leaves which is a lavender-blue, named, according to my reference book, the violet cortinarius, and good to eat—surprisingly enough. Color is no criterion of what is poisonous. The deadly amanita does not have the flickering blue-green color of something low and ominous, nor is it a dangerous red, a signal for all but the most reckless to keep off. Some of the reddest mushrooms, in point of fact, are the best to eat. But the deadly amanita is almost tempting in appearance. It is white and succulent-looking, and to eat enough of it means death.

A strange thing, the mushroom, of short annual appearances (though the roots, or mycelium, are perennial), of quick growth and quick decay. Some of them are already turned into rotten dark brown, nearly liquid heaps. Others will gradually dry up and disappear, but now, on this tag end of a moist season, they are the local bounty. They have curled edges like cabbage or dead oak leaves. They take the form of single stems and fronds like seaweed. They are fringed, scalloped, round or flat, thin or fat. They bunch together at the base of an old stump, or they climb the side of a tree in shelves. Their heads take the form of lima beams, or floppy rabbit ears, fans, umbrellas, trumpets, shaggy hats, or cottage roofs. They are scaly, rough, smooth, or silky. They have thin stems and dainty heads like flowers; or both head and stem look like one great overgrown protuberance. Here and there, coming through the leaf litter, are yellow bunches of coral mushrooms, so called because they have the look of branched coral; and in the deep shade they seem almost luminous. In fact, whether or not any mushrooms do have a luminosity, like some fungi, they have a glimmer of decay about them in our imagination. They are of the earth unearthly, in spite of the fact that many of them provide substantial beds for insect larvae, that they are good, if sometimes treacherous food, and that they can raise the top off a road.

This year has also been rich in Indian pipes. This is that unreal, pure-white plant, which, in more mythical times, has been called the corpse plant, or ghost flower. It blooms by itself, though out of the moist woodland humus like the mushrooms, lacking chlorophyll as they do. There is some dispute apparently, consistent with the Indian pipe's ghostly nature, about what it really is. Some books refer to it as a "saprophyte," which means a plant that absorbs its nutrition from dead or decaying organic matter, but in others it is called a "parasite." A parasite gets its nourishment from a living host. The Indian pipe has a very small mat of rootlets where the thick stems join together at the base of the plant. If you dig it out of the ground it looks as if it were resting on bare knuckles. These roots, according to the botanists, have an outer layer of funguslike tissue, which means that the fungus rather than the roots has actual contact with the soil. So it sounds as though the Indian pipe, being dependent for its food on the fungus and not the soil or humus, were a parasite. Another alternative, if the fungus gets any nourishment from the plant, is that they live in a state of mutual association, or symbiosis. Thus science, still trying for exactitude, and the Indian pipe, still unaccountable. It seems to be on the verge of several worlds rather than an integral part of one, a plant you might meet in a dream.

Other old and once popular names for it are: Dutchman's-pipe; fairy smoke; convulsion weed; eyebright; bird's nest; and American ice plant. It was called ice plant, according to Alice O. Albertson in her *Nantucket Wild Flowers* (1921), because "it resembles frozen jelly and is juicy and tender and dissolves in the hands like ice."

One contemporary authority calls it "clammy," which is accurate enough, and keeps it in the realm of ghosts and chills, but I think it was an exaggeration to say that it dissolves in the hands. I find it solid enough, not fragile or perishable to the touch. Its stems have a fibrous, tough core, which is sometimes hard to tear. It also has a pungent, woody smell, though this probably comes from the soil it grows in.

All the same, it is an elusive, beautiful flower, a miraculous specialty. Coral pink shines almost translucently through the stems, which are covered with tiny white bracts, or scales, taking the place of leaves—scales of a tiny albino fish perhaps—and the bell-like flowers hang their stiff white heads straight down, with pink seed pods standing up between them, round, decoratively grooved little crowns. When the plant dies, it stands for months as a thin, brownish black string, having turned from beautiful ghost to lifeless reality.

Over the mushrooms and Indian pipes, in subtle relationship to them, the leaves are losing their green chlorophyll and revealing the other, more stable pigments that last out long enough to make the familiar glory of the autumn. There is not so much a general "dying" in the fall, as an adjustment. Insect eggs are in the bark or ground, the mushroom spores are being carried through the air, the grasses are heavy with seed, acorns drop to the ground. One day last October I was hit with a shower of acorns from the white oaks. This year, since oaks fruit heavily on different years, I notice more acorns from the black oaks. How fast these acorns get to work! A little curling, probing, adventurous sprout comes from the nut, and in a short time has grown several inches. A few manage to take hold before the ground is frozen. A multitude of others provide food for squirrels, chipmunks, or blue jays. The measure of these arrangements is complex and elaborate. Between the leaf of a tree and a mushroom, worlds apart in function, there are connections of rainfall, temperature, or sunlight, in a context continually new, and though the ground colors fade, sunsets, seas, and inland waters will take over their active play.

That great bonfire of a maple tree—one special to my boyhood—that I used to marvel at in the New Hampshire fall, is here
replaced by second- or third-growth oaks. I now live in a stunted
land; but as it is the sea which surrounds it, so, in its long low
stretches, its glacial hollows and running hills, it rides ahead like
open billows. The early splashes of color come from the red of
the sumac and the purple-reds of the huckleberries and blueber-
ries. Then color begins to spread through the oaks, that war with
yellow-green pitch pines for living space. Yellow or red streaks
show in the leaves of the white oak, orange in the waxy leaves of
the post oak, brilliant red in the scarlet oak. Then deep reds, ma-
roons, cowhide yellows and browns pervade them, and our
woodland surroundings seem full of a beautiful propriety, a
beauty in necessity.

Occasional copses of beech trees are shining with gold bronze;
and tupelo, or black gum, trees, with scraggy, undulant branches,
have little leaves that are a blazing, livid red. Over bare hillsides
the "hog cranberry," or bearberry, a perennial ground cover with
shiny leaves, is hung with cherry-red fruit. The cultivated cranberry bogs show broad stretches of purple-red, shaped, depending on the area, in squares, circles, or oblongs, all, if well cared for,
neatly ditched. The tidal inlets and marshes run with flaxen and
gold, spotted at their edges with light festival red from the berries
of black alder, a form of holly.

These flaming revelations signal the trees' reactions to the de-
crease in light's intensity, or the colder temperature of the soil.
The leaf decomposes. The tree withdraws and makes ready for a
leaner season; but it is too big a display for mere "adjustment."
You will not find the category of color in a historical dictionary or
the encyclopedia of social sciences, but in this temperate zone at
least, it is now an integral part of the history of change, and of
natural society.

There is a deep little hollow nearby called Berry's Hole. Many years
ago it contained a cranberry bog, and it is still wet bottomland with

water around its edge, and a center choked with moisture-loving shrubs and reeds. Frogs take advantage of it, as well as water insects and their larvae. Wood peewees nest around it in the springtime. Now it is radiant with its special version of the fall. In the middle of October, sheep laurel is still green on the surrounding slopes, through the purple huckleberry bushes. I walk down them into a raining screen of leaves. Berry's Hole is circled by red, also called swamp, maples, and their red and yellow leaves, light and delicate compared to those of the oak trees on dry slopes above them, slip down constantly through the bright air, drift, eddy, and finally touch the ground, or fill the brown water with loose-lying, sinking rafts of color.

A green frog leaps into the water with a squeak. I notice a box turtle on the bank, with its head determinedly locked in this time. Its markings, on an almost black shell, are dashes of yellow, and a rich reddish orange that reminds me of a Blackburnian warbler.

Response to color is response to energy, the radiance and the reflection of light. I close my eyes after looking across the sun and see red, the color of warmth and desire. Around the eye of Berry's Hole is the red of blood and the yellow of the sun.

An Old Place, an Old Man

WHEN THE FEEL OF WINTER COMES, IN NOVEMBER or early December—though by astronomical calculation winter does not start until December twenty-second—when the first hard seal is set on the ground, and we are settled in with a new plainness, then it is not difficult to bring back yesterday and its country living. Winter's role in the year's wheel is an arresting, for the sake of renewal, a sleep, or half sleep, for later waking. It has its own suspense and violence, its roars and silences, like the other seasons, but in general its order is of a different quality, having an inwardness and resistance, a bare, gray need to keep things inside and hidden down. This is the time of year that shows a plain connection between human beings and their land.

I see last leaves whipping around the hollows off an old Cape road, or walk through the now more oblique rays of the sun that yellow the sandy ground held by thin, waving grasses, gray beach plum or bayberry bushes, and I recognize what has been left behind.

Here, surrounded by open slopes, is an abandoned house site, now a cellar hole, walled by square blocks of glacial granite. Orchard grass, timothy, and redtop still engage the old domesticity. Inside their circle you can see where children played, water was fetched and carried, chickens fed, and voices raised. There are yucca plants close to the foundations, and a rose or two. I transplanted such a rose a few years ago, and with added nourishment it turned from a slight, single-petaled flower to a great bunch of pinkish-purple fragrance.

Unlike some abandoned farm sites in other parts of New England, there is nothing left here to show what the inhabitants did. There are no harrows, stone bolts, yokes, or farm implements, not even any pots and pans. The stones are left, and the faithful grasses, and beyond them the crunchy, gray deer moss, and beard grass of indigenous fields. It was a small place, of bare subsistence. Whatever the qualities of the people who lived there, they left simplicity behind them. Not too far away, a bulldozer is making a desert with giant scoops, high-tension wires are marching by, and a plane rips the air overhead. We are encroaching in our oblivious fashion, without delay. The new domesticities may occupy only a tenth of an acre each, but they engage all lands. The old domestic wildness cannot be replaced. It was a lodgment limited by need, gray outside and dark within, perhaps unbearably close and confined at times, but with a knowledge of its earth.

It seems to me that as the world has grown outward in recent years, even *I*, a comparative newcomer to Cape Cod, have lost some local life to memory. When you live in a place for the first time you see behind it to its roots and grain, before the storms of circumstance blow you away from it. I remember a few old men who seemed so representative of the old Cape that it will never be the same now that they are gone. The loss is of a country speech, the flavor of a flesh and blood nurtured on locality. What has replaced them can be defined in terms of California as well as Cape Cod, which means no detriment to either, for what we are now obliged to consider is locality in a wider field. But those old men were born as we may not yet be born, sturdily, in custom and resignation.

Nathan Black died in October 1957, at the age of ninety-two. He was born in 1865, the year Abraham Lincoln was assassinated. He was a near neighbor. His land abutted mine, and since he was the proprietor of the Black Hills Barber Shop, I could walk down through the woods to get my hair cut, for the price, in a trillion-dollar world, of fifty cents. He was a heavy man, with bright brown eyes, and a head of curly white hair. He fitted the open Cape Cod weather, or the weather fitted him. I am not sure of the distinction. Nearly ninety years of change, of natural cataclysm, of both peace and abysmal war in the human world, had left him in the same place, with the same measure, outwardly at least, of stability.

When he left his place, or the customary orbit of work and old friends that constituted his life, perhaps to drive out on a new highway or to the chain store, he may never have stopped being surprised. I remember his looking at me with a kind of amused questioning—but no alarm—and saying something about no one belonging here any more. The new population didn't quite make sense to him.

In the way of old countrymen who knew their boundaries, he was tough and unforgiving in his role of landowner. He had his rights, "By gawly!" and he would know when someone did him wrong. He held on hard, and I suspect there were neighbors who felt the possessiveness too strongly, but this being none of my business, I will go in and get my hair cut.

The shop, with a tool shed under the same roof, where "Nate" used to grind knives and axes, stood, and still stands, across the yard from the house where he was born. There are some other gray-shingled, outlying buildings on both sides of a dirt road that runs through scrubby woods and hollows, dry hills sloping down to marshy bottomland . . . wood-lot country. One December day I rapped at the door, and he put his jacket on and walked across the yard with me, where two white ducks were parading and some red chickens giving the frozen ground a going over. The old man bent down a little and spoke to his dog Bonnie, a cream-colored spaniel, which had just wagged up to him: "Did you get it?"

Then, to me: "I lost an egg. Picked up five eggs, out of the hen yard this mornin', and came back with four. Maybe there was a hole in these old pants of mine."

The barber shop was small, long and narrow, but he had a stove in there that kept it warm. There were some old magazines on a bench against the wall, with a black Homburg hat hanging on a peg. It had been given him by an old customer, a wealthy man who had lived on the Cape during the summer and had come in to have his hair cut for many years before he died. There was a photograph on the wall of the two of them with an inscription underneath that read: "Established 1884. A satisfied customer is our best advertisement." They were standing out in front of the shop, smiling in the sun.

"Feller came here yesterday and I had to clip him in the kitchen. Shop was too cold," Nate said.

The calm of the place was comforting. It came, I suppose, from an acceptance that emanated from him, and brought in many old friends, who would sit down to say: "Nate, just thought I'd come over and pass the time of day."

Whatever he had to say about other people left them without the honor of human circumstances. "Pretty close, he is," he would say with a little laugh, or "I guess he had a shade on" (a Cape Cod expression for being drunk). "Guess you can't hold on to nothin'," he said about some local theft, in a way that insisted on not being roused beyond necessity.

His origins were out of a kind of history of which there was very little left intact except himself. He once showed me a tintype of his mother, a handsome girl named Bridget Malady, who had emigrated from Ireland in 1862. His father, Timothy Black, was born in Yarmouth, on the Cape. At the age of ten he signed on as a cook aboard the packet which sailed between East Dennis and Boston, and seems to have spent a good deal of his life on inter- mittent voyages at sea. He was also in the butchering and slaugh- tering business with his two sons. In the autumn they used to butcher eighty-five hogs or more, at the rate of three a day. And in some rough but related way, Timothy Black started his son in the barbering business. Nate remembered how his father used to cut his hair in the kitchen, long before the Black Hills emporium was established: "I used to sit there while he was sort of pummeling at me on the back of the neck. By gol! I sure did cringe when he was chopping me with those women's scissors."

While I, seventy or eighty years later, was sitting in the barber's chair, getting more expert and calmer work done on me, I assembled a little of the past. In the nineteenth and early twentieth centuries an expedition to the post office or the store took up a large part of the day. That was the time when you could hitch the horse up to a post and stop for a long chat, "having the capacity to waste time" as I heard a Texan phrase it about some of his countrymen in the western part of the state. People walked between their houses—there are foot paths still showing—on barren hills. They had small herds of cows that foraged on the sloping fields. Families used to picnic together by the ponds, and there were barn dances on Saturday nights, which were sometimes the occasion for a rip-roaring fight. I have heard it said that Nate Black was the strongest fighter in the region, when outraged beyond his normal patience, but he would reveal none of this prowess to me.

The Black family also held dances in their kitchen. The father of the house played the violin. On such occasions they would have plum porridge suppers, or they served crackers, milk, and raisins, and sometimes hulled corn.

He was of a piece with his surroundings. I think of many things he talked about while I was having my hair cut and they all meant the gray, sea-girded land, and a human closeness to it. I think of the deer that ate his beans, of his duck that was carried off by a fox, of foxes being reduced in population by the mange, of a watering place for horses by Cedar Pond in East Dennis (a beautiful pond with ranks of dark cedars backing it up, and now being encroached upon by house lots); and he talked about the big eels waiting to eat young herrin' (or alewives) at the mouth of a pond, and of sounding the depths of Round Pond here in West Brewster.

And then there was his dog which had to be chained up because it got so wildly excited chasing rabbits through the woods that it was constantly lost, having once been picked up nearly ten miles away; and the coon that climbed a tree after a hen; and his little granddaughter wanting to shine a flashlight through the window one night and take a picture of a coon she saw outdoors, because it was "such a pretty-looking animal."

There also come to mind the fishing boats all-over white with screaming gulls, that he once spoke about with real excitement, and, of course, the yearly work on his cranberry bogs . . . he and his tart and lively wife used to pick them together; and the shifting price of cranberries, and his wood lots, and who was after him to buy some of his land.

"Yes yes" he would say, in the Cape Cod fashion, and always, when a customer was leaving the shop: "Come again."

His wife Emily died two years before him. Some time before that I stopped to talk with him when he was scything the family plot in Red Top Cemetery, which lies at the junction of two country roads, on a little hill or high knoll up in the sky and the ocean winds. He told me two women had come up one day while he was there and said: "What a nice place!" He and his wife are buried there, in a place which has no more permanence than any other, but for them and by them had the simple power of acquaintance.

Deeper News

I READ IN THE PAPERS THAT SPRING IS BEGINNING to show its vast capacity in the nation behind us, with tornadoes in the west, and floods to the south. The way is being cleared with a violence.

And here, heavy fogs invest the Cape during the early morning and at night. On the night of the second we are lashed by a savage gale, carrying wet snow and rain, and feel a searching, bitter dampness. The next morning the sun comes out with promise and radiance. There is a faint new fragrance in the air. It would have been nothing but that—a sense of mild relief after the pressure of a storm, but for another piece of news. At 1 A.M. the Coast Guard had received an "incoherent" distress signal, though without exact location, from a vessel somewhere on a twenty-five-mile stretch of shore between Cape Cod light in Truro and Nauset light in Orleans. It was found before dawn, an eighty-three-foot trawler, which had run aground off South Wellfleet. Out of a crew of seven, the reports say, two are drowned, four survived, and one is missing.

They were returning to Boston with 38,000 pounds of fish, after fishing west of Georges Banks. During the night, through a thick fog, a thirty- to forty-mile-an-hour wind, high waves, and heavy rain, the radar stopped working and the crewmen were unable to see. The "Back Shore" bar, on which the trawler ran aground, is an old graveyard for ships. Modern equipment has cut down greatly on losses, along with some of the old safeguards against them. Many lighthouses are no longer manned by lighthouse keepers and their families. Great beams of light swing out over the dark sea and back again with inanimate, unmanned precision. Members of Coast Guard rescue crews may no longer be men born and bred here who know every inch of their beaches. In fact, they are more likely to come from a different state, and to be stationed temporarily on the Cape, so that a man hunting for a wreck may not have too exact an idea of his location.

During the afternoon, after I hear the news and drive to see the wreck, a southwest wind blows over the cliffs that stand above the Wellfleet beach, and clouds swirl up across the blue emptiness. Cars line both sides of the road. A thin trickle of people walk along the heights, sands held by yellow grass and purple patches of bearberry, and there are others far down the long beach where the trawler lies, heaved over to starboard.

From morning news accounts and a scatter of talk the story of the doomed ship and the rescue comes to me a little, from under its nighttime shroud of fog and heaving waves. After the radar quit and the vessel ran aground on the sand bar, the crew made a futile effort to get her off. Then the radio failed. The ship was being knocked around in the thrashing darkness. All attempts failed to put dories overboard. And the seven men went into the pilothouse, where they stayed for some five hours. When day broke, the tide was changing and the seas seemed bigger than ever. The men were battered and exhausted. The trawler's decks were awash, and they thought she was beginning to break up. The captain then ordered the crew over the sides, at which time the ship was some 600 to 700 yards offshore.

A local family, a man, his wife, and twelve-year-old daughter, proprietors of summer cottages above the beach, were awakened at four forty-five in the morning by two coastguardmen who had seen the wreck and stopped in to use the phone. While one of the men drove along the heights and trained the spotlights of his jeep on the wreck, the other, accompanied by the family, walked down to the shore. The fog had lifted a little and they could see white spars rocking above the water, and what looked at first like debris, being washed back and forth against the shore. Forming a hand-to-hand chain, the four rescuers then managed by just standing out far enough in the icy water to pull three men in. More Coast Guard personnel came later and rescued the fourth. The survivors were terribly numbed by the cold. One of them had to be forced into walking so as to save his life. "How much further?" he kept mumbling, as he stumbled around in the sands, held up by the mother and daughter. Later, the flesh of these survivors was found to be black and blue from the pounding they had taken on board the ship and in the surf, flung against the sands.

Two other crewmen were found dead on the beach. Another local resident saw one of them where he lay at the bottom of a ladder that reached down the cliff: "A big man, between thirty and forty. He had coveralls on, but no shirt."

His wife says: "I'll never complain about the price of fish again!"

There are plenty of fish in evidence, all for free, although not a single one is taken away. The boat's catch must have been broken into and scattered by the surf. Every ten yards or so along the wide, shelving beach are dead fish, lined up as if they had been placed there—a market display, for no taste but dissolution. Gray haddock cleaned by the fishermen's knives. Rose fish, pinkish, orange-red, a sunset color, with fringed fins, and enormous jel-lied eyes rimmed with white, like goggles.

A hatch cover floats loose in the water, and a pair of yellow, oiled fisherman's overalls lies on the sand.

The boat, which was shoved and lifted by the seas until it now lies a few yards off the beach, is just ahead. We curious onlook-ers walk toward it in growing silence. The surf waters are break-ing on the beach beside the strong, humble craft, inactive, done, pounded down. I can make out her name, *Paulmino*, along the bow. She is banked over hard, and the waves, still fairly high, back and fill around the stern. They well up, then ease away again. Where water sloshes amidships there are tattered nets and bobbing cork floats. The steel masts stand with ropes and stays unbroken, and the high, white pilothouse is intact, where they spent their terrible night.

I walk away from that scene with a question. Surely they could have stayed on board and survived? But time is not waiting for could-have-beens. The sea rolls by. The stars burn and roar in their distances. Immortal death, an ending, but the source of all questions and the answer to them, roars on too without reply. Men in their death, or fish, or birds, are the same. They share in universal soundings that no mortal fear escapes.

from

The Great Beach

(1964)

An Unimagined Frontier

*O*NE AFTERNOON IN THE MIDDLE OF JUNE, I SET off from Race Point at Provincetown, carrying a pack and sleeping bag, with Nauset Light Beach in Eastham, twenty-five miles away, as my destination, and my purpose simply to be on the beach, to see it and feel it for whatever it turned out to be, since most of my previous visits had been of the sporadic hop, skip, and jump kind to which our automotivated lives seem to lead us.

The summer turmoil was not yet in full voice but the barkers were there on behalf of beach-buggy tours over the dunes, and a sight-seeing plane flew by; cars drew up and droned away, and families staggered up from the beach with their load of towels, shoes, bags, or portable radios. The beach did not contain quite the great wealth of paper, cans, bottles, and general garbage that it would later on, in July and August, but one of the first things to catch my eye as I lunged down onto the sands was an electric-light bulb floating in the water, a can of shaving soap, the remains of a rubber doll, and a great scattering of sliced onions—probably thrown off a fishing boat.

The air was dancing with heat. The sun seemed to have the power to glare through all things. With the exception of a camper's tent on the upper part of the beach, and a few isolated gray shacks perched on dune tops behind it, there was nothing ahead but the wide belt of sand curving around one unseen corner after another with the flat easing and stretching sea beside me. Two boys waved to me from where they were perched high up on a dune, and I waved back.

Then I heard an insistent, protesting bird note behind me, and a piping plover flew past. It was very pale, and sand colored, being a wild personification of the place it lived in. It suddenly volplaned down the slope of the beach ahead of me, fluttering, half disappearing in holes made by human feet, side-winged, edged away, still fluttering, in the direction of the shore line, and when it reached the water, satisfied, evidently, that it had led me far enough, it flew back. These birds nest on the beach above the high-tide line, and like a number of other species, try to lead intruders away when they come too close to their eggs and young.

With high, grating cries, terns flew over the beach and low over the water, occasionally plummeting in after fish. Among the larger species, principally common terns, there were some least terns—a tiny, dainty version of the "sea swallow," chasing each other back and forth. They have the graceful, sharply defined bodies and deep wingbeat of the other terns, but in their littleness and excitability they seem to show a kind of baby anger.

Also there were tree swallows gathering and perching on the hot, glittering sand, and on smooth gray driftwood just below the dunes. It was a band of them, adults, and young hatched during the early spring, chittering and shining with their brilliant blue-green backs and white bellies.

It seemed to me that out of these birds—my unwilling or indifferent companions—came a protest, the protest of a desert in its beauty, an ancient sea land claiming its rarity, with these rare inhabitants, each with its definition and assertion, each having the color and precision of life and place, out of an unknown depth of devising.

Behind the beach at Provincetown and Truro are eight square miles of dunes, making a great series of dips and pockets, innumerable smooth scourings, hollows within wide hollows. Standing below their rims are hills, mounds, and cones, chiseled by the wind, sometimes flattened on the top like mesas. These dunes give an effect of motion, rolling, dipping, roving, dropping down and curving up like sea surfaces offshore. When I climbed the bank to see them I heard the clear, accomplished notes of a song sparrow. There were banks of rugosa roses in bloom, with white or pink flowers sending off a lovely scent, and the dunes were patched with the new green of beach grass, bayberry, and beach plum, many of the shrubs looking clipped and rounded, held down by wind and salt spray. The purple and pink flowers of the beach pea, with purselike petals, were in bloom too, contrasting with dusty miller with leaf surfaces like felt, a soft, clear grayish-green. Down at the bottom of the hollows the light and wind catching heads of bunch grass, pinkish and brown, waved continually; and the open sandy slopes were swept as by a free hand with curving lines and striations.

A mile or so at sea, over the serene flatness of the waters, a fishing boat moved very slowly by. I started down the beach again, following another swallow that was twisting and dipping in leafy flight along the upper edge of the beach. On the tide line slippery green sea lettuce began to glimmer as if it had an inner fire, reflecting the evening sun. I stopped somewhere a mile or two north of Highland Light in Truro, built a small fire of driftwood to heat up a can of food, and watched a bar appearing above the water as the tide ebbed. Low white waves conflicted and ran across a dome of sand, occasionally bursting up like hidden geysers.

The terns were still crying and diving as the sun's metal light, slanting along the shore, began to turn a soft yellow, to spread and bloom. They hurried back and forth, as if to make use of the time left them, and fell sharply like stones into the shimmering road of light that led across the water.

Where I live on the lower Cape, that part of it which lies between the Cape Cod canal and Orleans, the land heads out directly to the sea, toward the east from the continental west. Cape Cod Bay lies to the north and Nantucket Sound to the south. The arm of the upper Cape turns in the Orleans area and heads up on a north-south axis, the head of it, or hand if you like, curving around so that the sandy barrens in the Provincetown area are oriented in an east to west direction again. I am used to looking toward Kansas to see the setting sun, and from the curving shore line at Truro I had the illusion that it was setting in the north and that when it rose the next morning it appeared to be located not very far from where it set, a matter of ninety or a hundred degrees. In fact it does set closer to the north at this time of year, and along the flat ocean horizon this becomes more clear to the eye, as well as its relative position at dawn and its arc during the day. On the open beach in spring and summer you are not only at the sun's mercy in a real sense, but you are also under wider skies. In the comparative isolation of the beach, which is convex, slanting steeply toward the water, and therefore hides its distances, I felt reoriented, turned out and around through no effort of my own, and faced in many possible directions.

Shortly before sundown a beach buggy, curtains at its windows and a dory attached, lumbered slowly down some preordained ruts in the sand, and then a smaller one passed by at the top of the low dunes behind me. Fishing poles were slung along the outside of both machines. It was getting to be a good time to cast for striped bass.

I sat on the sands and listened to the sonorous heave and splash of low waves. The sun, like a colossal red balloon filled with water, was sinking in to the horizon. It swelled, flattened, and disappeared with a final rapidity, leaving a foaming, fiery band behind it. I suddenly heard the wild, trembling cry of a loon behind me, and then saw it fly over, heading north. The wind grew cool, after a hot day when the light shone on metallic, glittering slow waters, and sharp, pointed beach grasses clicked together, while I watched the darkness falling around me.

A small seaplane flew by at low altitude, parallel to the shore. A sliver of a moon appeared and then a star; and then single lights began to shine on the horizon, while from the direction of Highland Light an arm of light shot up and swung around. A fishing boat passed slowly by with a light at its masthead and two—port and starboard—at its stern. A few night-flying moths fluttered near me. The sky began to be massive with its stars. I thought of night's legitimacies now appearing, the natural claim of all these single lights on darkness, and then, making my bed in a hollow just above the beach, I lowered down into infinity, waking up at about one o'clock in the morning to the sound of shouting, a strange direct interruption to the night. It was the loud implacable voice of the human animal, something very wild in itself, filling the emptiness.

"For Chrisake bring her higher up! I can't have her dig in that way." The tide had come in and someone was having trouble maneuvering his beach buggy along the thin strip of sand now available.

The light of dawn opened my eyes again before the sun showed red on the horizon, and I first saw the tiny drops of dew on tips and stems of beach grass that surrounded me. A sparrow sang, and then, somewhere behind the dunes, a prairie warbler with sweet notes on an ascending scale.

When I started walking again I caught sight of a young fox. Its fur was still soft and woolly and its gait had a cub's limpness where it moved along the upper edge of the beach. I wished the young one well, though I suspected it might have an uncomfortable life. In spite of an excessive population of rabbits, and their role in keeping it down, foxes have not been too highly regarded on the Cape. In recent years they seem to have been a skinny and somewhat dilapidated bunch for the most part, suffering from parasitic skin diseases, and ticks in season. I once saw a fox out on an asphalt road sliding along on his chin and side, shoving and dragging himself in such a frantic way that I began to feel very itchy myself. I have heard them referred to in a scornful way as "spoilers," fond of scavenging and rolling in dead meat. In other words, they are smelly, diseased and, to add another epithet "tricky," not to be trusted.

Yet this cub exploring an early morning on the sands had a future, however limited, and I remembered the lively trot of foxes when they are in good health, and their intelligence and curiosity, and simply their right to whatever special joys they might inherit.

I carried a pair of field glasses with me, along with the somewhat thoughtlessly assembled equipment I wore on my back and which seemed increasingly heavy as time went on. When not too conscious of my burden I would use the glasses to bring an inland or offshore bird closer to me. I noticed five eider ducks across the troughs of the waves, a remnant of the thousands that winter off the Cape along with such other sea birds as brant, Canada geese, scoters, mergansers, old squaws, and various members of the auk family. I passed a dead gannet lying on the sand. It had been badly oiled, reminding me of the hazards of jettisoned tanker or freighter oil to all these water birds which land on the sea to rest or feed.

There were a number of kingbirds on the dune rims, and they kept dropping down over the beach in their special way, to hover with fast wingbeat and flutter after flying insects. I heard the grating call of redwings, indicating marshy areas inland of the beach, but the cliffs above began to increase until they were 100 to 150 feet high or more, and the sun was so fierce that I had little interest in trying to scale them to see what was on the other side.

I plodded on, noticing very little after a while, my attention blunted, reduced to seeing that one foot got in front of the other. The more level upper parts of the beach provided fairly good walking, but the sand was soft, and to relieve my aching muscles I would then angle down to the water's edge where it was firmer, and there I was obliged to walk with one leg below the other because of the inclination of the beach. So I would return to the upper beach again and push ahead. I walked on, very hot and slow, seeing no one for miles until I came up to a group of bathers below a road and parking lot giving access to the beach, of the kind that are scattered along its reaches; and there I refilled my canteen at a cottage and went on.

I found that if I rested too long during this hike I had little desire to go on again, so I confined myself to an army "break" of ten minutes every hour. Renewed walking unlimbered me a little and the wind off the water cooled my sweating skin. I listened to the sound of the waves. In addition to their rhythmic plunge and splash, their breathing, they clashed occasionally with a sound like the breaking of heavy glass, the falling of timber, or a load of bricks.

I passed what was left of two shipwrecks during the day, a reminder of the dangers that still face ships along this coast with its fogs, its shifting winds, its storms, the hidden, treacherous offshore bars. The sands often reveal the timbers of old ships. One day their ribs, sodden and dark, barnacle encrusted, may reach up out of oblivion, and not long after that the water buries them under tons of sand. From them a local history calls out for recognition. Thousands of ships over three centuries wrecked on shoals, engulfed by violent seas, men with the dark of doom in them, to drown or to survive, and only a few timbers left to declare the ultimate dangers and their terror.

I was not in Death Valley, or on a raft at sea. My walk was not unusually long, and I could leave the beach if I had to, but the enormity of the area filled me more and more. It had so much in it that was without recourse. Its emptiness, the great tidal range beyond it and through it, the raw heartbeat of the waves, the implacable sun, established the kind of isolation and helplessness in me which the commerce and community of our lives tries so hard to disguise. Even the birds, I began to think, were more secure than I. They had their strong bright threads of cognizance to the areas they came to, the water, the sands, the marsh. They were fixed in entity and grace, eating what was theirs by evolution to be eaten, using land and air in the ways that had come to them, knowing this place and all places like it in terms of its bounds and boundlessness, meeting its naked eye in the ways they had been sent to do.

I started off in the morning admiring the brilliance of the sun, the small shadows from the dunes and across the beach, through driftwood, isolated beach plants and tidal wrack, with the wide flooding of light ahead and the variation in reflected light across the sea. I felt the sea moving quietly beside me. The waves heaved and sighed and spray was tossed lightly above the sand. Everything was continuous, untroubled, and deliberate; but as the day wore on the sun became my enemy, and I had very little rage or resource in me to fight it with. I was not fitted to environmental stability, like a bird, or fox or fish. I found myself in an area of whose reaches I had never been wholly aware, and in me there was no mastery. The sun was not only hostile. It was an ultimate, an impossibility; and the waters beside me began to deepen from their pleasant daytime sparkle and freshness into an incalculable realm which I had hardly entered. I was touching on an unimagined frontier.

I spent my second night on the beach a few miles from Nauset Light where I left it the following morning. It was in the South Wellfleet area, and as I started to sleep on the sand a little above the high-tide line, I remembered that this was about the same place where a fishing boat had been wrecked two years before and two men drowned. I had seen the boat, with its cargo of fish, and some of the men's clothing strewn along the shore, and I had heard a little about the depths of their ordeal. Their story haunted me; and then I began to feel that I might be caught by the tide while I was asleep. There were only about twelve feet between the bottom of a steep cliff and the high-tide line. I would soon be lying on a narrow shelf at the sea's edge. So as the vague thought of being engulfed began to invade me, I took up my pack and sleeping bag again, retraced my steps down the beach, and found a way to the top of the cliff, where I spent the night in another hollow.

The light of dawn, lifting quickly out of the sea, flooding into the range of low-lying land, woke me up again, and it signaled to the birds, who started singing in all the thickets and heath around me with a sweet, high, shrill intensity, a kind of automatic worship; and after a while they quieted down again.

Little dirt roads dropped back from headlands through green slopes covered with bearberry and patches of yellow-flowered

Hudsonia, or "poverty grass," and there were hollows dipping back inland, and woods of stunted pitch pine. From the top of the cliff I watched the sun starting to send light running across the blue table of the sea, making it glitter and move. The intensity of light and heat began to grow steadily as I walked down the beach again for the last stretch toward Nauset.

The beach is not so very far from where I live, or for that matter where anyone lives on the Cape. It is a few miles down the road, beyond the trees; and yet when I came back from my walk I felt as if I had been at enormous remove from my surroundings, caught out where I might have feared to be. The long line of sand and surf, the intensity of the sun, the cover of stars had come close enough to put me in council with that which had no answers. I was in awe of nature; and I understood that the sun and sea could be our implacable enemies. It was in this context that I saw our human world as subject to a statute that it never made.

Who Owns the Beach?

*I*N THE "OFF" AND EMPTY SEASON, AFTER THE TIDES had erased all signs of a hundred thousand human feet, it was hard to believe that the beach could be owned or claimed by anyone. It took on the air's cold or warmth, receiving, passing things on, from one day and seasonal mood to another, not as on the land with its plant and animal reactions and obstructions, the hiding; shadowing; coming forth intermittently; but in bold and naked sight, reducing weather to its single qualities.

One day the Cape would be sunny and comparatively warm, and on the next in would come the authentic northern wind, the polar air, roaring and sweeping around with fierce abandon, riotously hard and cold, freezing the ground, cutting at a man, diving on him with an icy weight. The winter wind is so definite when it comes, overwhelming a fairly moderate climate, where roses often bloom late into the fall and hollies grow, as to make you think of icebergs, sliding down from the north unexpectedly to stand hundreds of feet overhead. The sky, threatening snow, writhes and purls up with gray clouds spreading fanwise like auroras, and in the evening the sun goes down with a coppery band on the horizon overhung by a bank of steely-blue clouds as menacing as a shark.

And the great beach received what came to it, retaining its primal right to a deeper breath and regularity, a harsh "poverty-stricken" environment where man has no lease worth the paper. It did seem utterly deserted, although the herring gulls and black-backs flew up steeply over the wind-buffeted waves, then banked and glided away, and draggers occasionally moved parallel to the beach bucking the choppy seas, their lines out astern. The wind threw stinging clouds of sand ahead of it. Except for the fishermen and the gulls, it was an abandoned world, glistening wide and cold, lost to importance and sense so far as human society was concerned. For many there is no force quite so inclusive as his own.

Since the beach is comparatively empty and isolated during fall and winter, the sight of life on its sands may seem as rare as a rider approaching you across the desert. I remember what an extraordinary thing it seemed one afternoon to see a tiny red crab moving very slowly along, high-legged over the bare slopes of the beach. I identified it later as a species of spider crab. Green crabs, rock crabs, calico crabs, and others are common along the protected shores of the Cape, but out on this stretch of beach they are rarities. This baby, with its beak, antennae, and eyes backed and covered by a knobbed and spiky shell, seemed like an exotic from another world, which in fact it was, having been flung in by the surf from rocks and seaweed forests in the waters beyond it. It not only added to the beach, but to me, since it made me realize that these sands were only shelving off into further dimensions. The beach is a repository of freight, wreckage, and lives from foreign lands.

This also happens occasionally on land. We all know that the sea is out there, that the wind swirls over us, and the storms carry more traffic than planes, but strangers sometimes appear as if to prove that no place is what it seems to be. One spring a vermillion flycatcher suddenly appeared in the neighborhood. I saw it in its exciting tropical gaiety as it flew down next to a shining patch of spring rain on an asphalt road. It is a native of Texas and New Mexico. Black or turkey buzzards ride the great airs of spring and sometimes fly northward, wheeling unexpectedly overhead. In November of 1962 I saw a black stork, *Ciconia nigra*, which had somehow managed to make it all the way across the Atlantic Ocean, perhaps managing to stop for rests in such areas as Greenland and Newfoundland. It landed near the Coast Guard Station, now National Seashore Park headquarters, at Eastham, in an exhausted state, to be picked up by the Audubon Society and later transported to the warmer climate of Florida.

The black stork breeds from Central Europe to Korea and China, and it winters in Africa after a long round of migratory journeys. Its advent was greeted with a certain amount of mild curiosity and even some jokes in the local paper, one of which had to do with its liking for Cape Cod scallops on its arrival. What better reason for coming here! (The truth is that like other newly captured birds, it had to be force-fed.) In any case it was a rare event, joining Cape Cod with Africa, and to see it was equivalent to seeing an antelope on Route 6. With large strong wings, attenuated red legs, a long, stout pinkish bill, red around the eyes, it waited in captivity with what seemed to be an air of great sadness, transplanted as it was, taken in to a gray, cold land without any sound but engines, human voices, and the wind, without any greenery but the thin-needled pines; and it roosted silently, twitching occasionally in its inactive unused state, an unwilling, unwitting Marco Polo in New England.

This is a narrow place, restricted by nature and by men, but foreign lives still fly to it like sparks in the air, and the sea beyond it takes things on their way with more room than analogy is yet aware of. What the sea sends in, like a dead skate, a starfish, horse mussel, or finger sponge, seems perfectly familiar as fish, marine, background animals, but they are also genuine primitives, remote not only from human physiology and complete understanding but from that part of the earth's surface that we inhabit. In fact many of the hints of marine life that are either brought up along the beach, or that appear in offshore waters, like a whale or a dolphin, have a theatricality, an off-stage hint of a wealth of other acts, tricks, and forms still to be seen. The simple, primal watery element has embodiments of use which are comprehensible and have been studied for a long time, but these are endowed with physical natures and capabilities that might make an air-breathing, earth-bound human quite envious.

During a violent coast storm, with winds up to seventy and eighty miles an hour, an exhausted harbor porpoise was cast up on a bay beach recently, and there it died. I confess I had never seen one out of water or even close to me before. For all the pictures I had seen, and all I had read, nothing prepared me for such perfection. Its round body, four to five feet long, was butt-ended at its head, in which there were small eyes, and small teeth in the jaws. It had just as much of the quality of flow as a raindrop, and at the same time was a solid packing of energy. Its skin graded down from the jet black of its back and upper sides through streaks of gray like rain along the sea down to a white belly, and without scales, it had a thick, smooth satiny polish like ebony or horn, perhaps reminiscent of synthetic rubber or plastic but of an organic texture which neither of those products could equal. The porpoise had a single fin on its back and a tail that could strike vertically for power and thrust. Its body was fairly heavy, weighing about a hundred pounds, but everything of speed and liquidity and dashing, leaping strength was reflected there. It lay on the upper part of the beach, conspicuous among the long piles of storm litter, the logs, pieces of broken dories, and thick seaweed, spectacular in its simplicity, a black and white that made me think of breaking waves in the night sea. I saw it curve over the surfaces of the water with consummate grace, slide away, and disappear.

"Where did you ever see more of nothing?" I was once asked as I looked out over endless dry Texas plains billowing like waves. Nothing or everything. Who knows? Who knows what the emptiness leads to or contains? The beach lies open. Its sands and rattling stones lead back through ages of weathering and change and are at the same time part of the wide give and take of the present.

The tiny spider crab, though isolated on the beach, was also a link with a teeming offshore existence, which hid in shadowy worlds of kelp and rockweed, or floated and roamed by with a free energy that was in complete denial of our tightening fall and winter world. Backed by a cliff, walking on sands shadowed and cold, faced by the churning waves, it is hard to believe in a life so rich. There are no rocky shores revealed at low tide and streaming with weed to prove the temperate fertility of the sea. The beach is a transition zone between one environment and another, but except in those areas where the cliffs are reduced to low sand hills, protecting a marsh or estuary behind them, the transition is a sharp one, the sands dipping from the inconstant sky to the constancy of salt water.

Along those stretches of beach where the sea has taken stones and boulders and deposited them offshore, storms sometimes bring in fairly large quantities of seaweed, which need beds of stone for their attachment. The fucus or rockweed, the laminaria or kelp, and some of the "red" algae like Irish moss which are among the more common kinds found along the beach, have no roots, since the plants take all their nourishment from the sea water that surrounds them, but are anchored by holdfasts, stubby structures which in the laminaria may look like the exposed, above-ground roots of some tropical trees, and in the fucus a round expansion of the tissues at its base, which is strongly and tightly sealed to the surface of rocks and stones.

Everything about these weeds, with divided, narrow, or tapering fronds to resist being torn by the waves, with bladders serving as floats, with gelatinous surfaces, with hollow stems, are eloquent of the nature of salt water, its ebb and flow, its depths, its capacious circulation. The seaweeds found on the beach, black, thin, dried out, or fresh and slippery, olive green, brown, or red, having been torn loose by a storm, start growing beyond the violent action of the surf, and grow for the most part to a depth of some forty or fifty feet. Different varieties like different depths, but since they are not free floating unless torn loose they are not found beyond the point where rays of sunlight, necessary for manufacturing food, cannot reach them.

Over and beyond them, in surface waters where the light penetrates before being absorbed, is a vegetation, varying in abundance according to place and season, but of incredible numbers over all, the one-celled microscopic organisms that are the basic food of all the seas. The seaweeds are simple and primitive in structure compared with much of the plant life on land, the more hazardous, contrary environment, and the members of the phytoplankton (the planktonic plants), even more so, although the diatoms, which form a large part of it, show a variety of outer form. Each diatom has a skeleton, made largely of silica, an outer shell hard enough to resist easy dissolution when the plant dies. It is formed like a pillbox, or a casket, or it is shaped like a quill, a ribbon, or rod, or it is joined with others in beads and chains. Each is minute, an etched, crystalline perfection, and each is lost in other billions, which we might only see on occasion as a green or greenish-brown stain across the water.

The shells of dead diatoms rain down through the water and form thick deposits on the floor of the sea. The cliffs above the beach are full of them. Cities have been built on their fossilized shells. In their number the diatoms balance the magnitude of the sea. In size they are basic to the existence of the minuscule animals of the zooplankton that feed upon them, and are eaten by large animals in turn. A diatom's delicacy and sparkling beauty as it reflects the light could indicate that universal productivity must start with a jewel, and perhaps end with it too.

That which is minute, like the diatoms, or cells, which are the basic structure of life, is a clue to the significance of things, leading from the simple to the complex and multifarious, but finally rounding us back to where we started. A man himself is the unique single cell with its own nature. Each life has its irreducible quality. I have been told that if you look at a diatom through an electronic microscope, from one increased magnification to another, you can see all its protuberances and layers disappear, and finally a sparkling crystalline form is revealed, like a cosmic surprise.

I suppose it is part of my fate as a large and clumsy animal of the mammalian order, crashing through the underbrush, knocking down trees, and displacing earth's other inhabitants, to miss a great deal, at least with my unassisted eyes. To learn about some new form of life which I may have been passing by for years is often something of a redemption. I can then say that we have not yet been so run down by our own traffic that we have lost the capacity to see.

Not long ago a colony of bryozoans was pointed out to me, at least the gelatinous crusts of the compartments in which they lived, like little tufts and fringes attached to the fronds of seaweed cast up on the beach. They are tiny colonial animals that make cups and compartments joined together in branching stems, from which they send out little crowns of delicate, filamentous tentacles waving in the water. There are three thousand marine species of them, growing in different forms, and having different surfaces for their attachment. I had thought previously that the little pale-colored, branched tufts were a part of the seaweed. Now another small marvel had appeared on my horizon.

The beach was empty where I walked, except for bird tracks, tidal wrack, driftwood, bits of shell, or a finger sponge in evidence of the life alongside it, and depending on the warmth and receptivity to life that the season held, excepting also whatever microscopic animals might be crawling over wet surfaces around the sand grains. Again, emptiness, or poverty, is always qualified. After all the copepods, the nematodes or thread worms, and other groups unseen or unknown to me might be underfoot in vast numbers; and as I continued on there was no counting the number of little holes in the sand made by beach fleas or sand hoppers. As the autumn deepened I supposed they were unoccupied and deserted, since these beach dwellers, as I had heard it, should have been tucked away in their burrows by this time, with the door shut above their heads, waiting for March and April to bring a warm sun which could tease them out of dormancy. But one bright morning in the middle of November I saw a great many of them hard at work.

At first I noticed thousands of little mounds on the surface of the sand in a strip some six to fifteen feet wide along the upper part of the beach, following in general the outlines of the previous high tide. Where a log or shelving bank was in the way, these mounds, and the many holes accompanying them, about knitting-needle size, were concentrated on the seaward side. I noticed that shore birds had attempted to pluck the occupants from their holes and had reached down two to three inches. I scooped out the sand where a hole was, spread it around, and revealed a little animal not over a half inch long, with two large eyes covering the sides of its narrow head. The eyes were not only conspicuous, they were also startlingly white; and the sand-hopper's body flattened on both sides, was a mother-of-pearl, somewhat translucent. This odd creature, one of a family in the order of amphipods, is called *Talorchestia megalopthalma*, a title that gives special credit to its eyes.

I put my pale-moon animal back in its hole, but to be held and thrust against its own volition apparently immobilized it, so I let it go free down the sands. After a second or two it made a few big and seemingly crazy hops—on sidelong springs like a toy—down a line of mounds and holes, popped into a hole and promptly disappeared.

I noticed that little spouts and bursts of sand were coming from many of these holes and with a little patience I could see some of the hoppers coming up as if to look around, as is customary with gophers and chipmunks, and then turning around and going back down again. What they were doing of course was a major job of digging, passing the sand up from one pair of legs to another and throwing it out the hole with a jerk. There was hardly time or inclination to pause and look around the far horizon. It was work that had to be done unceasingly, between tides and between seasons. Perhaps, if tomorrow brought consistently freezing temperatures, they might not appear again in any great numbers until spring; but their usual daily round meant frenzied feeding at low tide and after dark when no winged predators were around, followed by another return to the upper beach and another furiously energetic period of digging homes for themselves. Terrestrial animals, which might drown after a period of immersion, and yet bound on this strip of sand to the tides, they had a more legitimate claim to the beach than most of us.

Looking down at them, or in on their busyness, I had an extraordinary Gulliverlike feeling of encroaching on a world to which I did not belong. It was one kind of an eye looking at another without any sense of whether it was seen in turn or not, in a dichotomy of function, race, size, and place. It took the beach out of my possession. This was a place of other-world connections at which I could hardly guess. Do we need to wait for the men from Mars?

These are extravagant animals, with their grandiose if relatively blind eyes, with their feats of digging, their hunger dance. In a sense they have a very narrow range, between upper and lower tide, between one season and the next, between feeding and digging on their strip of sand, between hiding and emerging, and their life span is short; but what a use they make of it!

Talorchestia megalopthalma is now on my life list, as the "birders" put it, a pearly prodigy of moon leaps that may, for all I know, be the beach's foremost citizen.

I also caught a glimpse of another little animal as I turned over a piece of driftwood. It had numerous legs (seven pairs in all, I have learned), and a flattened body, though slightly rounded on top, and oval in shape, reminding me of a pill bug or sow bug, one of my most familiar landed neighbors, which can be found under almost any boulder or log that provides shade and moisture. The marine, or beached member of the family I met, was grayish white in color, and apparently had the same preference for moisture—if not too much, since it evidently lived at the high-tide line, and was "terrestrial" like the sand hoppers. Some of these isopods swim in the open sea, others live in shallow water, or at the low-tide line, and most are scavengers, feeding on dead animal matter.

All these and countless others are symptomatic of a tidal range, an ebb and flow that extends between sea and land in terms of millions of years of emergence and adaptation. In them the two worlds find their division and also their meeting and intercommunication. Their characteristic areas, their "life zones," from the tropics to the poles, all require extremes of risk and of the struggle to survive it. In one place or another they dance to the inexorable measure of things, limited in what they do but exceptional in their way of doing it.

On this beach, so unique, so well defined, and at the same time so widely involved, every upward surge of the waves and every bubbling retreat sinking through the sand, every range of tide, from the new moon to the old, every storm, every change in the season, every day and every night, is embodied in existence.

I would think it presumptuous of me to claim any more on behalf of a bug or myself than we could in our honest natures fulfill, but faced by the shining tides of life, I am sure we have great things to do.

My translations are on this beach. I am still a part of its measure, and when I forget those overwhelming controls that human power insists on, and all the artificiality men use to overcome their natural limitations, I begin to partake of this miraculous context. It is a cold beach, a bitter sea. Covered with cold, the sands impersonally receive the shadows moving over them tall and wide, gradually shifting and easing over slopes and shoulders toward the surf with its continual lunge, its pull and push, displacing the pale light that stands over the beach and gives it a hard winter brightness. The waves pour and foam and bubble up the beach and recede with a rainlike glistening and seething that sinks in, leaving dark stains behind. The middle part of the beach shows long thin lines like scars where the last tides came, part of the never ending drawing and erasing on this tablet of the sea's art. It is all clean, and naked, defined, and at the same time rhythmically boundless, providing everything that comes to it with an inexhaustible dimension. It needs another language, and at the same time no language could really encompass it. In this bold breath and silence moving up, scene shifting, always starting again, there are decisions of sun and waves, of wind and light, that leave me with a true silence, a great room to fill, though it is in my blood and veins, the roots of me to feel, and any companion whom I meet must be in an ancient earth·sense completely new, with a freshness made of a million years.

from

❧

The Congressional Record

John Burroughs Medal Address

Address by John Hay, acceptance of John Burroughs Medal, presented by the John Burroughs Memorial Association, April 6, 1964, in the auditorium of the American Museum of Natural History, New York, N.Y.

J AM VERY PROUD OF THE HONOR YOU HAVE DONE me, especially for the company it puts me in. When I was first called a naturalist I was pleasantly startled and also a little disturbed by my inability to measure up to what I felt, and still feel, is a title that requires high standards of knowledge and effort. Let us keep it that way if we can. We cannot all have the kind of training we should like in order to analyze the living world, but we can think of it in terms of its own heights and depths, its everlasting offerings. The naturalist has an obligation to the context of nature, and I should add that neither he nor anyone else will ever understand it unless he makes a personal commitment, out of his own experience. Nature is not a matter of mere tranquillity, a kind of weekend reassurance for a city crowd, a retreat, or in terms of society, an object of use. Whatever quiet it has is the quiet of the sea whose partner is violence. Whatever re-assurance it may offer is the kind of reassurance vast energies offer to lives that are always subject to chance and exhaustion.

I think that the world of nature has to be approached with re-spect and anticipation, not so much in terms of the knowledge behind us as the knowledge ahead. In this a naturalist has the role of a leader, not as an expert necessarily, or a representative of sci-entific mastery, but as one who has practiced living with nature, and who has exposed himself to it like John Muir lashed to a tree so that he could experience a storm. He must encourage us to use our basic senses.

John Burroughs told his readers to have sharp eyes. The people, I have known, who were directly influenced by him were unani-mous in emphasizing how he encouraged them to see. Cultivate sharp eyes and ears, he told the children who came to him, and watch for the unexpected. I think I would add, on behalf of his good friend Walt Whitman, learn to include. A friend of mine, who is a distinguished author, told me that the writings of John Burroughs were one of the delights of his youth, that he was so soaked in them that the local countryside became Burroughs' country, and in fact still is; but above all that, he learned through his books to look at things.

To see, and then to interpret takes practice, and practice in depth. I was thinking the other day about the alewives, the fresh-water herring that migrate from the sea to spawn, thinking in fact, that neither I nor anyone else would ever finish thought with re-spect to them. We keep on and on, applying new hypotheses to their behavior in order to try and come up with some simple so-lution. For example, how do they find their way during migration? Why do the young leave fresh water when they do? The more ef-fort we make, the more we know, knowing at the same time that there never was a final, simple answer to things. The schooling fish circle together as they spawn, migrate, or feed, and so do we, in quest of fulfillment, or understanding, circling in depth, together with the spinning globe. The more we practice, the more we in-clude. It is an education. It is a universal necessity. We invariably fall short of the goal but we are always given the equipment with which to start or start again. Failure and renewal are inherent in evolution. Nature gives a basis for both pessimism and optimism.

This is not the relatively pastoral world that John Burroughs knew. I do not have to go very far into modern anxieties and rifts and complexities to emphasize that in some respects we are more isolated from nature than we ever were, isolated as exploiters, divorced from obligation to what we imagine we have conquered. Also, in honest greed and fascination we build myths of space, knowing that space may destroy us. In other words mankind is still carrying out its own exclusive experiment.

On the other hand we may now have the beginnings of a new sense of mutual obligation as part of a smaller world, and if that is too much to expect, at least a sense of universal participation. Science, as if to compensate for our crowding, has shown us new depths and distances and it has innumerated more fellow lives, human and nonhuman, and added more detailed variety to those lives than we ever dreamed possible. Science, which is no more of an "it" than nature is, but part of man's activity and associative thought, has also given us a world which is both forward and backward in time, taking some tradition and continuity away from us, but releasing us from too narrow a view of the present.

All this transformation of human perspectives is the result of some large and precarious steps in scientific thought. As individuals we might take a few large steps ourselves in order to keep up, in order to use what science has given us. We have a continual right to see the universe for its creative grandeur, manifested in us and in everything around us. Instead of spending all our time running around in a technological squirrel cage attending to our own needs we might use technology to look beyond ourselves. That is a precarious activity, as life itself is precarious, but it also has an element of identification and love.

Whatever we do or don't do, energy manifests itself through every inch of the earth, the great process continues, the earth shifts and cracks, the winds roar, the sea erodes the land, the red wings migrate in the spring, the swallows mate, the peepers start their annual symphony. There are laws pertaining to abundance and poverty, to providing and spending, which work themselves out in the circling and schooling of natural lives. All manifest action, the hawk using the currents of the air, the fish in the water, is incomparable. Nature gives us new dimensions, even of pity and terror. Its real depths are beyond our control. I suppose that is one of the reasons why we are always taking up arms against it, almost in anger, while knowing somewhat perversely that there is strength in conflict. What we call "natural resources" of course is likely to mean the things that are most useful to us. We destroy or alter the landscape for our purposes and learn too late just how much we have damaged or impoverished ourselves in the process. We take a chance that nature's primal energy will sustain us. Perhaps it will and perhaps it will not. In any case it survives our claims upon it.

It seems to me that what there is in nature that is not directly controlled by man is just as important to him as what he can exploit. The other lives in the natural world bring life to us. Learning to see, to look at things, may help take the man-centered world away from its own image.

Nature makes science possible, it brightens the arts, its tides are in all experience, and in timeless nature there is no turning back, no nostalgia for anything. Not that we can reject the past, since it is a part of us, but our balance is in the present. We may admire a man who writes with lonely enthusiasm about life in the woods, or what is left of them. We want the challenge of simplicity back again. We want the old associations, away from urban demands and cruelty and noise. But our woods, for which we are directly responsible, are here and now. The universal waters surround us, now. From the atom to the galaxies we are involved as creative beings, trying to understand, trying to see. Our relationship with nature is not ended, only transformed. Ultimately the two of us are not to be separated. In this alliance, the mystery and significance of things are still ahead to learn. Finally, we can't diminish nature by writing it with a small n * * * we can only diminish ourselves.

from

In Defense of Nature

(1969)

A Dependable Endurance

Early days must have been incredibly difficult. As one resident of Rose Bay told it, "They used to get letters from home but they never answered them because their people didn't want them to go away. They thought if they'd write back and say it was so hard, why, the people'd say they had no business to come over there, and if they said it was so good, others might come. They had terrible hard times."

—Helen Creighton, *Folklore of Lunenberg County, Nova Scotia*

1

*M*ORE OFTEN THAN NOT, I SET OUT, AS MOST of us do in the roaring twentieth century, not to walk from my house into the trees, but to open the car door. I have to begin, whether I like it or not, with what the car enables me to do. It is a symbol of society's technical domination. The highway on which it takes me out—where I have been racing half my life—leads to our means of subsistence; and it "gets you there," wherever "there" may be. Whether it has helped us communicate may be open to question. In any case, accepting it as a need, I also mean to get out of the car and stray off the highway when I can. I look for side routes that invite me to their openings, like those dusty roads whose meanderings are no longer considered vital enough to save.

I take to the road and walk down to the shore, to see those waters marked by nothing but the world winds and our onetime lord the sun. Perhaps I can claim some old attachments there. Perhaps there are old designations in me that have gone unnoticed. I make the assumption that any detail in the sky, any angle of a bird's flight, or motion in a wave, any object still not wholly felt or seen, may mean an untapped source for me, as not merely an observer but a life, in as original a sense as all other lives.

I know that man, in population, in power, now influences everything. I know that there is nothing he does not have his eyes on, nothing he does not have the capacity to move or put aside, but I also know our omnipotence has not given us much confidence in and of itself. We find we not only have the means to destroy nature but our own world too. We find that our overwhelming position does not turn us into great communicators so much as bypassers. A kind of hardening and codifying of our methods and achievements seems to have detached us from the sources of life. Direct experience of the natural earth is becoming rare. Perhaps the world of nature, because of what was once one of its own familiar predators, must now have to hold its secrets more closely than ever for survival's sake.

Still, I believe, as I set out once again, that the earth is in us, come what may, and that it has more saving examples in store than we realize, or even understand. And I suspect, as I push the car up to the speed limit, that men need something more than speed to get them where they need to go.

I drive through the city, the great smoking heap of civilization, with gas in my nostrils, a roaring beside me and overhead, the human imagination and order embodied all around me as cars, planes, factories, concrete hives, miles of glass, countless lights, a huge fantasy-filled horizon spewing out poverty and grime on its fringes, belching tons of waste into the atmosphere. This order may contain power on its own, charged by what it takes and consumes, a vast greed, hardly aware of where the original fuel may have come from that fires its furnaces. But I know that wherever man took his violent path in the first place he is inextricably a part of universal energy, and there is no way out.

We have not conquered nature, any more than I have conquered myself. Life unfinished is the rule for man or trees. What I go looking for is not nature under man's control but a wider, lasting range—that which we will have to live with in order to avoid a life in isolation, that which belongs to us only when we go out to meet it.

Americans have certainly gone far since yesterday, when this continent meant an almost impenetrable shoreline confronting a few men in a wooden ship. It does seem strange that just behind all the headlong and scarcely understood exploitation of energy, the rush not to be late, the readiness to be run over, this was a rough, raw, untamed land to which the earliest voyagers came like wolves pawing gingerly around a cache of frozen meat.

Suddenly, in the age of crescendo, we seem to have jettisoned several centuries of New World history which for terror, conflict, and cliffs of human experience have never had adequate embodiment in our literature. Perhaps sometimes, when the wind is blowing from the right quarter and the surf roars, you can imagine cries of rage, distress, greed, and protests to the Almighty, but the echoes seem to be growing fainter every day. It is true that the woodlands are coming back in many areas, and that there is still a residue of farmland, of barns and the stone wall culture, gaunt and at the same time redolent of all seasons, comforting; but the pastoral strength of our recent past does not mean a great deal to us. We have an inheritance in America of leaving continuity behind before it has a further chance to develop, and in part this has been because a vast new continent gave us space to fill, and kept us going before we even knew we had to stop. It was in part a conquest by right of the conquered. In that sense, we had a close, warring relationship with the land, before a later day when it was not so much fought as covered over and ignored.

The past meant war, an all-out attack on the dark riches of a new land. In Maine and Canada, still relatively untouched by urban sprawl, evidences of their Antietams, their Verduns and their Okinawas are plain to see. The battlefields show us great areas of bare rock-bones, partly covered by alder, gray birch and goldenrod. In other regions just the powerful beauty of woods and shore is eloquent enough about what the would-be conquerors faced when they arrived.

On some of the less protected shores facing the North Atlantic great round boulders jostle each other in the surf. Stormy seas pound on upthrust blocks of rock and toss spray over the shoulders of granite sloping down to the water. High curtains of rain or impenetrable snow move across the hills above cliffs and stony coves, and the wind shears through the tunnels of the spruce. Three hundred and more years ago the dangers of the sea were commonplace for most Europeans. It was a familiar realm, in legend or reality. But what lay behind this somber, shrouded coastline, those precipitous, gray and dark green heights with plunging wave lines below them? Some men landed and made their independent way. And some were landed, like those seventeenth-century German settlers who were promised milk and honey before they left their homeland, then fleeced of their money and crowded into ships where there was often so little room and food as to result in famine, cannibalism and suicide. Aside from the actual hardship of immediately scraping into the rocky topsoil of Maine for a living, what did they feel with the weight of a colossal, still unconquered land at their backs? The unbroken forests were full of unknown dangers, and to many they presented a witch-haunted, horrifying darkness. In some parts of America the settlers laid the land completely bare to the pitiless sun simply because they hated and despised the trees, even blaming their shade for sickness and death. The trees were felled from the Atlantic to the Pacific, thousands and thousands of square miles of them, not only for the need of cleared land, building and firewood, but also because they stood in the way and had to be fought to the limit.

The American landscape rolled on ahead—forests, rivers, plains and lakes, mountains and deserts—open, grand, invigorating, sometimes menacing, stormy and wide, rich in hazards, rich in detail, and every new battle or meeting with it meant that the experience of the natural wilderness had added to our stature. When the war was won, the experience was ended, but we are still trading on its impetus. We "conquerors" will get what stature we can, though it may be spurious, from universal possession.

The land has new proprietors; and will they ever know it well enough? Will they be able to value the earth not only for its products, its man-made triumphs, but for what it is? We are not so nearly on speaking terms with nature as we used to be. Common naming, common names, are less familiar. Timberdoodles, shitepokes, ragged robins, skunk coots, wall-eyed herring and quawks are disappearing into books. How can the three-quarters of our population that lives in cities replace such terms, and all the humorous, rough, gentle, accurate acquaintance they imply? Common naming means a common recognition that numbering will never find. The object needs a person, to be personified.

The natural environment lacks the security of our once familiar speech, and we have also become less amazed, perhaps in the process of this loss. The earth no longer comes before us in a new aspect with every hidden flower and every earth-regenerating clap of thunder. We have left a great deal of awe behind us. The fact that we can alter and remake the environment almost at will has deprived us of much of our original surprise in its manifestations, even though it kicks back at us from time to time. To be a "free agent," in idea if not in fact, is to be tempted into monumental carelessness.

It is becoming rare to find communities still founded on a common experience that grew out of the land they settled in. To the north, in regions which are gradually less populated as you progress, the old ways may be easier to recapture, even to the superstitions. The harsh, dangerous, seagoing life of the New England seaboard and the Canadian Maritimes once encouraged a wealth of belief in mirages, presences and strange disappearances. Like the Indians, the local people used to believe in charms and countercharms, and they swore by stories about "forerunners," supernatural happenings that told of a coming disaster. Underneath common reality, in the air, superstitious feelings were handed down through local generations of people, almost electrically communicated.

It may be hard for a contemporary man, rid of most superstitions (if not tribal routines), to believe that places existed not long ago where ghosts were real. But when I heard a Canadian say, "Every time I see a dead person I have to wash my hands before I can eat again," I felt that I was back in the subsistence struggle and the world of the spirits.

Superficially, the north country looks as though it were just as much affected by human presence as any other place, but it still imposes a climatic rigor, a semi-isolation, with a will of its own. During my sporadic trips there I have often had a sense of primal age, held in its own right by bold, raw rock, cold, swinging seas, a silvery sky, whose force now and force behind seem to be as ready to have men relate themselves to the sky by myth and magic as any scientific progress by plotting arcs into the unknown. Nature to the south is often disguised as "vacation land." In the north it requires some attention to its own authority.

One afternoon, in the northern part of Cape Breton, I walked off a side road to look for a beaver dam up a small stream that ran through a meadow and marsh backed up by a bowl of hills. It was in early spring. The snow which lay over the forested banks on either side of the little valley was still deep. The season's air was cool and circumspect, but there were signs of a gradual release. Patches of snow were melting away in the sun in the more level and open areas along the stream, revealing last year's leaves and patches of moisture-soaking moss. Fleas, gun-metal gray, flocked over sun-warmed snow. Where the stream's rounded white covers of snow and ice were melted, the golden-brown waters rushed down, and in side pools there were water striders flicking and twitching over the surface, making little leaf-like dimples. I heard a hemlock bough jerk lightly behind me, and turned, thinking of a bird, to see only that the bough had been released from a burden. The spruce and hemlock, with their rough bark, and their needle-lattices that shaded and saved the snow on the ground, were letting it slip slowly from their branches. Below them were clumps of alder with hanging gold-tinted catkins.

The stream's cold waters poured on. In open areas the trees spired against a radiantly blue sky, and light breezes blew over the ground. A wild woodland robin screamed and fled away ahead of me. Then I saw the big paw marks of a lynx in the snow and I began to track it up the bordering banks until the drifts were too deep. On my way back I was followed by a golden-crowned kinglet which seemed to have no fear of me at all. It kept flitting over my head, flying quickly around the clearings between the trees and coming back again, expressing itself in high, thin notes all the time, a tiny olive-green bird, with light gray underparts and a stripe on its head like a flick of fire.

A little later I found a few beaver-chewed logs lying loosely over the stream, with clumps of brush fixed to them, but not the animal itself. Everything I saw, or that met me, seen or unseen, in that short walk, brought a recognition out of me, clear and positive in depth. I saw intricate alliances of crystal light in the needles of the evergreens, over snow running through sun and shade, across flowing banks and ravines, cold pools under the ice, warm ones in the sunlight, over craggy shadows, open yellow grasses, past waters mellifluous and laced with light. I thought of all the visitors here, the lynx with its silver eyes, the deer that stepped in on slender legs to drink, a snowshoe hare, or a tramping man, throughout the extremes of the seasons: a fury of flies, water roiled in flood, the massive snow. Kinglet or water strider, lynx track and catkin, the stream and its traces, the rooted trees, the little fish or migrant birds, came to this place or lived here; and all made it live, each to its chance, in the balance of chances. In this small valley was a power and surety that met all random events, all accidents, as they came on, and it was no tyranny . . . fragility, sensitivity, connectedness, were a part of it. This also meant inches, feet, acres joining thousands of miles of procedural events, an orderly provision in which every action was accepted into space. With the black, inquisitive little eyes of the kinglet glancing at me quickly, I had thought to myself that in the perfection of this place you might as well live eight minutes or eighty years. When the stars appeared at night over the hills and the spruce, everything I had seen, from point to point, in significant detail, seemed to join those flaming stations of light, as inadvertently as breath.

It may be true that we can only be taken up into the precision and wholeness of nature on occasion, often by accident, and sometimes as a result of practice, preparing ourselves for whatever openings may come. If we are only fractionally committed in the first place, that may be the best we can expect. Men go their own way, and nature's "blind" entities do not always seem to be relevant to human endeavor. We drive through valleys and rip through woods on journeys to which we can always attribute a human end, seldom stopping to ask our way of things that can obviously give no answers, except by our leave. We have our terms, as nothing else does, our own conscious ability to explain success or failure, our supernatural methods to help us command our surroundings. We pass by a nature that continues with this seemingly cool, ageless use of elements, the kinglet, the water and the moss, and to personalize them, in an age of man-centered progress or apocalypse, may seem irrelevant, even trivial.

In other words, for reasons of indifference, for reasons of self-preoccupation, for reasons of haste, men act as if they only met nature when they were ready to. But when I watched the kinglet, or the wind shake the evergreens, what did I have to start with except what was theirs to give *me*? How, also, could I know them unless we were together in a realm of knowing, unless our world was mutual? Our perception of things depends on what they are, in their essence, not on man's disposal of them. Alliances, between men, between men and nature, do not last in one-sided terms. In order to know any other part of being, I am obligated to give way. When night falls, how can I truly answer its silence but by silence? When the stars began to shine and frost settled down over the ground in Nova Scotia, and a world in unity seemed to appear before me, what did I have at my back but a dependable endurance that supported everything without exception, and no one for his arguments, or his special virtues?

2

> For the squid, whose nature is to come by night, as well as by day, I tell them I set him a candle to see his way, with which he is much delighted, or else cometh to wonder at it, as do our fresh-water fish. The other cometh also in the night but chiefly in the day, being forced by the cod that would devour him, and therefore, for fearing of coming so near the shore, is driven dry by the surge of the sea on the pebble and sands. Of these, being as good as a smelt, you may take up with a shove-net, as plentifully as you do wheat in a shovel, sufficient in three or four hours for a whole city.
> — "A Letter written to Mr. Richard Hakluyt of the Middle Temple, Containing a Report of the True State and Commodities of Newfoundland," *Hakluyt's Voyages*, 1578

I have to travel at intervals just to prove to myself that the valley with its intricate alliances or an Atlantic cover rimmed by the glory of high weather is still there, though I do not always go on my own terms. It might be better to give up the car and walk permanently, but I have my attachments. The ganglia of communications have me by the neck. Never out of reach of a newspaper, TV set, plane, electric light, telephone, or perhaps an unseen tapping device, I have a modern helplessness which often stops me before I start.

Contemporary travel has a curiously anesthetizing, self-enclosed quality. You can go several hundred miles in the wrong direction, as I once did to my embarrassment, and if you get the next flight back, not lose more than a couple of hours. The fantastic but hardly noticed speed, the dark-suited passengers reading the stock market quotations as if they were not flying over the edge of a great sea or complex landscape at all but were in a city bus—even the possibility of an unregarded death, makes travel not so much a matter of bypassing time and distance as losing track of transitions. We take our cities with us and join them together as we go. It amounts to a new kind of insularity. Speed past sound, forced immediacy, puts all the world in the same room.

Have we become so megalopolitan as to lose our innate responses to whatever distinctive part of the earth we call home? Fiddler crabs have been transported from one coast to another, with entirely different tides, or put in receptacles of still, nontidal water, and their behavior has continued to be timed exactly to the tidal rhythms of their home flats. Then, gradually, though they were as insulated from the outside as a scientist knew how to make them, they sensed the atmospheric changes around them and adjusted their reactions to the lunar periods with which such changes are rhythmically allied. Insulation, self-installed, seems to work better with us in keeping us detached from the inner rhythms and senses of this planet. We seem to have lost the kind of inner timing which makes the plant react to the changes in the season, which sends the migrant herring or salmon to find its home stream, or the tern to leave a northern coast and fly down the shores of an entire continent. We still have the tides in us of our natal blood, but I sometimes wonder whether our conscious correspondence with them has not been left behind.

After one such trip I got into my car and drove home. There was a smoky sunset on the hills, wind stirred the pines beyond the city. I saw a rare man out walking by himself in a field, and I felt that this natural, landed part of things, with all its relative speeds, from a turtle to a hawk, was not only like an old culture left behind, but that it had become fictionalized.

On the other hand neither jet nor rocket can reduce the earth's surpassing age. Perhaps they even emphasize it. One spring I flew in to Newfoundland, over the water from Cape Breton, past miles of drift ice that hugged the coast. On the approaches to the great island itself, the sunset made a blazing coppery path across ice and sea, a series of amazing spots and shines. The mountains inland from the coast were like flat-topped piles of brown earth, veined with stony streams, sometimes radiating down to ponds and lakes. It was a landscape interminably grooved and grained, and bore no resemblance to the aerial views between Boston and Washington, where you look down on a man-scarred earth, the thin, worn lip of land along the sea covered with grids made by houses and roads, smoking with the human atmosphere. I had never seen such irregularity. It was earth stress and change in relief, an old world bitter and mighty, and, as night came on, cavernously dark.

After a short spring visit, I came back in July. One late afternoon at Cape Spear, which faces the open Atlantic south of St. John's, the headlands were almost completely closed in by fog, though I could see a few kittiwakes flying close by inshore, and swinging down to fish. (The kittiwake breeds on clamorous, fog-shrouded islands off the coast, along with other seabirds, but it is a true ocean wandering gull which spends the rest of the year far at sea. Newfoundlanders call it "tickle-lace" and "lady-bird." These small gulls are pearly gray and white with sharp black on their wing tips and banded tail feathers, and when they fly over the water fishing, wing-rowing neatly and quickly, dipping and turning, they belong to the word *grace* like no other birds I ever saw.) Once a minute my ears were split by the bawling, bass note of a foghorn close by. On the short-summered land various kinds of heath were only just in bloom. There were tiny pink flowers on mountain cranberry and low-bush blueberry, white flowers on the Labrador tea. I heard the alarm note of a trim, tail-wagging water pipit as I climbed a boulder-strewn hillside full of buttercup and clover. In and out of the rocks and the wisps of blowing fog, underneath and beyond me, I felt the ancient landscape, the flow and tilt and weight of millions of years.

This coastal ground and the ground beyond it had been scoured by glaciers like no other I had seen. Some of the mountains were already eroded to the butt before the glaciers came and now looked like piles of rubble, thinly covered by vegetation. The sea's edge at the outlet of rivers and streams, or former streams, was full of the wash of loose earth and stone. Shattered slate and sandstone fell down the eroded slopes. I had been shown one high wall above a cove, whose sheer face had marks of ripples made by the sea 600 million years before. In other areas volcanic rock and sandstone were oddly juxtaposed. Without having any precise knowledge of geology, I could see enough to be deeply struck by the unimaginable stress and at the same time tidal order of earth processes—growth, fire and ruin in a mountainside, on the classic scale. We move together on a violent shore.

There was a silvery light over the great rounded boulders where the surf washed back and forth with a kind of lazy largesse. Kittiwakes showed occasionally through the fog. Then the wind changed and it began to clear toward six o'clock. A short rainbow, shaped like a horseshoe, appeared over the water. I had heard this called a "fog eater" by a Nova Scotian coming over on the ferry from Maine. "You see one of these," he said, "you feel good. It's going to clear." And as the "fog buster" (another version from Newfoundland) shone out and the curtains of fog began to lift, I could see the steady drifting by in wide and easy circles of the gulls, diving as they went, and beyond them many more making white rafts on the water's surface.

Then, in a direction where there had been nothing to be seen all afternoon, the outlines of a big, deep Newfoundland dory appeared, and in it were three fishermen casting handlines over the side. I could not help thinking of the long history behind them, of the thousand years and more, starting presumably with the Norse, that European fishermen and explorers had touched on this coast and grappled with it, with a rough acceptance of extreme endurance, through ice, fog, shipwreck, famine and drowning, of which most of us can have little conception. Hakluyt's *Voyages* speaks of the Newfoundland "Cod, which alone draweth many nations thither, and is become the most famous fishing of the world." And there is mention of the Banks off the coast where: "The Portugals, and French chiefly, have a notable trade of fishing . . . where are sometimes an hundred or more sailes of ships: who commonly beginne the fishing in Apriell, and have ended by July. That fish is large, alwayes wet, having no land neere to drie, and is called Corre fish.

"During the time of fishing, a man shall know without sounding when he is on the banke, by the incredible multitude of sea foule hovering over the same, to prey upon the offalles & garbish of fish thrown out by the fishermen, and floting upon the sea."

(Not long ago in Normandy the discontinuance of the Pardon of the Newfoundlanders was reported in the news, and another direct link, in custom and religion, between man and his earthly food seems to have been lost. This rite, also called the Pardon des Terres-Nuevas, used to be performed for Basques, Bretons or Normans from as early as the sixteenth century, and probably before that. It is recorded that the Spanish were employing experienced Breton pilots to take them to the Grand Banks in 1511. Each year the fishing boats were blessed and the townspeople made a procession to the shore before seeing their men off across the lonely, gray steppes of the Atlantic.)

And now, as if to show its own lasting continuity, the big body of a cod plunged straight up and dropped back heavily into the water, where the wind made silvery and dark patches, rainlike on the clearing surfaces of the sea. Beyond it I saw that the fishermen were pulling in dark bodies of codfish hand over hand almost continuously, throwing out their lines and quickly hauling them in again. In the middle of this display of inshore bounty, of the advantage taken of the sea's intermittent giving, a big old man in the boat saw me watching from the hillside and waved over, with a great smile on his face. A new moon appeared in the sky and a fiery red sun started to disappear behind the coastal shoulders jutting out into the sea.

There was a calm wordlessness over the water, a savage evening brightness, the presence of quick life, quick death, multitudes of fish, birds, and fishing men brought there by inexorable greed, balanced by the ages; and it was not something we ask for necessarily, as part of the acceptable world, but I took it as an offering, in answer to all need. In this exposed country, at the sea's eye, in the sea's hand, the underlying wildness, the undefiled depth could show itself. I felt that I had been profoundly welcomed there. I was at home.

The Eye of the Heart

And when he came upon a great quantity of flowers he would preach to them and invite them to praise the Lord, just as if they had been gifted with reason. So also cornfields and vineyards, stones, woods, and all the beauties of the field, fountains of waters, all of the verdure of gardens, earth and fire, air and wind would he with sincerest purity exhort to the love and willing service of God. In short he called all creatures by the name of brother, and in a surpassing manner, of which other men had no experience, he discerned the hidden things of creation with the eye of the heart, as one who had already escaped into the glorious liberty of the children of God.

—Brother Thomas of Celano, *The Lives of St. Francis of Assisi*

J GO DOWN TO THE TOWN LANDING AGAIN ON THE shore that has opened itself to me over the years and been an introduction to the earth. I hear the thunder of water, the thunder of a plane in the sky. The sun's radiance, though less direct now that summer goes, still warms the shallow seas. There is a brave honking of Canada geese over the land. Migratory birds skim along the shoaling sands. Here where there is an open balance of many worlds, I can also sense the massive interventions of mankind, our terrible amputations and distortions. But the tides change with their wonderful rhythmic grace, and life moves with them. As the tide began to ebb during the afternoon, with a simultaneous beating in and pulling back of low waves, a hundred gulls flew out from the salt marsh creek back of the beach, crying, moving back to waters now getting shallower, where they could more readily find food. It was a correspondingly rhythmic, well-timed, steady move. And so, these backings and fillings, the going and returning, ripples in sand, a roaring sunset, a gray and showery dawn welcomed everywhere. Spring followed an ice age, the tropics arrived, a new ice age will be accepted in its time. The earth-tried enormous balance puts the whir of a fin and the shock of a hurricane together, and accepts all sinewy, kinetic, visionary response, and the inner darkness of sense as men know it—and the deliverance from sense.

Nature is something I have never wholly seen before. That is more than an assumption, because I doubt that there has been a day in all my natural life that mere repetition was all that was provided me, in spite of monotony, in spite of my own readiness to sleep rather than act, or actively receive. In the second place, whatever happens to me by night or day, at whatever age, comes not altogether of my own volition. The real nature of causation is largely unknown to us. What part are we really playing in the creative universe? Behind the beauty, the savagery, the minnow, or the leaf, there is that which plays with *us* like light on a wing and is just as uncatchable.

None of us seem to get the chance to see enough in order to rightfully enlarge our lives before their end. But we have a history in us which is of the earth, and nature gives us clues to its capacity, and signs now and then of the incomparable form and passion in which we take part. I remember, when I was in Nova Scotia, heading for Newfoundland, that I passed by a woods fire on the way to the airport. It was only a small fire and the local fire department had almost managed to put it out. The men were concentrating their hose on the ground at the base of a tall spruce, the last to go. The fire shot up in a deeply roaring, devouring orange-red wave. Then it topped the tree with a final rush and fury. A one last crackling curl into the air and it was gone completely, leaving a tall, smoking black stick with naked branches behind. In a country of frequent forest fires, this was not a memorable event, but for me it provided an added, elemental statement, flung out against the background of an ancient world.

Exaggeration, so many artists say, is a necessity in expression. The wild, the mad, the hyperbolean puts the passionate point across. But we are deceived if we think that our exaggeration goes any further than in nature. Follow that fire, that wild heave of wind, the enormous cloud range on the horizon, the evenings of burning cold, mornings a cave of darkness, days with hissing snow, all expressing the inexpressible, and how far do you get? The brush has barely touched the canvas.

I do not live in a backwater, not in *this* world. This is a shore, not of a pond or marine embayment, but of the globe. Man has made it that way. You have to give us some backhanded credit for universality if only in the sense that we occupy the entire globe, and cannot leave each other alone. And not too far from me is the city I came from, which is a mystery in itself, though an often tortured, smoking, grasping one. How did the unbelievable quantity of material that makes up those vast towers ever get into the city in the first place, under the cover of darkness?

I came out of the dark mouth of the subway in late evening and watched the sky turn sulfurous above a city square. It was like an artificial sea. White and scarlet signs, fat with glass, hung overhead, and I walked past yellow caves with music jangling at their entrances, through waters of light. During the day rivets tapped up and down on steel spines, trucks fumed and ground their gears, brakes squealed, there were sounds of upheaval and crashing as walls were building up and tumbling down, and in between, those stops and silences in which heels are heard clicking on the sidewalks. The city is a storm, a place of floods, a flood of lights, of intense, competitive friends, intense loneliness. The city is a tide, though without much mathematical predictability, and what spreads out from the city and touches all the natural world is not so much a remoteness, an artificiality, as a power, even a massive kind of blindness which takes its impetus from relentless social conflict. In the city, "Know thyself" becomes "Know thy world," or take the consequences; and, theoretically, what happens to the osprey or the peregrine is out of the picture. But if you believe that true bonds in nature are not external, then our meetings with it are on the central square, or 37th Street (where I grew up), as well as on this beach being cleaned by autumn winds; it is only that our human commitment and its terminology are in dire need of extension. Perhaps we lack the images whereby to save the natural world through our own organic and moral connection with it—at the very least the old pastoral images will have to be reconstituted. This may be in the hands of science, of psychology and biology, but in order to bridge the gap between science and the general understanding, natural phenomena need to be treated as of a life to a life. Our overriding concept ought to be that in the wholeness of the living environment there can be no exclusions.

Extra-human, extra-natural terms divide us from compassion. We have a death-dealing capacity that is without parallel; and, having to a large extent disorganized the gradual, assimilated experience which bound man to place, we have thrown events not only into the hands of unpredictable change but into the unknown capacity of mankind to keep control without appalling tyranny. We are governed by our obsession with means. We have been treating the earth with a recklessness which is no tribute to human genius. The almost total poisoning of the natural environment is only being postponed by fragmentary efforts.

The great danger in a revolutionary world that takes us with it in spreading mobility, forced communication and unprecedented speed, uncertain of the outcome, is that we will take our own risks and live out our own violence as we can. In other words, we may risk the habitable earth for the sake of mere impetus. Perhaps the awareness of disaster will prevent us from bringing on our artificial ice age which could postpone spring for ten thousand years.

Perhaps we can, by conscious, continual effort, keep turning the bow aside to save the ship. We will have to try, in this one world. We have now come to the point where we meet the living earth either in terms of fundamental conflict or fundamental cooperation. All our pillaging and presumption have brought us face to face with ultimate limits. We have pushed ourselves and the rest of life on earth to a point where one step more could mean survival or extinction.

On the other hand, the revolution we are now making only increases the frustration, the greed and longing in our lives. I am still passion's slave. I still cannot fully discover why I act the way I do. I am still frightened by my human reach and its ties with human misery. I know by an experience I never conceived that I do not, and never have, lived to myself alone. And there, next to me, as the east wind blows in early fall, a season open to great migrations, are those lives, threading the air and the waters of the sea, that come out of an incomparable darkness, which is also my own. To claim a false connection from a distance would be to fall prey to a far worse fate than being born and growing old. Universal inclusion is the best and worst we will ever know. In John Donne's words, spoken in St. Paul's Cathedral: "As the Lord liveth, I would not have thee dye, but live, but dye an everlasting life, and live an everlasting death. . . ."

Off over the shoals in the bright afternoon, now that the tide has nearly ebbed and shallow waters run with schools of small fish, the gulls are flocking and dipping in, crying out in wild, shivery tones. The wind makes the green and gold marsh grasses hiss, nod and sway. The clouds over the sea look like fine filamented seaweed swaying lightly in the water. A flock of terns, lined up into the wind on the banks of the outgoing creek, suddenly fly up excitedly at nothing more than a sudden small wave, a rush of water in the current running by them. Then they fly down again, facing up the sandy slope, each in an orderly spacing with respect to the other. Those which were first to land are nearest the water and the rest take their positions above them.

The water flows by, with waves in the sky and in the season, part of the wheels of the year, and when the tide turns again it is

scarcely noticeable. Whatever instability may occur in natural circumstances, or is introduced by human agency, motion itself is
the great stability.

In the late afternoon, several hours after the tide has turned,
and the waters that run along the sloping beach are glinting with
copper and gold, I hear the sound of fish. Saltwater minnows by
the thousand, flipping at the surface, running through the grasses
just off the beach, make clicking sounds like grasshoppers in a
meadow.

Do men say that fish run without them, and that the tides ebb
and flood with an indifference? Are we, in our overwhelming responsibility as the bearers of consciousness, seekers of meaning,
without a nod or shake of the head from the universe? But nothing we can ever do is diametric to the sun. We may drive ourselves through power and confusion beyond the outer limits of
universal tolerance but the tides continue.

Perhaps this smacks of cold physics, but to share (and that is
what the natural environment needs of mankind—at the very
least an effort toward mutual accommodation) may mean that we
have to find new ways to tolerate the inescapable. After all, these
global waters are where we came from. Out of these primal
bounds and allowances the mystery of knowing emerged. Out of
this life-sea came a being that could express the incredible idea of
God in his hawk-headed heaven. Our limits and our possibilities
have not escaped their universal origin, their ties in love. Life al-
lows only so much, a certain number of seasons for any man. We
are limited, but in major terms. Cosmic participation calls for
scope. Reality circumscribes us, and at the same time not only
awareness but the experience of living takes each of us on a great
journey into space and into a profound, painful acquaintance
with the relentless standards of growth and survival; and these
are mere words compared with their potentiality. In us there is an
infinite play in depth, of reckless encounters, brave effort, hope-
less ineptitude, weakness that leads to murder and self-murder.
But this is in the order of space, where we live on one earth and
its many seas, room from which we will not soon escape.

It is strange, I think, to have survived myself. It is strange also to have come safely through terror and constriction, the tyranny of human means, the fear we have of our own attributes; but something more than getting through has brought me to this shore. Life is endured, and it also steers me. I am kept in a certain organic and spiritual frame, held in cosmic dignity even in my failure at dignity, and this is human, and natural too, as nature is the context for an inexorable discipline, in which I and the frog have our special character and our mortal ends.

Through the inescapable meetings with what we are, or what we may not be, there is all human experience for any man to know, and a way, I think, to meet the rest of life on earth. There is no discrepancy between what makes me go through the same inescapable problems as my fathers, and the vast energies that are put into the readiness of the seed, or the sending of a mouse or bird through a short hard life for the sake of its race. These necessities come out of those down-under continents where indivisible existence was generated. If nature is inside me, with its grace and inevitable demands, I can hardly deny it without excluding myself from most of earth's intentions.

This season in its flowing power is a measure of the whole earth. This putting forth of the gentle and implacable together in the realms of nature, the violet and the shark, of innocence to the ends of maturity, of rising up to send abroad, is part of world weather. And all the sacrifices made along the way are an immolation at one with all identity. Nature is life's creation, life's spending. No amount of intellectual despair, nihilism or sense of worthlessness in men can alter their basic dependence on regeneration, that which sends every beauty, each excellence, in each detail, into everlasting fire. We will not survive without the seeds of grass, and the mass of minute animals twitching in the waters of the sea. We belong to these multitudes; all that is lacking is our commitment and our praise.

It may be that nothing is predictable but the precarious nature of human history; and this may be what the universe provides for us. From these endless conflicts, that tear us apart and throw us together, future standards of cooperation may be born, even out of a need that seems pitiless. We change after all, out of deeper, universal changes, unseen fruitions, the coalescing of elements out of disparate parts; our acts materialize out of an ageless adventuring. But our place in this universal equilibrium needs realistic allegiance, and the exercise of sight, in all humility. In the face of perverse human will, armed with superhuman powers of destruction, we have little time to wait.

How can we be optimistic about a technology that merely speeds us beyond our inherited capacity, in terms of genetics and physical attributes, to survive on earth? We cannot change the environment past the degree to which we are able to change ourselves. We cannot adapt to continual alterations of our own making that destroy our sources in natural energy and diversity. It is already obvious that technological changes are at variance with our ability to keep up with them, that we are falling into violence, mistrust and confusion. We are in no position to boast about a manipulated future. The pride we need is something else.

A viable future needs its champions, those who will defend not only their own self-interest but function and belonging in nature. The future can be an entirety or a fragment. Divisions can breed divisions, as enemies breed enemies, until at last the universe will restore unity in what might be a catastrophic way.

Man against the natural world is man against himself. In spite of our rational endowments, we are now acting toward our earth environment with the random ferocity of bluefish attacking a school of herring. The equivalent greed in nature at least acts on behalf of fecundity. What is eaten up is a measure of reproduction, but we, with our limited and short-term means, are unable, all by ourselves, to make up what we consume.

Somewhere along the line, the demand exceeds the supply. Starvation and violence occur. This happens in human society. It is happening with respect to man's relationship with nature, now; and so long as we treat nature as a commodity instead of a life-and-death companion, the worse things will be.

As an old countryman in Vermont once said to me: "Ain't any of us know too much." That seems to be the soundest philosophical position a man could take, but, as he was talking about himself and a college professor at the time, I think he was really saying that each man has his validity. Each man has his democratic validity on behalf of his world, and how much he can speak, live and act in terms of its potentiality, but that world in isolation from nature is a world devalued. We cannot live in the full use of earth and earth's complex, expectant, vast experience and deny it at the same time. Worth is defined by participation.

The problem of man's undertaking his own evolution, the risks involved in human achievement and assumption, are not the whole point. The whole point is that we depend ultimately on an everlasting drive for unity whose wellsprings we did not create but can only draw upon or try to re-create. The whole point is the human commitment of human experience to universal nature and all its lives. We cannot divide one from the other, or neither will be sustained. When I look out on the rippling landscape and breathe the lasting air, walking in the light of earth and sun, I am a central part of the globe, humanly claimed, and I also depend on a reservoir of knowing and being forever incomplete. Buried deeper than our microscopes can see, there is a well of flux and motion, incomparable elaboration, a consuming joined with a proliferation, out of which all things are born, are required to be born.

So I go down to the shore again, not only as the old clammers did, day after day, with their own company, but in sight of our crowded world. There is no escaping from our fierce ventures, win, lose or draw, no escaping from resurrections, not only of the seed but human trouble, risk and brutality. These sands not only bear lone walkers and the tide, but all mankind. At the same time, we are also what we choose, by cultivation and association. The natural horizon has in it something that is rarer than sight. It is the source not only of taking and fear but of an unlimited potential beyond the survival of man or fish. We have to keep up with that potential not only in terms of our assumptions about it but in terms of how much we can cooperate, discriminate and cherish.

The earth insists on its intentions, however men may interpret them. Unity and use is what it asks. And use is what may be missing. To the degree that we become disassociated by our power to exploit from what it is we exploit, so our senses will become atrophied, our skills diminished, our earth-related vision hopelessly dimmed. Without a new equation in which natural and human need are together in eternal process and identity, we may be lost to one another, and starved of our inheritance.

from

The Undiscovered Country

(1981)

The New World

". . . a plain wilderness as God first made it."

—Captain John Smith

J WAS AN OUTSIDER, COMING BACK TO A COUNTRY I had been born in but had hardly been given enough time to know. So were we all, displaced persons after a period of war that had engaged the entire globe. It had been an apocalyptic separation from the sun and rain, from all the timeless rhythms that brought back the birds and the sweet spring colors on the trees, that kept the low waves rippling along the shore.

One day I watched the sun setting over the water and listened to the wailing gulls, with no sense that having moved to this place I was really planted anywhere. I felt permanently uprooted, the subject of a civilization that had discovered how to circumnavigate the earth in an instant and almost how to circumvent all the exactions of nature. We had learned how to blast our way through life and death, although we seemed to have very little idea of how to deal with the consequences. I was stranded on the beach, the victim of an age that consumed its own history, part of the tidal wrack and litter flung in from all points of the compass. Despair took me. I flapped on the sands like a fish out of water. "Hold on. Help is not coming."

Who was I? Where did I live? One night I dreamt that the house we had newly built, perched on an inland ridge overlooking Cape Cod Bay, was floating out in the middle of the ocean like a raft, with storm waves breaking over it, and the floor leaking. All the new highways then being constructed did not seem to lead me anywhere, but confined me to islands between them, waiting to hitch a ride. The seasons might have been reduced to unseen intervals, dates on a mechanical calendar. How and where should I start again, facing this monotonous, windswept plain, with no guidance? The sea was wonderfully indifferent to my complaints.

One cold and windy day, I stood on the wharf at Provincetown watching a dragger unload its catch. As the crew sorted out and cleaned the cold, slippery bodies of cod, haddock, and flounder, their hands were meat red. The white fish skeletons were the leavings of a vaster appetite than even fishermen knew, and the gulls, practiced for ages in this kind of trade, were wheeling and crying overhead. So it had been for thousands of years: the original exercise, the inescapable condition. And although our age seemed to have cast itself out beyond all moorings, this was where the New World came into view again.

From where we lived, our eyes swept down over the tops of oaks and pitch pines until they met the circle of the bay, a kind of great bowl of seawater investing the contours of the land. At low tide, sandy flats extended for nearly a mile out toward the last retreat of the waves. It was a wide, elastic range exposed to all the weather, every extreme of temperature and condition throughout the year. The watery shallows swept across tan-colored sands covered by ripples made by wavelets during the advance and retreat of the tides. Some sections were made up of a mosaic of short, curling wavelike forms, and others had long, fluted, undulating avenues crossed here and there by bird tracks. Everything suggested travel, sweeping away, sweeping back in again. The waters pulled outward toward the depths, and, as part of a global exercise, periodically turned to rise toward the shore.

When I walked out over the flats, to stay there at times for as long as several hours before the tide turned and sent me inland again, the life forms schooling or twitching in the depths beyond were not only hidden. I had very few names to give them. And the endless tracks over the sand, the innumerable little holes, the castings, and the debris of weed and shells with the many lives that attached themselves to it belonged to another kingdom I had only begun to be aware of. It was a first opening into original space. In the sense that I was largely ignorant of what to call its occupants, it was a mystery. On the other hand, I saw that it was also ours, the neglected space in ourselves.

When you stand on the beach, you can see above five and a half miles out to the horizon, before the round world seems to drop off. On ocean voyages, it is a matter of moving over the earth's curve, checking your course as you go. Before I became aware of these facts, I remember traveling to England on a small liner at the age of seven. I remember an endless range of waves, rocking in deep green, stomach-sinking troughs; I saw rolling plains of ebony, lead, quicksilver, gold, and jade, swelling and heaving under the sky. Now and then I caught sight of a roving seabird; now and then a roving rain lanced down through the cloud countries overhead. I sensed that ocean travel, all the way around the world, meant a moving-on-forever, over the backs and flanks of the waves, up and down, not lost, but out the other side—an outward passage such as a child could take for granted.

So, in this country, by the sea, I looked to that other side again, as if I could leap all the intervening years and accept the first, nameless condition where death and life are held in one. This oceanic anonymity had called forth fear since the world began, but it reached for me. And as I followed the flats out, jumping their ribs and lanes, I felt they might lead me to any number of countries I had never known before.

The tide was the framework that governed the shorebirds, crabs, gulls and clammers, and other people I met out there meandering, circling in the right proportion, as if to discover and be discovered. We could not escape it. All the same, in spite of their recurring, accurate rhythms, tides crossed time. They certainly had only a passing connection with my watch, which was geared to the great business of the human world, and they ignored the modern obsession with being in such a rush—to what end? I could see that if you wanted to understand the action of the tides you probably had to start by slowing time down, so that an hour became a day, a day a century. So I kept watching those graceful, inexorable turnings. On the incoming tide, I stood in the water as it began to trickle in, with bubbles and foam on the tidal lips, a filmy sheet transporting fine grains of sand and light debris, running between the ripple marks that braided the sands. As the water deepened, small bunches of rockweed attached to isolated rocks and stones began to lift their golden skirts, and thin, green ribbons of eelgrass floated and streamed like weather vanes in the direction of the shore. These great repetitions gave me another lease. They opened life to the enigma of beginnings. What was the real power, under our global pretensions, that ran the year?

Wandering, over the sands and inland across the bubbling marshes, and into the woods and thickets, became a way of seeing. "Man has but a dim light in him," says St. Augustine; "let him walk, lest darkness overtake him." But only to walk in a straight line, even for Christian reasons, is not necessarily the best way to travel. Fish, gulls, and weather circle on, in the endless process of becoming, and through that motion we discover the unexpected, which we might otherwise pass by.

My new neighborhood was not just the countryside, which our society sees with dominating eyes and determines to change for its own good, but a land, or lands, of the universe, peopled by lives that came to the present out of unrecorded time. Out on the flats, and no less inshore, I could expose myself to currents of unfailing energy, while light and water kept flowing past, and feel a wealth of other senses moving with me. Every life was taking advantage of its time. In learning to recognize these members of a greater community, not only by their labels, as objects of natural history, but for their connections with myself, I started to make some progress. I pushed out the boundaries that had confined me, and it began to be an open world again.

Homing

WITH AN ASSURANCE THAT CAME OUT OF unending exchanges with space, the alewives, the bird migrants, even the local trees that swayed and changed with the rhythms of continental weather, would ask me, as the seasonal tides went by, if I had learned where I was, and I had to answer: "Not yet." My sense of location was still at a rudimentary stage, and I might have lost all confidence in improving it if I had not decided, after another restless period, that it was better to stay put than to run off. The twentieth-century traveler does not soon come home to roost.

Certainly, if I had paid too much attention to what the economy said about the land I moved to, I would not have stayed there very long in any case. First, it was only an abandoned woodlot, full of scrub trees, and worth only twenty-five dollars an acre at best, and years later when the real-estate market and the developers began to take hold it had turned into a potentially profitable investment, which might have kept my family secure somewhere else for the rest of their lives. Either way, it had a cash exchange value that never indicated it was worth living in for its own sake, or even tell me where it was except on a map which ignored the landmarks. Maps, it occurred to me, could not be read by the real pathfinders in this region. That alewives should migrate from some unknown distance at sea to a narrow waterway like Stony Brook was one of its best possible identifications. I wondered if any of us cared about it to the extent that they did. And if a pitch pine found Cape Cod to its liking, or a white pine was such an ancient believer in New Hampshire that its progeny sprang up in the myriads as soon as we had abandoned an old pasture, then we ought to be consulting them about home territory. We had moved to a country that was constantly rediscovered and claimed by beings with universal guidelines. The one thing they could never do was devalue the place they lived in or returned to. That would surely mean the obliteration of their lives and their directional knowledge.

In a world that tells you where is everywhere, it is no simple matter to get your bearings. Although I still had a few human neighbors who were sticking it out and seemed to know the points of the compass, I was not at all sure that they would be able to hang on long enough to supply the rest of us with guidance, and as it turned out, they hardly managed. Yet the fish and songbirds came in from great distances, the mayflower found the appropriate place by old paths and abandoned wagon tracks to spread its leaves and hug the ground, and the sharp, pointed beach grass held down the dunes with flexibility and pride, making windblown compasses on the sand.

That same science which could send a camera off to take pictures of Mars, and, later, Saturn, millions of miles away, also told me that a mere beach flea was capable of performing some amazing feats in its own right. There is a little pearly-white creature that lives on the beaches feeding off piles of rotting seaweed, and its name is *Talorchestia megalopthalma*, for its white, protruding eyes. This beach hopper has to live in a humid environment, because though it lives out of water it still has gills. So it feeds at night, to avoid drying out, and burrows in the sand of the upper beach during the day, a hole it abandons to dig another the following night. The eyes are apparently used to ascertain the altitude of the sun, the place of polarization of light in the sky, and the position of the moon. This creature, with its odd, sideways hop, can leap fifty times its own length, which seems to make it a champion among animals. All of which is scarcely an achievement of mind, but it is of such embodied genius that the earth's progress is measured. I could not help being impressed by whatever oriented that little animal, whose house was a temporary hole in the sand, to reference points far beyond its immediate horizon.

You have to suppose, with or without much knowledge, that we don't attach ourselves to a place merely to get away from another one. While human culture seems to be acquiring the role of a substitute for nature, I suspect we also learn from whatever reaches are left inside us to match the earth's, and whatever of its sensual messages we innately receive. Otherwise, why should we roll in the first snow, or rejoice all over again at being visited by the fragile, white blossoms of the shad blow in early spring? Have we not experienced them before?

The first week my wife and I moved in to our newly built house a flock of geese greeted us by flying past the window during a snowstorm, and for some years deer would step out in the late afternoon to browse in a field not fifty yards from the door. In the growing springtime the tender oak leaves hung before us in all their light and shimmering curtains of pink and silvery greens, and I knew scarcely the first thing about their ecology. In fact, when I first started reading about that new discipline, the idea that each life was so aptly fitted to its environment was a little difficult for me. Influenced by a world flung out in all directions, I must have had the notion that anything might be anywhere. Still, I sensed that we were in the right place when we finally moved in, like those alewife fingerlings that head out to saltwater from the outlet of the ponds they were hatched in. They have never seen the sea before, but its image is in them.

I could now watch the passing weather touch and define the place I lived in. I could reassure myself that we had built at a centrifugal point, which migrants from hundreds or thousands of miles away flew in and identified. I could begin to see that the common forms around me, such as the countless blades of grass, the geometrically distributed leaves on a tree, the barnacles flicking out their feathery feet down by the shore, were displaying the great co-equality of life. They acted as receivers of the sun and of global currents in the waters and the atmosphere, each a reflection of surpassing complexity. Every life that touches on another, or becomes part of another, keeps the earth's fluidity in being.

To locate ourselves, we needed to be located. If the warblers failed to arrive in May, how would we recognize our station between the continents? When we left home we could quickly join the highways and airlines of the world. They had succeeded, along with all forms of modern communication, in making a good deal of local, which is to say connected, travel unnecessary. Despite the telephone, which crossed many voids, there were areas between us and our neighbors, near or far, which we no longer needed to explore, because they were so easily and quickly passed. This also amounted to a loss of local hospitality, in terms of people who could help you on your way and give you directions.

Yet those "compulsive" birds and fish, like the ever moving and changing clouds, kept homing in, roaming and circling, to turn the land and its waters into a center for universal travel. I had to inquire why it was that many of these other forms of life still knew their way across the surface of the globe through such an amazing variety of sensate abilities, while we who were supposed, by all accounts, to share in life's multicellular, neurophysiological connections, and were long-distance fliers into the bargain, seemed to be losing that innate sense of where the earth's great headings were. It would seem that the intellect that probed these matters was in need of more companions.

A phoebe showed up from South America, wagging its tail, pretty much on time by comparison with the year before, and seemed to say, in its dry little voice: "Here am I, ready to nest in your eaves. Let me stay." And I felt that any fool would who knew how much we stood in need of directions from such a reliable partner.

As time went on, I learned to recognize the terns and plovers, the yellowlegs, the sandpipers and songbirds, when they came in off the flyways and sea-lanes of the continent during the spring, while the wintering eiders and brant geese flew away to northern breeding grounds. Some passed through, while others stayed, taking part in a dynamic employment of the rangers of land and sea. Many shore dwellers knew tidal time as intimately as we know night and day, and they knew sidereal and sun time and could find their way accordingly. The long-distance migrants could take advantage of landmarks, ocean currents, and the wind, and they were able to use information about the earth's magnetic field. They carried earth's directions in them, ancestrally, genetically. Young sooty terns fledged in the Dry Tortugas off the southern tip of Florida migrated in their first autumn all the way across the South Atlantic to the Gulf of Guinea in Africa, which they had never seen before. Nor did they have the benefit of adult leadership, since the adults left their breeding grounds after nesting but appeared to go no farther than the Gulf of Mexico. The young did not fly directly. The route they took was apparently 20 percent longer than that which could be traced on a direct line across the Atlantic, and it was the most favorable one, facing them with less resistance from prevailing winds.

This inherited sense of direction plus the native ability to fly great distances was not a random business but was tied in with the fact that populations had to be homogeneous but dispersed at the same time, consistent with the breadth of the ocean and the periodic nature of its food supply. Still, it seemed astonishing and exciting that a young bird, only a few months old, could take off across the Atlantic without any prior knowledge of where to go, a kind of ancestral daring in nature to which we were only half-awake. Was it right to call them limited because their journeys were only unconsciously motivated? To say that human beings needed consciousness to survive while birds did not seemed to put their use of the unconscious on a more accomplished level than ours in some respects, or to make us more wholly conscious than we seemed to be.

The green turtle could find its way from the coast of Brazil to tiny Ascension Island in the middle of the Atlantic, 1,200 miles away, where they nested. Said Archie Carr in his book *So Excellent a Fishe*: ". . . it really seems impossible that turtles or terns could ever gather at Ascension—and yet they do." Take into account the theory of celestial navigation as it might apply to turtles, or of inertial-sense dead reckoning, or piloting with landmarks unknown to us, or response to the Coriolis force, and then logically knock each of them out, as he did, and you were left with the irreducible fact that either all these factors were involved or that there was some sense in them that we knew nothing about. The great mystery in terns or turtles was their inner synchronization with the changing conditions and ranges of the planet. That may be why some of us, still circling, backtracking, confused by our own directives, might be envious of them.

What did these consistent periods of arrival mean, as I began to note them down in the local phoebes and swallows? Nothing fixed, in a particularly useful sense. (We like it that way, but may be the poorer for it. Besides, the swallows of Capistrano were late last year.) Migrations usually came in waves, and those that were "on time" might be only the vanguard of more to follow. They might be pioneers who were more adept at arriving when expected because they had done it before, which certainly seemed true of the alewives. Many migrants were lost along the way. Many were thrown off course by storms, or moved in the wrong direction by contrary winds, or, if they were fish, by ocean currents. Migration implies searching, or even hundreds of miles of drifting, for some marine species, as much as a fixed and conscious directional movement from one place to another, though some migrants, particularly birds, could be amazingly sure and direct.

Some of this I learned through observation, and more still through natural history and popular science. But it was not only the coordination of these animals with earth's conditions that lifted me beyond the facts, but also their often mysterious affinity with its elemental reaches, like an arctic tern traveling up to twenty thousand miles a year between the Arctic and the Antarctic, a bird that experienced more daylight than any other creature on earth; it was a bird of light, engaged in an ancestral practice that challenged the planet.

On a whole-earth scale, the timing of these migrations was headed for timelessness. I had been too long confined to dates. (Would I never swing off the undeniable security of the calendar?) Days, on the other hand, days in space, days under the sun, days and nights, shadow and light, forever passing over us, trying out, were the measure an unemployed migrant might be looking for. The need to seek and be centered was as vast as geologic time. And all factors came together on some day in early spring when I heard the high, sharp whistles of a yellowlegs along the shore, announcing its arrival from the southern hemisphere. What could a poor calendar do in the face of that? The bird came in and set me free again.

In part because I was none too practiced in finding my way, easily lost one morning only a few hundred yards offshore when the fog suddenly rolled in, and none too sure of my bearings when I strayed too far from the asphalt, I knew we had much to learn from these explorers, since explore they did. If they were "simple," then so was I. You could doubt, even if we eventually discovered the precise mechanism through which birds found their way, whether we would be able to exploit it, as one account suggested, for our own purposes. By the time we got to the point that we needed some computerized device borrowed from pigeons to tell us how to get to the home loft, it might be too late anyway. Our brains would have lost connection with our legs.

It could be said that we were turning into perpetual migrants with no recognizable place to go to, continually exchanging houses and land, so that Cape Cod could be the same flat, insulated place we were trying to make of Arizona. All life explores its environment, but we seemed to be doing it to a fare-thee-well. I suspected that we needed to return to places we had long since forgotten, such as those the fishes knew.

In response to inner command, not only baby fish or sea turtles but also human beings might still have a sense of the way to head when faced with unknown waters, but we had lost faith in it. Perhaps we were only neglecting directions we felt we no longer needed. Still there was a residue of old seas in us. It stemmed from an ancient part of our natures that we were a little afraid and turned a little wild when watching hordes of fish move inland, or saw the unfolding of a leaf as a new event, off at the edges of experience, or felt the diving of a young seabird from its breeding cliffs for the first time as uncanny in its depth. Nothing was yet found.

I stood on a cliff above the open sea and felt that there was something of me running through its currents and its eddies. I watched continual explosions and disappearances taking place in those rolling waters threaded by sunlight, where unseen legions of fish were roaming, muscularly vibrating under the surface. At times, from a boat offshore I had seen long windrows of foam where bait fish were being chased to the surface, firing the waters with their motion.

It was over the offshore waters too that the white gannets with their six-foot wingspread wheeled from high in the air and then pitched in, sending up jets of spray. Those strikes, those recognitions, went on all around me, and though I had traveled far and wide myself I had hardly begun to recognize them; but they come back, if we are on hand to receive them, repeating their directives for our benefit.

There was, for example, the reappearance of my turtle. As a boy, with the wish in me to capture, I kept a painted turtle in a pen, and it surprised me by laying eggs, thus revealing a secret identity. The eggs were eaten by some marauder, though I had desperately wanted to see them hatch out, and later on the turtle died of unknown causes. I suspect it had something to do with mismanaged captivity. I gave it a formal burial under a big sugar maple that stood over a rock wall. I also carved my initials and the date on the plastron, or undershell, of another one. I can still feel the black, low, shiny-smooth, hemispheric shell, like a water-worn stone, and the little black legs with clawed feet that felt as soft as the pads on a puppy. Red-orange, yellow, and black are first colors for me. Then, many, many years later, with all kinds of human displacements and holocausts in between, I met it again as it ambled slowly across the grass out in front of that same tree where I had buried its compatriot. And I thanked the turtle as an old friend, not only for the pleasure of meeting it again, but for bringing me back into one of those mutual, lasting circles never stopped by the passage of time. It was like another lease, smelling of apple blossoms in the spring, the way they were and would always be.

Though I had a late start in learning my directions from the life around me, the lesson of the turtles was reassuring. They were educators who knew how to take their time. Someone once carved their Cape Cod initials on the shell of a brown and black and yellow box turtle I met while it was peering up and moving slowly ahead through fallen leaves, and so I found it to be twenty years short of the century mark.

That box turtles did not travel more than a few hundred yards or a quarter of a mile from their home territory did not mean that they lacked a deep sense of location. When displaced, which happened when the ignorant and innocent took them away from their native areas to city apartments, they were completely disoriented. So I was grateful that we had box turtles around us, with their scraggy yellow necks and the reassuringly antediluvian look in their little eyes, to help place us, or, for that matter, advise us to be satisfied with where we found ourselves.

We needed one kind of turtle to tell us how to cross time in one place, as well as another who was an expert in crossing the seas. This homing business ought not to be wholly entrusted to human beings with nothing more than mechanisms to deal with it. It ought to be left to the professionals, such as turtles, frogs, toads, and salamanders, as well as birds who, in the art of wings, could come and go over thousands of miles. A study of California newts by Victor Twitty—*Of Scientists and Salamanders*—showed that when displaced from their home creek they returned to it, through forests and gullies and over a mountain ridge a thousand feet high. This was their breeding stream. On the other hand, since some of the males captured along the way showed no signs at all of sexual development associated with impending breeding activity, it seems that their ability to home in in such an impressive way had more to do with the right place to live than the right place to breed.

Toads have returned to breed in ponds that have been destroyed by road building. All landmarks were wiped out, and still they possessed their wonderful sense of where home was, or ought to be, in a featureless new landscape.

The homing instinct in these creatures of slow travel was invisible to us, and we did not seem to get close enough with the kind of biological tampering that suppressed their hearing, their sight, or sense of smell. Could we not ask the same kind of investigative question of ourselves? If we were still capable of homing in, after having strayed so far away, it might very well prove to be an attribute which was essential to our future; and we would do well to start practicing the art; though if I were sufficiently relaxed about finding my own way, or not losing it, I might not trouble myself about such things, any more than an experienced fisherman does who steers his way unerringly through fog to his home channel. If toads retained an image in their heads of where a central place was even after it had disappeared, a similar faculty could be useful to us who had erased so many landscapes at will.

We needed a whole earth and a whole sea to find out where we were and dance to its measure, either with the wonderfully swift and graceful style of a tern, or the gait of a turtle, but it should not be too hard to find if everything around us embodied it. Even the common periwinkle down by the shore could claim a kind of global conquest, taking its own good time, like a box turtle. One early spring I found innumerable black specks in the wet sand of the beach. With a hand lens, I could see the round forms of these snails, each not much larger than the wet, pearly quartz grains that surrounded them. The cohesive, rounded surfaces of these grains seemed to give the tiny creatures a temporary medium for growth, before they were large enough to separate and start their slow tracking along the edge of the tidal shore.

The edible periwinkle was not an original native of America but an immigrant like the rest of us. It evidently came over with the Norsemen in their long boats to Newfoundland many centuries ago, but did not cross the Gulf of St. Lawrence to Nova Scotia until 1850. After that it made steady progress, to New Brunswick in 1860, then Portland, Maine, where it was discovered in 1870, and New Haven, Connecticut, in 1879. It had reached the prodigal resort of Atlantic City by 1892, and finally got down to Cape May in 1928. The periwinkle is now found as far south as Chesapeake Bay. So this dark-shelled creature, with its slow roll and two black antennae pointing forward, finally rounded a vast stretch of the North Atlantic for as far as it seemed useful to go.

Symbolically the migrants are also in the stars, sliding across the waters of the sky, traveling past each other, moving on great circles the way the periwinkle did. They made up a heaven of directions for ancient civilizations, extensions of human realities. The Toltecs of Mexico wore a snail shell on their heads. The shell of a snail was an enclosure like a house that held a life inside, and also symbolized birth as the insignia of the moon god. The moon itself was connected with water in the minds of the people, and its hieroglyph was a water vessel. The Mexicans associated the moon's blue light with turquoise. It was also a prototype of growth, and of change in the weather. Even now, if you walk down to the shore and watch the shining moon reflected on the waters, that magic symbolism seems as appropriate as what can be seen through the accurate eye of a telescope. And those who finally landed on the moon to report that it was a pitted wasteland which looked like a "dirty beach" did not alter its regality.

The shell, matter enclosing spirit, was the insignia of the great god Quetzalcoatl, who disappeared in the direction of the East and the land of the dawning sun. It was said that he would one day return like the rising of the morning star in the East, where the moon, with which the star became mythically unified, had died, and would be reborn in the form of a slender crescent tilted in the sky.

The snail was identified with the winter solstice, and the slow-moving turtle with the summer solstice, at a time when the sun seems to stand still. The Mayan month Kayab, when the summer solstice occurs, showed the face of a turtle. The Mayan name for them is *ac*, or *coc ac*. The sea turtles, loggerheads, which are sometimes found stranded and frozen on our shores, and the greens, are also represented on their temple buildings, and when you look up at the constellation of Gemini you can see three stars, which they saw as having the form of a turtle.

Starry nights, moonlit nights, with the sea breathing in the distance, its tremendous gravity poised beyond us, its waves belting the shore. If I know that Cancer the crab scuttles across the tidal flats to its designated part of the sky; if I know Pisces the fish swims off light-years away, I too can follow, from one home to another. To be head-taut with the stars around you, foot secure on soil and stone, to know your direction and return through outer signs, is as new as it is ancient. We are still people of the planet, with all its original directions waiting in our being.

The Prodigal Style

THE SHORT LIFE OF A SHREW OR A CHIPMUNK, the ephemeral lives of the insects, the long life span of a human being, which tempts us to lengthen it and conquer fate, are only intervals, punctuations of an immense passage. The miseries and accidents we meet have an intensity that often fools us into thinking we have never lived. The laws of survival are harsh, and at the same time the lives that practice them are moved toward the open ends, the outcomes, spring risings in the sea. We inherit a sense from nature that regeneration never stops for mortality. Otherwise, why do none of us, in spite of everything, really think we are going to die? Immortality lies buried in our thoughts.

Cheating finality, the light flows and dances across the tablelands of the tides, where the gulls hover on the wind. The rushing, rolling, realigning waters work their way back in, and then withdraw. Under bold blue skies, or gathering and shifting clouds, the coastal waters carry and distribute their probing lives.

Flowers responding to light, barnacles flicking out their feathery appendages, fish rising to the surface, or butterflies lazily waving their wings embody the great, volatile transformations of the world around them. The hurricane is in the flower. Subtle changes in light govern a starfish or a bird. Alterations in pressure have immediate effects on the sense organs of a shrimp. The fireflies that bob along through a summer night, or those planktonic creatures that produce a similar bioluminescence in seawater, embody an extraordinary magnitude of effect. In fact, the sensitivity of living things in response to their surrounding environment is nothing short of miraculous. The secret of ultimate power that we sense in living responses and in the changing wheel of the year is what the human race has been playing with, so as to endanger the planet. We deal in nonreturnable risks. You wonder, since we can scarcely know how to disentangle the processes of our own thought, let alone solve the mysterious spontaneity of life, how we are ever to know enough so as to survive our own acts. Does the innocent warbler have more experience in the matter than we do?

Equating ourselves with living things that have such a close affinity to this prodigal and at the same time fragile and acutely sentient style is not, in Robert Frost's phrase, to institute "downward comparisons." The crucible of light, earth, and water ennobles us all, and it does not seem to matter that neither the average person nor science is able to catch up.

As William Blake put it, should there not be "senses unknown" in the living universe, trial approaches unexplored, unsuspected energies, conjunctions unheard-of, forever and ever, "trees, beasts and birds unknown: Unknown, not unperceived, spread in the infinite microscope"?

Late one winter day as it verged into early spring, I watched one of those quick-moving weather fronts that have the kind of fire in them that seems to need a special quality or state of the atmosphere to set it off. The temperature had dropped to twenty degrees the night before. During the day, the wind blew strong from the southwest, beating against the rollers coming in from the open Atlantic and breaking on the outer shore, so that their great manes plumed up and sprayed away. By late afternoon the temperature had started to plummet again and the wind blew from the north, while fast-running clouds let down showers of snow and sleet.

The bay waters to the north were violently roughed up and studded with whitecaps. Waves tumbled, rocked, and splashed along the shore. Standing at a distance, I could see their white shapes heaving just above the far rims of the salt marsh, where the gulls seemed to be flinging across the sand dunes, making low arcs in their leaping. The grasses tossed and swayed, and they carried a fire on their blade which they caught from the sunset. The sun's western reaches were of a golden salmon color, of a metallic brilliance, making a deep, pure gash in the sky. Overland the running clouds were pink as flamingos, gray as a mole. The whole sky in its freezing beauty crossed all known boundaries, leaping like the gulls from one sea to another. This was light I was unable to catch or see, integral with a motion I could only conceive of, part of the incredible speed of planetary bodies, a beauty made of an infinity of variables. But it is of such a furious unity that we, a feather, or a leaf are made, no matter how far we stray.

What any region has to have to ensure its stability are these practitioners of alliance. What are the north woods without a wolf? was the question Aldo Leopold asked. Having exterminated the wolves in the northeast, we think we are managing very well without them, but somewhere along the line eradication has its vanishing point and terrible logic, not only for the plants and animals that disappear but also for the places they inhabit and define.

What would our woodlands be without ruffed grouse? One flew into the window and broke its neck. After due deliberation, we plucked, roasted, and ate it, a consecrated host, made of sunlight and trees. The brown back of a male grouse is flecked with gold points. The wings and tail feathers are of a warm orange to reddish brown, blends of simmering light. When the bird thunders up and makes a wide circle through the trees, you can see the banded tail as a signature of gravity with respect to the leafy ground from which it just shot up. Its feathers are a great art of woodland slopes and hollows, the triangulation of trees, their shadows and fallen branches, and nothing but the woods themselves could tell you the secret of their making.

I will never forget the plumage and coloring of the arctic loon I once saw on a June trip to Hudson's Bay. Thin, cold air rode off the waters along the primevally rocky shores while bands of clouds, the color of coal smoke, drifted slowly over the ice floes. In the light of the icy waters the stout-bodied loons that were swimming there showed a glow on their silvery heads at a distance, an electric bloom, and there were white stripes descending wavelike down their dark necks, while their broad, black backs carried white markings like veins of quartz or ivory teeth.

A feather is a global recognition point; its wearers take earth's various surfaces upon themselves. In their art you can see the perfect meeting between light and air. The glossy feather I just picked up off the ground fell from a crow, and it is pure black on the broad side of the shaft, bluish, as seen in full light, on the narrow. A blue jay's feather is iridescent, the result of a structure that reflects the light. They are intensely visible constructions for races that depend much on visibility during display or in finding each other over open distances, as gulls do. They are also a matter of life and death, in concealment for themselves or in hiding their young.

Feathers are a supreme craft, straying off into the realm of incalculable genius. Who would think of putting those scarlet spots on the tip of a waxwing's primary feathers, or adding a halo to an arctic loon? The contour of a feather and its lightness are made for the flow and stress of the atmosphere. Its colors, sometimes drab and nondescript, often highly elegant and subtly shaded, are suited to the earth's variety.

We make blends of color, of course, and find endless uses for it, whereas birds are unable to change their uniforms. Perhaps I am more flexible and have a greater freedom of choice, up to the point, at least, where I face a traffic signal. But I share reactions to color with other animals out of an interior eye that was never self-originated. As I walk across the salt marsh again, passing through last year's dead cattail stalks and the new green shoots, a redwing not far from me suddenly spreads his shoulders and puffs out the chevron patches on its wing. The flashing red line with its white border stands out like a sunset low on the water, producing a sudden reaction in me. I throw back my own shoulders for a second in time. This is the color red, meant, like fire, to produce an unqualified response in any color-conscious creature capable of it.

Red goes deeper still. Being primitive as well as civilized, I look at the leaf surfaces next to me, seeing the red veins in a pale green leaf, then watching a tiny red mite crawling down across them, as one pulsing vein to another. One night I had a dream in which I said: "If I am part of East and West, I go down as the sun goes down." I go down, or rise, with the color red, the primordial one, fire and blood in the sky and the waters of the sea. Through that fundamental color, with all the feelings of glory or disaster it can summon up, we share with a mite or a redwing.

If the human eye sees "only" 15,000 tints out of a range that extends farther than that for some other eyes, if a fish is so much a part of its waters that it often seems to swim through them as one reflection to another, if the blue jay's feathers are only blue, lavender, and iridescent because of the way they refract the light, being in fact brown, then what we see in them are magical adaptations achieved through infinities of choice. The earth takes care of the truth in sight.

One day a fine, wild wind such as we get in spring and fall came in out of the North, with the sun shining through drifting clouds along the white and blue surf so that it blazed, primarily with an amalgam of gold and silver, but with any number of mercurial colors as well, and I thought of fish again. Where the broad reach of the thrashed waves lay directly under the rays of the sun, from my relative perspective, the light in each section like the schools that roamed under such waters all over the world, was supreme, unalloyed, impossible to adulterate, dim, or tarnish, and the mere expression of scales on a fish's body was a symbol of that brilliance in affinity which characterizes all things under the sun.

This high magic, this universal bonding, is not only in the light but in the provisions for life. What we euphemistically refer to as the balance of nature is really a continuous balancing act of surpassing scale. All phenomena are engaged in it. It uses unnumbered copepods in the ocean, seven trillion spores in a puffball of average size, billions of spores in a mushroom, four million eggs laid by a female codfish. A vast production in nature compensates for vast attrition; but in some species numbers are so delicately proportionate to their losses that they are nearly impossible to interpret. Why should a sea turtle lay an average of one hundred eggs? How did that pivotal figure sustain it in the great context of the oceans and their shores, at least before man's world came in to upset the balance? Has it been the turtle's destiny to bear in itself the right reproductive counterweight to the energies of the globe?

The sun, the wind, and the animals liberate and distribute the seeds whose mission is to plant the earth. So living things act in terms of what lies ahead of them, each race a power in the face of all the great forces that contend against it. The alewives leap, again and again, up impassable falls during their spring migration in a heroic expression of need and desire. Shorebirds and terns try again after their eggs are washed out by storms. The trees put out their intricate load of new leaves so as to take on the global measure, with a wilderness style that has hundreds of millions of years behind it. There was a time, perhaps because of the narrow terms of the world in which I was indoctrinated, when I could hardly guess I was surrounded by such extravagant statements.

Late May into June is the time of year when the pitch pines loose their pollen in clouds, so that a yellow wind passes across the landscape. It is a fact, easily found out, that this has to do with the reproduction of a pine tree, but I confess it took me a long time to look into it. So I hesitate to condemn those citizens who have been looking for a scapegoat for this phenomenon. There is a suspicion in town—it has been reported to the police—that the yellow lines now spreading across the surface of our local ponds come from paint, not spilled accidentally by some sloppy house painter but by vandals. You can also find it covering pools after it rains, coating porch floors, and invading living rooms, to the exasperation of their owners.

Pine pollen is not known to cause hay fever, though many are convinced that it does. Some people are almost as alarmed as they were a few years back when the gypsy moths were chewing up oak leaves in one of their periodic invasions. It was said that our children were endangered, for reasons that were far from clear. We did the children far more potential harm by dousing the town with thousands of dollars worth of pesticides, at a time when the gypsy moths were reaching the end of their population cycle in any case. The following spring there were those who attributed the brilliant green of the grass and the foliage to the fact that they had been sprayed the previous year, diminishing nature's role to a wonderful degree.

Despite contemporary myth and madness, the yellow wind still belongs to our world, to sex and attachment, breath and continuance. If you can make that difficult stretch between hearsay and the tree standing right next to you, then there is a visible reason for it. The male cones on a pitch pine, which develop as numerous small catkinlike clusters, produce the pollen they let loose in May. Each grain is minute, visible through a high-powered microscope, being about one-twentieth of a millimeter, and it is a geometrical figure, crystalline in shape. This dust of golden spores is released on the wind, which carries it for great distances, in forested regions for hundreds of miles. The purpose of each grain, a messenger of heredity, carrying chromosomes, is to reach the female egg in a female cone, which starts off as a little rose-red blossom, to develop the following year into a slim, light green, tapered structure covered with studs, and usually growing on the upper branches of a tree. This cone opens to receive the pollen in the spring, then closes again, but the spores that enter it do not fertilize the egg cells for thirteen months, so as to result in a mature seed. After that the cone becomes brown and woody, maturing at three years and ready to release its seeds. Exceptionally hot weather or an occasional fire will hasten the process. (The pitch pine itself is resistant to fire.)

The little male cones drop off in a few weeks, sooner in open sunlight than in shade. The tide of fertility they release is so extravagant as to be past counting, and most of the pollen grains never reach their destination. In more advanced plants the sexual cell of the male is enclosed within grains designed to be transported, but the pitch pine sends its pollen particles out on the wind and they reach the female organs by luck.

This incredibly ancient method has been called primitive by a popular theory of evolution that thinks in terms of a progression toward increasingly complex and less haphazard ways of doing things. At the same time, the yellow wind blows from origins we can only conceive of. Other plants employ endlessly ingenious and complicated means to the same ends, but that fierce spending in a pitch pine has the original voice which the human mind has not yet evaluated. And why should not the world have *started* in complexity?

Nature's inspired provisions for regeneration are on a scale that we may be trying unconsciously to reduce, in order to save us from its implications. Sacrifice, not only in pollen grains, or in the vast number of marine organisms that make up the food of the sea, but in all life, is the rule. Thousands of warblers die during the spring migration. The normal mortality of young terns, without the factor of human interference, is 80 percent. Of 80,000 eggs produced by a single female alewife only one hatchling may survive to leave the spawning grounds for the sea. Here is what N. B. Marshall says, in his *Life of Fishes*, about the chances of a mackerel in the marine world: "South of Cape Cod, the catches of eggs in 1932 indicated that some sixty-four million million eggs were produced by a spawning population composed of one thousand million mackerel. During most of the larval life, the mortality was estimated to be 10 or 14 percent each day, but was considerably more (30 to 45 percent each day) in larvae measuring from eight to ten millimeters, at which stage they were rapidly acquiring their fins. By the time young mackerel were about 50 millimeters long and about to end their planktonic existence, something of the order of one to ten fish had survived from each million of eggs that were laid."

Although we depend on it for our very being, it is hard at times to see the vast expenditure in nature as much more than cruel and unnecessary waste, and we see ourselves in its victims. Why should the dead tern chick, or the trembling baby rabbit lost from its mother, or a cub seal dying of internal injuries, not have been given its chance? Why the terrible anonymity? It might seem unendurable that unnumbered innocents should be born into a world that promises them nothing but abandonment. The earth has a savage heart, and that which nearly matches it is a wayward savagery in ourselves. But who can run away from the great terms of existence and survive in spirit? If I can move one essential step further toward that universal capacity, even in fear, then my life may gain in something more than an isolated sense of itself. "Va com Deus" ("Go with God"), said the Portuguese captains, as the men lowered away in their fishing dories from the ship's side. It is well to honor the dignity of fate as we set out.

For all our dam building against nature, we can hardly avoid sensing its inevitable processes in ourselves. We know that the artificial lengthening of our days fails to cheat death. We know that nothing stops deterioration in our bodies or our machines. What else could bring us, all the same, to mutual love and need, but this universal inclusion? Love your neighbor so as to share mortality. Accept the endless eggs and seeds for their immortal habit, in which we are equals with the frogs, the flies, the plankton, and the pine. No life under the sun is inferior to that of the human species. All have to prove themselves. Who is going to ride out this storm but all its riders?

I go back to the great seasonal passages again, which is inevitable for someone who has lived with their variety for so many years. The seasons have to turn into something more than the four quarters, or how should we recognize their freshness in ourselves? They always predict an entire change. All life pivots on their tidal moods.

One year, on another day when the last of winter seemed to be behind us, I watched the sky curdling, heard the wind picking up, and saw a few snowflakes running before it. According to the radio, offshore winds were blowing at twenty to thirty knots, and small-craft warnings were in effect. In a few hours a tree-cracking wind was having its bold, free way, and I drove off to watch the waves on the outer shore. When I reached it, a green and white surf was boiling along fifty miles of the great beach. The waves had been turned into spume-choked flanks of water heaving back and forth, churning up massive volumes of sand.

The wind stung my face with driven sand and my eyeballs with sleet. The surf munched and licked away at the base of the sand cliff where I stood, and in one place a crack started to appear. Then a whole section slumped, slid down, and fell away, to be transported by the currents along the shore. Where low dunes, rather than cliffs, confront the sea, the surf sweeps up their face, falls back, does it time and time again, eroding and reducing them, so that the top of the foredunes, which usually make an overhanging bank, are incorporated into the downward-sloping beach itself, resulting in a long, steep profile. In some areas, storm waves cut through these dunes into the marshes behind them.

I returned after a night of booming depths running riot along the shore, with salt spray being cast from one side of the Cape Cod peninsula to the other. Though the storm had begun to slacken, there were sudden explosions along miles of white surf. As the tide retreated, froth from the waves leaped across wet, dark sands. Higher up on the beach, sand grains of white quartz went whizzing and bouncing away. Great combers rose offshore. The surf still sounded like a hundred Niagaras. Sheets of foam ran toward me where I walked, and chased me up a dune.

Out of that cold belly came a sound I had heard before, a commandeering eloquence. A unilateral passion filled the atmosphere and rose beyond the horizon with the clouds. Under the mottled sky, with this great roaring beside me, I felt my tentative existence. I was no more than a jellyfish, a bryozoan or a hydroid attached to ribbons and stems of seaweed broken off by the waves, fragile laces of the sea. I was no more than a splinter of light struck off coldly silver and sulphurous waves. I raced back and forth with gulls beyond the surf. I was broken like the chunky, black and white body of a dovekie, or little auk, which I found half-buried in the sand. That roaring, loaded tumult could have pulled me in for good; but I knew that it was the right space, the only proportion to define the human spirit. Man's "divorce from his roots" is a terrible deceit. We have nothing less to fall back on, to live for, than this conflict in sublimity, which includes all races, all cellular communities, there being no special guarantee for Homo sapiens. I saw this—praise be—in the grandeur of the caved Atlantic.

Listening

A FTER WE LANDED ON THESE SHORES, THE nearly constant proximity of birds enchanted me, though it took me some time to hear their calls as a nonverbal speech, rather than as mere background music. When the songbirds moved in waves into the surrounding woodlands in the spring, to court and sing, it simply fitted the characteristics of a season that returned on schedule the way we expected it to. It did not occur to me at first that they were not singing just for the sake of it but that it had a meaning for them. So, with a little more exposure to their realities, I started to listen harder, as, in a sense, I had been listening to the silence of migratory fish.

When Herman Melville wrote *Moby-Dick*, he was not aware of the underwater communication of whales, which does not make his statement about the majesty of their silence less relevant: ". . . seldom have I known any profound being that had anything to say in this world, unless forced to stammer out something by way of making a living." It does look as if our ideas of what is of the most value to us in nature were primarily confined to matters of food and utility; so you have to suppose that we are missing something more important, or at the very least being inattentive to it.

We suppress too many of the sensory tools we need to counterbalance that artificiality which takes so many manufactured tools to maintain. At an early age, those senses for survival so vital to all other animals are stifled in us and later nearly atrophied for lack of use. Conscious prohibitions take over, about the use of our hands, our sense of touch; and what we listen to besides the immediate company is the human voice scrambled, rendered, and returned, in unconscionable volume. The noise level of machines in the background is so constant in most places that little else comes through, or is given much importance if it does. In other words, we do not need a bird cry to alert us, or the deep cough of a leopard. We have become, above all, creatures of sight who go through the landscape without enough native equipment to interpret it in any but its more subdued and altered state. We lose the instinctive grasp of what the earth is saying to us in its varied eloquence. Education, a new leading out, so as to bridge the gap between the ear and the song, the hand and the objects of its touch, the sense of smell and its natural choices, is perhaps the best we can do, but we have an extreme deprivation to overcome. We ought to be tuning up to what is around us, but our own static is too loud.

Instead of looking out and listening, which was our original need, we have our heads planted in a television set for much of our lives, and whether we will be able to find ourselves there seems doubtful. Television is a product of our conquest of nature, or to put it in a better light, it is a magic symbol of the conquest of loneliness, the awful prospect of not having any companion but your own thoughts; though I think television watching is in some ways a lonely occupation. Barn raising, feasts, dances, berry picking, gabbing "down to the store," clamming, and calling on the neighbors were more sociable. There is something about the attention we give to the machine that is abstracted and attenuated, like the airwaves it employs.

Here we are in our great indoors while the wild stars fling out beyond us. We are able to abide the weather unless the electricity or fuel give out, when we may expect violence, and we are provided with enough goods so as to be able to have Christmas at home many times during the year.

In the midst of these acerbic thoughts I am interrupted by the clamor of Canada geese, bugling on the outside of my inner ear. They may be warning me of eternity. I run out of the house and dimly see three wedges of them flying over, sounding their great gabbling calls as if from the frontier of another world.

Surely we shield ourselves from too much real, nocturnal information, as if afraid that the immense darkness might enter and overwhelm us. What would we do with the aurora borealis on the living-room wall? Hunger out of cosmic nowhere could turn a man into a mouse.

Still the spring birds consistently call around us, and are later succeeded by locusts, grasshoppers, and crickets, out of a reservoir of sound, of intonation, pitch, and emphasis more complicated in its makeup than the product of any instrument or set of instruments we can devise. I think that by starting to listen, even if we do not come much closer to relating to other languages in the process, we have a chance to rejoin the cycles of universal expression.

There is a dry field below our house, really a double hollow scooped out of the glacial moraine, with two adjoining bottoms, their slopes tilting up toward a ring of oaks, and it is covered with wire grass and bluestem, and patches of sweet fern and huckleberry. Luminous gray-green deer moss lies over it too, in clouds. At one time, I took a young ornithologist from the Cape Cod Museum of Natural History there, and we spent half an hour tracing and identifying a field sparrow that led us in circles with its climbing notes, until we finally spotted it against the dazzling sunlight, perched on a wild cherry, acting like the one and only claimant of that dizzy, aromatic field.

It is a field I have gone back to many times so as to listen to languages I cannot speak. Through practice, though not always with confidence, I have learned to identify white-throated sparrows, black and white warblers, yellowthroats, towhees, and others through their voices. In a few instances, I have learned to identify an alarm call or a territorial song fairly readily, though I have a long way to go. At times I fancy they are just singing in praise of the light, or congratulating themselves on having arrived. It moves me, in any case, to hear a singing speech that has resounded on earth's tympanum for such an incredible length of time. It becomes a mystic form of communication, though real enough. If a bird's pure voice may now be keeping up with the moods and motions of the planet better than I can, then I feel nothing but jealousy toward it.

When a wood thrush sings out of the evening trees, I go back to where I first heard the spiraling notes of hermit thrushes and veeries coming out of the white pines and birches bordering Lake Sunapee in New Hampshire. They gave us and our land a grace abounding. Their freshness is the same as it ever was, though their numbers seem to be dwindling, and it comes out of principles of harmony that we are as much dependent on as they are. Why should the song of a thrush be beautiful to us? In the first place, because we still have earth ears. Also, it takes the path of beauty, avoiding repetition and monotony, following the painstaking traditions of nature with such purity. Our emotions respond because we are there too, as more conscious creators, but never ranging so far from the deeper requirements of form that we are not aware of disorder when it occurs.

Those rippling, half-slurred, vaulted notes are not disembodied. They come out of feeling, live emotion. It seems that for many birds out in the open spaces, sight tends to be more important in signaling and recognition than sound. Many ducks, for example, can see each other plainly across open water, and a "quack" will do. But song may become more elaborate in the region of dense trees, where visibility is relatively poor. Thrushes in the forest engage in "advertising songs" to announce their presence. If a singing male is threatened by a rival thrush, intruding into its territory, it will sing louder so as to increase the "escape drive" in the other until it flies off. This may also result in the two of them engaging in competitive singing for a while, each trying to outdo the other. They engage in a kind of countersinging, which gets more and more intense and elaborate until one bird loses, so to speak, and flies off through the trees, though this occasionally ends in a fight, usually no more than a brief flurry on the ground.

Knowing that the beauty of their song is in part a matter of competition certainly does not spoil my enjoyment of it. I hear the thrushes as even bolder in their ardor and formality than I had realized, and in their intensity they seem to be competing, not only with each other, but with the rest of the singing world, calling out the kind of standards every serious musician understands. There is no backing away from performance.

Carl Jung wrote: "I regard behavior as a mere husk that conceals the living substance within." So what language should we know that corresponds to living substance? I hear it in thrush music through the convoluted chambers of my skull.

The closeness of birds to the light is very marked at dawn, when many kinds sing together. On the other hand, a chuck-will's-widow prefers moonlight. The ovenbird's flight song sounds in the evening, and the mockingbird frequently sings all night, when encouraged by the moon.

"At twilight," says Roger Pasquier in his *Watching Birds*, "the Eastern Wood Peewee sings a faster and more complex song than the familiar whistle given all through the day. Other birds have songs given only before dawn."

"Little work," he then writes in a tantalizing fashion, "has been done on whether the less frequently heard songs have meanings different from those the bird sings all day."

Whipporwills sing—*shout* seems more appropriate if you hear them through an open window at night—in response to the amount of light, like the woodcock, which starts its first evening call, according to William Sheldon's *Book of the American Woodcock*, when the light is on the average of ".71 plus or minus .26 foot candles." For three years, for whatever it is worth, I have marked down the date when I first heard a whippoorwill, and I find that it happened twice on April 24 and once on May 1, another example of hemispheric timing that never ceases to surprise me.

One evening there was still enough dim light that I could just make out a whippoorwill where it perched, or crouched on its short legs, along a rock above the garden wall, looking like a piece of driftwood on the beach. It gave out a loud, shrieking "whip!" before the "poorwill," and with each shriek its head jerked back violently. Since this performance is often repeated hundreds of times in succession, the apparent effort the bird had to make was surprising, unless I am judging it too much by the vertebrae in my own neck, which are poorly equipped for such an exercise. When it became aware of me it flew up quickly and silently like a great moth, a white necklace and a white patch on the tail showing distinctly against the gathering darkness. The time was ten minutes to nine.

Each spring a ring of whipporwills makes a loud and unrelenting clamor outside our house, and their wild, woodland mating call has always seemed as extravagant as ancient tribes howling under the blood of the moon. I have spent some wakeful hours counting these calls, and until recently, I was jealous of the naturalist John Burroughs' record of hearing a whippoorwill repeat itself 1,088 times. But one predawn I was awakened by a shrieking just outside the window and got out of bed to throw a stick in its direction. That worked for a few minutes, but the same bird, or another one, started up again at close range. Struggling to keep my sleepy head clear, and using my fingers for the hundred marks, I started counting, and this master shouter finally quit at 1,136, with no interruptions between phrases.

With this achievement behind me, I turned on the light to look at my watch. It was about five minutes past four and growing lighter, though the sun would not appear over the horizon until an hour later, this being the end of May. I heard another whippoorwill calling in the distance, but only for a few minutes. Then the passionate white light began to produce more responses: the rat-a-tat voice of a crow, than a catbird's chips, warbles, and scratchy notes, followed by the cheerful whistling of a tufted titmouse, and then the tin-horn sound of a blue jay. This celebration of the dawn took only about ten to fifteen minutes, and was followed by a period of relative silence while life prepared for the next wave and intensity of light.

The whippoorwill calls in its strange style out of some relationship with a chosen shade of darkness. It proclaims and hides at the same time, while the woodcock chooses an open clearing and stakes it out for nesting territory, launches mating flights, pitches tents, and raises flags. Its performance, like the whippoorwill's, is in accordance with the motions of the earth with respect to the sun, and takes place on the fringes of day and night. These ritualists attract me out, after supper at woodcock time, when the light is between 5.0 and 0.2 foot candles. Walking down from our little hill, following an overgrown cart track, I reach a bottomland covered with thick grass growing in a grove of locust trees, and there I have been able to wait and listen for them for many years. At times I have seen deer there as they bounded off through the trees toward a neighboring swamp, their white tails flashing.

About 8:15 of an April evening, with the light fading, I have often heard a woodcock ahead of me in the grasses, starting to sound its "peent," or what I have heard of as a nasal "zzamp." Then a small body comes hurtling low across the open ground, on a short flight, calling with a kind of buzzy snort, perhaps in warning to another bird. After about fifty peents, the first woodcock suddenly rises up on a slanting course through the dim light and commences to climb, hurtling up like a little whirling projectile, making twittery, warbling sounds. It loops off in one direction and then turns, making a spiraling hook as it goes, reaching a zenith at several hundred feet, to whip down toward the ground, with a "chip-chip chop-chop-chee" that sounds somewhat like the fast dripping of water in a well or underground cavern. It is the male who puts on this show, and I can only suppose that there is a female waiting down in the grass in silent admiration, unless she is suggesting that he ought to try it again: "Just another hundred feet." But it may not be the male's prowess that impresses her so much as his choice of the one and only nesting site. All the concentration and intensity that they put into these courtship flights go to that end which, in terms of its earth ties, is a sacred one.

The home grounds are still being attached and rightfully employed. The woodcock's twittering and blurting in the fields is an event I can look forward to so as to renew my own sense of the appropriate. I am astonished by whatever it is in that little being that could have such miraculous properties of touch with relation to the great world surrounding it. These often faintly heard, little-noticed reactions to the finest emanations from cosmic surroundings are in everything we too could be, everything we attempt. The power in it tempts us as much into conquest as receptivity. The mind that is able to track light-years out of sight goes with a will to defeat circumstances. And so we fail, time and time again. Human supremacy conquers itself.

Still, the old rituals prevail, holding past and future in themselves. Birds are still following them, while we threaten ourselves with exile. In a time-honored sense, they have as much right to the land as we do. They are ancestral claimants, with a profound sense of direction and internal ties to their natal sites. By comparison, we have almost abandoned the land and the lessons of birth and growth it can teach us. Our local history has become vulnerable, temporary, easily swept aside.

There is an eighteenth-century cottage near these mating grounds, now caving in, a roof with a sky view. It is sinking and sliding down in broken glass, wet plaster, rotten wood and leather, rusty nails, and old mason jars. An iron bed stands in one corner, with its rust-colored legs poking through what is left of the floor. You can hardly hear the human voices any longer. Local memories are losing their hold. But the woodcocks come in to identify the land, whose underlying wisdom survives. Nothing quite erases the tremendous, unseen energy of cognition.

from

The Immortal Wilderness

(1987)

The White Pelican

WHEN I CLIMB INTO MY CAR AND HEAD EITHER northeast for Maine or south toward Florida, I can avoid the dangers of biological flight between the Caribbean and New England. I can reverse my migratory heading any time I want to. This is the way freedom from elementary peril and need, freedom from nature, is supposed to have been achieved. But although I enjoy the relative freedom of owning a car and going where I please, I recognize that it was made possible by a civilization that is highly concentrated on itself. It may be, after all, that some of the anarchic and specialized ways of our society are biologically preordained. The ants go their own way, too. Part of the reason for their success, as William Morton Wheeler pointed out in his famous study, *Ants*, is due to the comparatively small number of their enemies: "As Forel says: 'The ants' most dangerous enemies are other ants, just as man's most dangerous enemies are other men.'"* So we do not really avoid danger; we just invite our own accidents.

*William Morton Wheeler, *Ants* (New York: Columbia University Press, 1910).

Like the ants, I have to stick to the roads we have constructed, a continental web of them. It is no easy matter to stop on some of the superhighways without high risk; but if I were unable to get out and walk somewhere along the way I might never see a thing. When driving, I am not aware, as I might be when trying to cross a highway on foot, that my car goes tearing by like a maniacal bee deprived of its senses. For the most part, I just tamely stick to the route and get to the other end of it, as part of a regulated environment, insulated from what it goes through. Travel does not mean going out over stormy seas to reach unseen shores, or fishing for our lives, but joining a network. So when I move out now and then, leaving the barnacles behind me, I take our messages with me, transmitted by the car radio. "Join us in this great crusade," says a built-in evangelist at the end of his harangue. "See ya."

Birds travel the earth as a different breed of searchers, at times on very direct routes between their wintering and breeding grounds, at times circling to find their way over immense distances. They have the planetary currents, the major tides of weather on their wings. They are often blown off course. The great space that is intrinsic to their lives is also the space for getting lost. At times, I wonder if that is not the kind I am looking for, not so much to get away but to enter in.

In 1974 a white pelican, which may have soared in from its breeding grounds west of the Great Lakes, having been forced eastward by a major autumnal weather front, spent much of the winter in the Herring River and reservoir area of the town of Harwich on Cape Cod. I first saw it just after Christmas, and it had frequent visitors for as long as it stayed. I last saw it well on in February, before the water was completely frozen over and it had to go somewhere else for its food. For a while, some fishermen who chopped holes in the ice, where they dropped in their hooks and lines, slung it a few fish, and the bird readily accepted them. It used to stand on a small, grassy hummock above the ice and preen. I watched it flapping and gliding on its nine-foot wingspread very high in the air until it became almost lost to sight. Clearly, it was a major, continental bird. When it flew up off the water, still open

around the edges of the reservoir, with a few herring gulls screaming at it in exasperation, its white excrement streamed down. It
had a long, pinkish yellow bill and pouch, yellow-orange legs and
feet, and the solemn look of a tragedian indifferent to tragedy. Trying to get a picture of it with my camera, I skirted one end of the
reservoir, stalking the bird through the woods and thickets along
the shore like a phony Indian; but it spotted me long before I
could get close enough and casually flew off to the other side.

I set off for the south on my own voyage at the end of the winter, feeling a little like an "accidental vagrant" myself, when I got
temporarily lost on the fringes of the great city I had once lived in.
I wandered in and out of a district of empty warehouses, driving
under half-built overpasses and down side streets that shouted at
me about all the tense concerns I might have forgotten by moving
to the country. What is nature but human nature? Then I joined a
jostling, semi-congealed mass of commuter traffic trying to work
its way beyond the city during the rush hour. Under these conditions, the automobile loses the freedom of the open road and at
the same time is one's security against chaos. Thousands of us,
crammed together, only drive and wait, in a kind of enforced patience. Perhaps fury and weariness just cancel each other out. All
the complex structure and greed of a civilization is concentrated
on an individual sweating out a traffic jam.

I can get inside a newspaper, or restrict my travel to an ex-
pressway, the manmade equivalent for the pelican way, or what
the Anglo-Saxon poem "The Seafarer" called the "whale-way over
the stretch of the seas," and experience the equivalent of shutting
myself up in a room. In traveling so as to make time, or cheat it
as much as possible, I become part of the spreading, gray-brown
discipline of the highway culture, spending each night at a
stereotyped motel, a traveling salesman for one of a thousand
products.

As I drove on, I thought of the pelican, soaring from midconti-
nent to the shore. It was quite a stunt, although the bird could not
be publicly acclaimed for an achievement that was not of its own
volition. No Lindbergh there, but the bird was a splendid voyager,

all the same, and a great many people came to see it, so that it could have enjoyed some notoriety had it been the least bit interested. Other migrants were in my head, too, like the terns that would start to show up along the Eastern seaboard in a few weeks. They might already be on their way from South or Central America, going low over the water, with a quick, sure beat to their wings, veering from side to side with a searching motion fitted to the ocean airs.

Smokestacks released huge clouds into the air. Miles and miles of power lines marched ahead. I passed rivers that were opaque, like blinded eyes, and filthy streams, the gutted dregs of what were once pure, receptive veins in the life of earth. Tidelands were being dredged for real estate. Great areas of marshland had been destroyed by garbage dumps, landfill, or phosphate mining, tremendous stretches of the shore were torn up, stripped, and ravaged for their resources of shell, gravel, and sand. Silt-covered marine habitats smothered the shellfish. Spilled oil had been incorporated into marsh sediments, bays, and inlets. In some areas there seemed to be little life left, only the semblance of a grimy beach facing oily waters.

It had become a conscious effort to find wildlife. It was not that all America had turned into Hackensack, New Jersey. You could find clean marshes, native birds, and the sea beyond if you looked, but it was as if they only existed on our terms. The engineers could will it that the Mississippi be confined to ten miles wide, as compared with its original, great course, because the needs of motorized river traffic took precedence over the river's mutual accommodation with the land. We could, in theory, dam the Grand Canyon; or reroute the water from Canada, if we risked the political consequences. The power that moved us only seemed to respect nature's give and take when faced with some absolute limit to its actions.

The revolutionary aspect of our society does not depend on our having sent George III packing back to the old country, but on its experimentalism. We follow invention, what seems to work for the time being. There is a heroic ignorance in us that insists on taking what it can from the earth, if only because taking has made us what we are today. A triumph over circumstance built this great traffic that can take us where we want to go, and where on the way every man can dine as well as a king.

In the famous dialogue between the Lord and Job, after Job has already endured so many tribulations that he has desired to die, the Lord, out of his whirlwind, puts a series of unanswerable questions to him. The poor man *has* to submit, although he is justly rewarded for it later on, when the voice, the unassailable bully, asks: "Where wast though when I laid the foundations of the earth:

"Dost though know the balancing of the clouds, the wondrous works of him which is perfect in knowledge?

"Hast though with him spread out the sky, which is strong and as a molten looking glass?"

Job survived the divine terror of God, the dark nature of creation, through the power of his humility. To endure as he did, to grovel in the dust, to be stripped of everything, had the end result of raising him in stature. He and his God, man's God now, were redefined. But if that Old Testament God has been replaced by man, what then? If such overweening questions were asked of many who ride the technological, industrial heap, they might well answer, "Sure. We were there. We know that. We can do all those things," and then sit back, although in some unquiet, existential limbo.

I sat in my motel room, trucks and planes droning, snorting, and making the ground tremble outside—my own blood trembling from my daily run in the car—while I drank a carbonated drink, read a syndicated newspaper, and shut off the TV to see a giggling image disappear down its throat. The thunder I heard was not the thunder of Jehovah; nor was I terrified like Pascal before the reaches of infinite space. As a matter of fact, the night was hard to see. Those stars by means of which birds may find their way over great distances were partly lost to view because of artificial light, smoke, and haze.

Where I stopped along the shores of the Carolinas, the wrens and cardinals were singing loud, and warblers were flying through lobolly pines, cabbage palms and palmettos, magnolia and holly. On Bull's Island, north Charleston, I saw a wild turkey, displaying before his mate in the spring sunlight. His bronze feathers glowed like a dull fire. Shoals of light shifted over his back, giving it a glossy iridescence. With his tail opened into a great fan, and his wings spread and fluffed out to the side, this old American strutted like a ship loaded with sails, moving through heavy seas.

Canoeing around a bend of the Waccamah River, I heard the hooting of a barred owl, and there it sat ahead of us in broad daylight, motionless in a tall, red-barked southern pine. That night I heard it again, through the sound of jet planes ripping vents in the sky, as it moved through the swamp bordering the river, from tree to tree. Owls have a deep sensate realm of their own, calling to each other and their surroundings, feeling the expanding and contracting circles of the dark.

In Georgia, a kingfisher dove out of a palmetto, splashed into lazily moving water, then flew up with a loud, rattling cry. It was one of those snaking, shifting, weaving rivers that go through brackish marshes where small fish leap like fired rockets between the grasses and then subside, while the long, gray twists of Spanish moss hang and rustle from the live oaks on the banks. A big pileated woodpecker hitched up the bark of a pine, an erect, black body with a flaming, scarlet crest, giving a raucous, clarion shout. They called it the "Lord God bird" in parts of the South. Warblers lightly buzzing and trilling veered in and out of tree trunks, catching insects, tied to each other by their calls and the threads of their quickness. A common egret, with classic white wings, black legs stretched behind, rowed above the treeline. Orange and black monarch butterflies alternately flitted and made short glides over open ground; and a wood duck I had surprised at a bend in the river stared at me with an untapped lightning in its eyes.

In many areas, where sights like this are not just a normal part of your surroundings, they have to be found in wildlife or conservation refuges. We come off our omnipotent highways and cities to parks and natural areas where we hope to "see nature" and enjoy ourselves. They are places, according to the great Dr. Freud, which belong to "the mental realm of phantasy. A nature reserve preserves its original state . . . where everything, including what is useless and even what is noxious, can grow and proliferate as it pleases."*

Freud was clearly more learned on the subject of human fantasy than in the realities of the natural world, which, either at a distance or close at hand, are beginning to seem more basic to the needs of a whole earth than the ends toward which we try to steer it. Those who are concerned with endangered species, and trying to decide which of them to save first, do not get much help from adjectives like *noxious* or *useless*. They face emergency questions about living things that are being isolated from their sustenance. How can they be evaluated, how can they exist, without the original, full range of life in which all divisions, all contrary elements, are included and reconciled?

Brown pelicans flew along the coastal beaches of the South, gliding effortlessly together along the surfline, but they had been much reduced in numbers at that time because of their vulnerability to DDT and its derivatives. Cutting across to Louisiana, I found that breeding population of these birds had dropped to near zero. The mighty Mississippi, constantly pouring vast quantities of chemical wastes and pesticides into the gulf, had poisoned their food supply and permeated their tissues, so that they had raised no young. They and the ospreys, the bald eagles and other fish eaters so affected have been coming back from the brink in recent years because of restrictions on the use of DDT—which has not stopped our colossal and widespread use, often untested, of chemicals.

Many of the competitive and "harmful" insects have become resistant to pesticides, as if obeying prior directions as to survival. Other populations come back because they still have the space, the food supply, and the regenerative powers of nature behind them, but we do not often know the reasons for it. What do we

*Sigmund Freud, Introductory Lectures on Psycho-Analysis, in Strachey, J., trans. and ed., *The Complete Psychological Works*, Part 3 (New York: Norton, 1976).

need to know? What are the right equations between life and space, attrition and abundance? It often comes as a terrible surprise when we inflict so much damage on living things that it becomes irretrievable. What could we "lords of creation" have possibly done? A good guess is that we have been neglecting creation. It is certainly very hard to talk about man's responsibility for nature when we insist on being oblivious to it.

None of us know enough about that awkward-looking bird the pelican. Still, we might find out, somewhere along the line, that it was a linchpin in the wheel of survival that includes the human race.

At the Corkscrew Swamp Wildlife Sanctuary, on the north edge of the Everglades, I heard a man cry out: "But, it's all so bloody alive!" as he looked at the teeming concentration of water plants, trees, birds, insects, lizards, frogs, and snakes. I might have been tempted to ask him whether it was so dead where he came from, except that I understood, having come in from some conquered territories, what he was talking about.

A swamp, from the point of view of people who "don't like nature," and there are many, is a sink hole made up of blind, mutual consumption, and the most direct equivalent of it in ourselves is a darkness with no promises; but it can also be a source of relief and joy, as we discover that the earth is richer than our compulsions make it.

It amazed me that a huge area like the Everglades, once synonymous with remoteness, the nearly unreachable wild, should have been so cut down, not only in reality but concept. The pressures were obvious, from the canals to the north that controlled the flow of that wide, slow-moving river toward the gulf, to a threatened jetport and a future city of a million people. Real estate development, the multimillion-dollar business of recreation, with marsh-skimming boats and other destroyers of remoteness, just the constant clamor of a growing population demanding to be let in everywhere, made me thankful for the national park. But the human tide is relentless and conditions us all. We were seeing wild America, if we saw it at all, not in terms of its supreme diversity and running skies but of the outline, the bare bones exploitation could make of it, more real than its own substance.

I emerged at the end of this trip to walk down a west Florida beach, in a resort area. As I was looking out over the marl-clouded waters, I heard a voice, in low desperate tones, saying: "I don't know what to do." So I walked over to a man I had only half noticed where he stood with a fishing rod on a concrete wall, and what should he be trying to reel in, like a great stone, but a white pelican, which had the lure and line slung around its wing. As he kept reeling in, the bird let itself be pulled in for a foot or so at a time, a dead weight in the water, then flapped up again; and so it went, foot by foot, or inch by inch; each short haul bringing it a little closer to the dock. Then a second pelican flew in and dropped down close to the other.

"Keep off, you," the man growled. He had graying, close-cropped hair, gaps in his teeth, eyes slightly screwed up, and a broken nose. He was a slim, slight, but rangy man, his limbs shaky from the ordeal—perhaps they were always a little shaky—and he was quiet and apologetic in a manner that seemed part of his nature, too. I liked him right away, and while he reeled in I waited, lying down on my stomach, for the docking of the pelican, which was finally pulled in close enough for me to reach.

"Take a hold of his bill," he said. "Not that it hurts much, but it stops him."

The bird's combined bill and pouch surprised me when I grabbed it, being as soft as chamois. Its white eyes were pink-rimmed and stared vacuously, and after the line was unwound it flapped noncommittally away—Lindbergh altered into Pagliacci.

The drone of engines; the grinding of gears; shore mud that smelled of gas; the ebb and flow of cash in voices everywhere; some loud kids and a quiet heron. The heron felt the sandy mud, its long, jointed legs and flexible, clawed feet lifting very slowly and deliberately. Stalking is the way to sense the ground beneath you, a delicate pacing, the steady feel of counter response in an incongruously long-winged frame. To find your food, you trace your way, a slave of patience from our point of view, but wise enough.

I saw a little migrant warbler come flying in off the windy waters of the gulf to land on the ground at the foot of a tree, looking genuinely distressed and tired, its feathers wet and ruffled. I listened to noisy willets where the tidal currents ran by. They had a near idiotic, brassy cry, flung off into the wind; while two hunter dolphins, wet flanks slip-streaming, arched in the rip tide, running together, their fins in a spliced play. A flock of white terns flew loose and easy over the water, dropping and diving as they went. A plover flew off and away with a sharp, sea-honed cry: "Keealee!" I watched the mating of horseshoe crabs on the beach at the high tide line, as the water was starting to fall back. Some got flipped over by the surf and had to wait for it to right them again. They were a gray-green color, unlike their brown relatives in the north, and their shells were encrusted with barnacles and slipper shells. Nosing into the sand, with improbable compounded eyes like windows encased in martial helmets, they shoved ahead and into the sand, clasping each other, hitching rides—slow, cold, deliberate sex, out of ageless law. They stayed at the high tide line while the surf still washed it and then began gradually to move back out into the water, being fair swimmers once they reached it, and disappeared into a Cambrian depth.

One afternoon, a south wind was roughing up the cloudy green waters and rattling the palm branches. Thunder boomed; low and heavy, it spread around. A grackle ducked suddenly under a bolt of lightning, and so did I. Then the rain slammed and spattered down, while vultures, terns, laughing gulls, ospreys, and herons flew just inshore to a mile or so farther back, lifting and dropping down to the measure of the receding storm. The terns ran before the wind like leaves in a northern fall and occasionally shook themselves in flight during the hard pelting of the rain.

As the dark clouds blew off and the sun came through, the birds kept circling overhead, riding the updrafts, drying their feathers and evidently enjoying themselves. The clearing off resulted in the most subtle color changes in the sky and over the water. There were dark green and copper openings through the clouds hanging above the shore, clouds of violet reflecting the sunlight, others keeping a darker gray from the storm. The elements had exploded like a wave losing its energy in falling on the beach, and every life responded.

I met my friend of the pelican incident as we were plodding down the shore, drying out. "Couldn't get away from *that*, could we?" said he.

While development was doing it best to conceal the natural state of Florida, the exercise of light was never stopped for a moment. I looked to its participants to see how it was done. Freud's fantasy lands were exiled from earth experience. Travels are universal, so the white pelican told me, or they have no meaning.

Open to the Sun

J FIRST WENT TO COSTA RICA BECAUSE OF THAT
small country's reputation for conserving its threatened resources. I also wanted to follow out some life lines I had
learned to look for at home, such as a tanager, an oriole, or a
swallow back for the nesting season from the Southern Hemisphere. They do not conquer distance so much as embody it.
They are more beautifully tangible than any map; and when I see
them fly in I have some assurance that the rain forests are still intact. When they fail to appear I worry about their future and our
own. Birds are indicators not only of the state of the lands they
come from but of how it goes with us who despoil them. Are we
becoming accustomed to emptiness? Are we leaving all the trees
behind us?

Exploitation was in the air as soon as I arrived at the airport in
San Jose, where I overheard an outgoing passenger, a fellow
American, telling how a friend of his had made a huge profit out
of an unprotected stand of balsa wood. This was largely a matter
of buying cheap, selling dear, and taking advantage of the greatly

devalued colone, the currency in that nearly bankrupt country, then several billions dollars in debt. To his credit, he looked a little embarrassed as he reported on this shameless operation, but un-embarrassed speculation goes on as usual, destroying forests and degrading soil, a process that has brought some countries to a kind of ecological death. Millions of people can no longer find enough sustenance in their own soil. Through its system of na-tional parks, Costa Rica has taken steps to save some of its her-itage before it is too late. Even so, it is said that at the rate the forests are going, all unprotected stands will disappear in a few years, a devastating prospect for a country that can boast two thousand known kinds of trees.

Tourists like me can skim like dragonflies between one resort area and another, although resorts seem relatively scarce in Costa Rica, or to those parks open to visitors. Then we clear out in a few weeks, leaving the country to its fruit and coffee plantations, its hundreds of thousands of cattle, its agriculture and expanding cities. You can soon see what population, industrial advance, and the exploitation of land is doing to try the country's resources to the limit, down to the last poor landholder facing the prospect of an acre of soil that has been finally drained of its life. But Costa Rica, unlike many other "Third World" countries, has been learning how to hold its own.

In the developed countries, through power acquired over na-ture, although derived from nature, millions can be deceived into thinking that the land is only a background for their material needs, and to be manipulated accordingly. For the developing countries, on the other hand, where development is still an unat-tained goal, or whose economic resources are limited, land is life and death, nutrition or starvation, expectations or burned out hopes. There is no way to disentangle local destinies from it. The land dies and the people die with it, often through social disrup-tion and assaults on each other. The symbol for a country that has lost its resources in the land is a gun.

Costa Rica, to its everlasting credit, has no standing army and has spent much of its income on health and education. It is essentially a nation of small landowners and has a reputation for stability, although its economy, like most others in the developing world, is dangerously unbalanced. It is a country devoted to the needs of agriculture, while it has become increasingly dependent on the industrialized world outside it. The tropical forests, which once occupied 99.8 percent of its land area, have been reduced by nearly 70 percent. More than half of this deforestation has occurred since 1959, because of the demand for land, a growing population, economic pressures, serious invasion by squatters, exploitation by cattle and lumber interests. Even modern timber companies employing professional foresters have been involved in the loss of the rain forests, in Asia as well as Latin America. They have often been less interested in the practice of sustained forestry than in securing their own investments.

Cattle ranching, in which many Costa Ricans take pride, has also contributed to the loss, not only of forests but of the grasslands that have replaced them. When this land gives out, particularly on the hilly slopes that comprise much of the country, the cattle ranchers have often let in local people, the *campesinos*, to practice what agriculture they can. The result, in a few years, is a soil worth nothing at all. Under optimum conditions in the tropics it might take two centuries to regenerate. The average Costa Rican eats rice and beans, while those of us who frequent fast food eateries eat the hamburger, luncheon meat and frankfurters. It may seem like an innocent American rite, but in effect our exaggerated demand for meat, not only for ourselves but our canine pets, has encouraged the extinction of species through their lack of habitats.

Costa Rica is a small nation, no bigger than the state of West Virginia, and all it has left of that dark and intricate forest growth that extended from Central America to the Amazon, that magnificent original, are representative samples, although they are rich enough. For an outsider, a species count of the tropical rain forest does not mean a great deal until you encounter the rooted reality; but the numbers, with all they imply about living forms, are startling. When I visited Corcovado, Costa Rica's first national park, I was told that of the four hundred kinds of trees that scientists had found there, a possible one hundred more were still unknown. In Costa Rica as a whole, eight hundred forty-eight bird species have been found, twelve thousand flowering plants, one thousand ferns and their allies, fifteen hundred kinds of fungi, an astonishing variety of insect life, not fully explored. What will the disappearance of the world's rain forest mean, besides more deserts and disastrous changes in the atmosphere, but the loss of a balanced abundance we cannot ultimately do without? There lies in those tall, vine-covered trees, the light-loving butterflies, the stirring soil, the intensity of birds, all multiply engaged, that wilderness power we denied too soon at home.

Costa Rica has already lost an enormous amount of soil, the guarantee of any country's vitality. According to the Tropical Science Center of San Jose,

> 17 percent of the country is severely eroded and 24 percent is moderately eroded. . . . Serious and widespread erosion (30 percent of the area) occurs on the Pacific side with another 30 percent moderately eroded. A rough estimate of soil loss is 680 million tons a year to erosion, of which over 80 percent is caused by overgrazed pasture lands. Since topsoil is essentially a nonrenewable resource, the soil loss seriously threatens not only the country's agricultural productivity, but the economic viability of hydroelectric, potable water, irrigation and forestry projects as well.*

It is a country defined by a great spinal column of mountains and a central valley where agriculture is practiced. The tilled soils also climb the slopes that characterize so much of the country. There you can see the gullies, a deep clawing into the ground, the giving way of an underlying balance, as well as brown fields terraced by wandering cows, or red earth marked by blackened stumps as memorials to the vanished trees. In some areas black weathered rocks give an additionally blasted look to the landscape.

*From *Country Environment Profile: A Field Study* (San Jose, Costa Rica: Tropical Science Center, 1982).

The traveler sees fires as he looks down from a plane, fires from the roads and highways. In March, during the dry season in Guanacaste Province, it looked as if the land were burning everywhere. Fires climbed the hillsides; smoke filled the air and darkened the sky. The pastures, once forest lands and already overgrazed, were being set on fire in the annual practice of burning off to prepare them for planting. How many years the soil, open to the fierce tropical sun and to periodically heavy rains, would hold out was problematical.

A rain forest has a fire of a different kind, annealing and regenerating, perpetuating those planetary energies that are fueled by the sun. The forest reaches upward toward the light. The trees are not sheltered from it, they employ and embody it, and every life they shelter shares in that exchange. The rain forests have a stability that has been millions of years in the making. The annual rainfall in Costa Rica comes to at least four meters and is not a limiting factor in the growth of the plants, nor is the temperature, balanced within the system. The principal, dynamic factor affecting forest growth is light. Forest nutrients are locked up in the vegetation and only superficially penetrate into the subsoil. The topsoil has only a thin layer of humus as compared with temperate zones. The leaves continually drop down to the forest floor, instead of seasonally, and they decay fairly rapidly. Nutrients are taken up by a tightly linked network of roots and associated fungi and transmitted to the growth of the trees.

Fire the rain forest, cut it down, break open the soil to the unshielded light of the sun, and its life forms are wiped out, or forced to live on a marginal subsistence level in whatever pockets of sustaining habitats remain. Every acre so destroyed can lose literally thousands of plants and animals. On the global scale at which this occurs, an instability results, of a peculiarly modern kind, the consequence of a planetary throwing out at human hands.

The loss of these great green reservoirs of life was happening at so fast a rate in Costa Rica that the nation, in very recent years, has undertaken to do something about it. As a result of enlightened planning and leadership, a system of national parks was founded in 1970. It had to be conceived and designed in large terms. The parks were not to be limited to sanctuaries, or isolated islands of life, but planned so as to contain areas of considerable size where native species could be free to develop and would not die out through lack of contact and genetic exchange with the surrounding world.

Costa Rica is a land of great diversity. You can stand and shiver in the high zone of the *paramo*, at an elevation of some eight thousand feet, a tundra-like region of stunted growth, inhospitable enough to be associated with *la muerte*, or suffer from the heat in the dry grasslands or swampy areas at sea level. The parks, designed to reflect that diversity, include offshore islands with nesting seabirds; coral reefs; beaches, such as the one at Tortuguero where the sea turtles come in to lay their eggs; mangrove swamps; marshes rich in waterbirds; grassy savannahs; intermittently active volcanoes; and forests ranging from moist to wet, whose various zones, at different elevations, contain species that are particular to them.

As it has in so many parts of the world, development, out for short-term gains, regardless of long-term results, often threatens the very existence of the wild and all its adventurous species. The exchange in space that is so vital to them is increasingly endangered by the Great Exchange Robbery of our times. It is no easy matter for a small nation, suffering from population pressures and incomes close to the poverty line, to resist. Since development for "emerging" countries is an ideal, it is difficult to defend conservation unless it seems to lead toward economic and social advantage. Conservation as an alternative to development may only look like another form of exploitation if it is seen as taking food from people's mouths, or money from their pockets. Yet the new program of setting parks and reserves aside, if it has not always had universal support, now appears to have gained growing understanding and acceptance. The people of Costa Rica, after all, have seen much of their land slide down hill, and its plants and animals disappear, and have felt the world grow emptier as a result.

The parks were designed to protect the nation's water supplies, pure water being one of the real wealths of a country not rich in the kind of exploitable resources that talk the loudest in our world. They were also meant to encourage scientific research and public education, to establish reserves of native trees for refor- estation, and to help in rural development. This national effort, which took a great deal of determination and common sense to bring about, has resulted in parks and biological reserves that comprise eight percent of the land area of the country. New ac- quisitions may bring this to ten percent, an extraordinary figure for any nation, especially one plagued by economic uncertainty. Proportionately, it far exceeds the investment of the United States in national parks.

This commitment to conservation is directed toward a people's attention to their own land and a recognition of it in themselves. The soil is the man, woman, and child, and the trees their fellow guardians of earth's identity. Five centuries ago, Leonardo da Vinci put the equation directly enough:

> Nothing originates in a spot where there is no sentient, vegetable, and rational life; so that we might say the earth has a spirit of growth; that its flesh is the soil, its bones the arrangement and con- nection of the rock of which the mountains are composed, its carti- lage the tufa, and its blood the springs of water. The pool of blood which lies around the heart is the ocean, and its breathing, and the increase and decrease of the blood in the pulses, is represented in the earth by the flow and ebb of the sea, and the heat of the spirit of this world is the fire which pervades the earth.

Sacred Places

*U*NDER THE HEADING *SACREDNESS* THERE ARE several references in the *Oxford English Dictionary* to real estate and property, which might reflect the religious yearnings of our economic system but probably has more to do with the rights it holds most dear. By contrast, the sense in which living things, plants, animals, mountains, springs, and forest trees, were once held to be sacred and associated with deities and ceremonial observances has been cast aside in favor of another, many-sided deity that has a tendency to crush its worshipers. No compromise has yet been reached between the scale of modern expansion and the worlds of nature. They must survive as best they can. It amounts to an imbalance that may succeed in destroying several million species and turning major parts of the world into deserts.

Human societies have never been able to conserve and stabilize their environments for long periods of time. It is as if we were not only ignorant of how not to let things go too far but had an often uncontrollable desire to commit sacrilege. Is it not typical of us that since the sea is a symbol of the infinite we should want to ravage it? This goes with a subservience toward authority that tends toward disastrous rigidity. It is a wonder that the earth has not shrugged us off by this time as a major irritant.

It has to be said that the Western world, in attaining its new power to migrate beyond its means, has seldom been at peace with itself. We are split between homocentric power and our origins in the world of life. While the universe endowed us with thought and consciousness, terror, greed, and a haunting sense of the shortness of existence go with it. How can the life of the planet and such a dominant but unruly creature coexist? When there were fewer of us, with less overwhelming power in our hands, we could attain an equilibrium between the earth and the human spirit, changing, shifting with the weather, but understood. We belonged within the earth's orbit, poised between light and darkness, and our senses could equate their risk or well-being with the other living things around them. Without that relationship we do not know the earth, and when its species go into extinction because of us, we have little in ourselves to protect them with. When nothing is sacred, nothing is safe.

(The extinction of species, now proceeding at a rate never before encountered in the history of evolution, is often ignored, in part because "we can get along without them," and in part because the idea is unthinkable. Extinction is anathema to most spiritual beliefs and unknown to children, as well as birds, which, if their sense of being could be translated into words, would probably declare their immortality, in keeping with nature's principles. It is interesting that two of the better known dictionaries of quotations have only one reference each on the term *extinction*.)

Many thousands of visitors to Costa Rica have seen the resplendent quetzal, *Pharomarchus Mocino*, a bird that is doing well in protected areas of that country but has a precarious status in other parts of Central America because of plume hunters and the destruction of the forests. While we outsiders see it as exotic, or something to be added to our life list of birds, the quetzal was sacred to the Maya and the Aztec. It is said that the Maya never killed the bird for its plumes but plucked them while it was alive, which had less to do with what we call conservation than with a belief that what was sacred could not be violated. Its beautiful golden-green feathers were reserved for rulers. In *The Ancient Maya*, Sylvanus Morley described the headdresses into which quetzal feathers were woven:

> The framework of these was probably of wicker, or wood, carved to represent the jaguar, serpent, or bird, or even the heads of some of the Maya gods. These frames were covered with jaguar skins, feather mosaic, and carved jades, and were surmounted by lofty panaches of plumes, a riot of barbaric color, falling down over the shoulders.*

On the assumption that their Spanish conqueror Cortes was a god, the Mexicans sent him splendid presents, including headbands of quetzal feathers and cotton cloth embroidered with them; and a cruel, deceitful god he turned out to be. Montezuma, forced to fill a room full of gold for his benefit, is said to have sadly protested that he would give it all for the feathers of a quetzal. Perhaps that was the point at which money began to degrade the New World environment, or at least take its visibly godlike qualities away from it.

The ancient god Quetzalcoatl was the rain god of the Toltecs, a deity associated with peace and plentiful harvests. Among later people he was the god of life, of wind and the morning star. His name is derived from *quetzal* (the Aztec *quetzallo* means precious, or beautiful) plus *coatl*, the Nahuatl word for serpent. On his back, in the culture of the Toltecs, he wore the brilliant plumes of the bird, and he carried a staff in the shape of a serpent. (Alexander Skutch, the naturalist of Costa Rica, has suggested that the union of these two eternal enemies, bird and snake, might be equivalent to making a single deity of God and Satan. The Toltecs may have been symbolizing an end to strife and the beginning of peaceful existence. In any case, the uniting of disparate elements into an

*Sylvanus G. Morley, *The Ancient Maya* (Stanford, Calif.: Stanford University Press, 1946).

ecosystem, as we might put it, seems like far less spacious a concept.) The word *coatl* also meant twin brother, which added still another dimension, combining, as the planet Venus did, the twin nature of a star of the morning and of the evening. So Quetzalcoatl came to mean the god of the morning, and the evening god was his twin brother Xolotl. What greater part could a bird play in the religion of a people!

The first quetzal I saw, on one of several trips to Costa Rica, was in the cloud forest reserve of Monteverde. It looked exceptionally tall and regal as it perched quietly near its nesting hole in a tall tree, with a long, curving train of plumes hanging down below the tip of its tail feathers. The green feathers on its back were iridescent, like spoils of light, and its crimson breast had all the openly defiant qualities of blood in the reflected rays of the sun. From the wing coverts, the most elegant green feathers curved over its breast on both sides. On the head was a crest of brushlike feathers that reminded me of ancient, martial helmets. The two very long, slender plumes looked like too much of an adornment for a bird that nests in tree cavities to handle. But, in fact, the male, when he takes his turn sitting on the eggs, faces outward, while the plumes are folded over his back, their tops often seen waving gently in the forest airs. "Solomon in all his glory was not arrayed like one of these."

The quetzel is a shining facet of the great civilization of nature, where the spirit of human life was once inextricable from birds and flowers and tall trees rising from buttressed trunks with branches smothered in bromeliads and epiphytes, a context of growth and sacrifice reaching through intricate shadows toward the sun. In an open clearing at the edge of the forest where the quetzal and his less extravagantly adorned mate were nesting, a wattled bell bird called with a loud, single "bong," which sounded less like a bell than a metal pipe being hit by a hammer. Inside the forest, nightingale thrushes hauntingly sang, like fine instruments being tuned up to some ineffable scale; and the last I saw of the quetzal was a shimmering waterfall of color plunging down off a branch to disappear in the darkness made by endless leaves.

To think of the dark and tenacious rain forests in terms of the diversity we say is necessary to natural systems is useful to the conservationist, but it is not enough. We who spend our lives guided only by terms and categories, endless facts and numbers, have not yet recognized the depths that would, if they could, help us out of our simplicity, the lack of diversity in ourselves. The great tropical message is inclusion. The forests, with their endless varied functions and differences in form, are statements as to the total involvement of life. They are the original grounds of life's inventions, a great drawing in of all kinds of possibilities, over endless time. Without them, we lose not only their incomparable species but the foundation of shared existence.

There is one great, constant element that is seldom, if ever, brought in when conservation is discussed, and that is the night. In spite of the fact that it is so common and inescapable, we have confused it with finality. We have hidden from it, tried to exclude it or cut down on its immense scale, profaned its majesty, called it bad names. That its immeasurable beauty should be included when we think of the value of lands, forests, and seas may not occur to us, but it is in them that the whole night is weighed, contained, and experienced. To lie down with the earth and deny the night is to lose what stature we gain through sharing it.

In the southern part of Costa Rica, in the Talamanca mountain range, is a magnificent new national park of four hundred eighty thousand acres called La Amistad. The name means "friendship" and comes from the original plans for a joint effort between neighboring Panama and Costa Rica. On its side of the border, Panama has not instituted any corresponding park lands, possibly because it imagines it has more important ways to use its money. In any case, I traveled to La Amistad with a group from the International Division of the Nature Conservancy, out of San Jose. It took most of the day to reach the park, and the roads leading into it were made slippery by showers of rain, red tropical earth now churned into ruts as deep as chasms.

That evening, fireflies ferried their very large, pulsing lights all around the clearing where we spent the night. At the base of the surrounding hills and the mountain slopes that rose beyond them, they were winking like campfires. After dark, a large brown and white moth visited the bunkhouse where we slept and lighted on the table. The design on its wings looked as if it had been taken from a native African basket, suggesting that all nature carried the crosscurrents of culture in herself. As I walked out into the night, I heard the waters of a mountain stream rustling by, and I felt the stars and the trees moving with the earth in its orbit, a beautiful interdependence. How wonderful it is to be part of the present mystery, the depth of a darkness never to be explained, out of the universe eternally timed. You pray never to be so far removed from the night as not to be received by it, this magic greater than all our fears.

In the early morning, when the stars were retreating, flocks of little green parakeets began to fly from one leafy tree to another, sounding like squeaky wire wheels. We set off on horseback to climb up to seven thousand feet or more in the mountains, riding cautiously up and down steep ravines along the way and forging rocky streams of purest water. On the lower slopes we had passed an Indian burial ground with one tall stone still standing in it, sacred death in the depth of the forest, where a tinamou, or *gallina de monte* sounded its tremulous call. The now displaced Indians and their lost culture played back the music of the birds with their flutes. To them, the jaguar, hawk eagle, frog, turtle, spider, or lizard were elements of the world of the spirit, and when they died they took these soul symbols with them in the form of golden ornaments. A totality from outside has long since made a clean sweep of those customs and beliefs; but the magic remains, in a beetle with a brown, varnished shell crossed by gold zig-zag markings, or the call of a thrush heard rising upward through the green sides of the mountain.

We had a cheerful, good-hearted guide named Salomon Romero, half Indian, who had spent much of his life in the *bosque* (wood, or forest). He had a family feeling for it. In fact, from the way he would transplant a displaced seedling on our route, such as a high altitude cedar, or a bromeliad, he seemed to treat it as his immortal garden. As we rode slowly up those slopes, past tier on tier of columnar, climbing trees, I thought that the tone of the forest was not of warring, predatory elements so much as an intensity of peace.

In the park that includes the volcano of Rincon de la Vieja (roughly translated "the old woman's corner," presumably by the chimney) evening's blue haze was settling in over the plains below it, while flocks of birds arrowed away overhead and dragonflies darted stiffly over open ground. Smoky clouds gathered over the summit and pit of the volcano, vultures glided toward it and then moved away. From the forested slopes came the shuddering roar of howler monkeys, and the clear, in-shadowed tones of forest birds. We also heard the calling of a quail, and since the wind was from the north, it was said to be a sign of good weather. After dark we found a group of luminous toadstools shining like the lights of some tiny, faraway village.

In North America, we are influenced by the extremes and conflicts in a weather system that ranges over many thousands of miles. The space we occupy is governed by storms from the Gulf and the winds off the glaciers, which may be one reason we can't keep still. Tropical rain forests seem calm and contained by comparison, growing in unchanging constancy. Each life seems not only to take on the characteristics of its surroundings but to be able to change with them, almost mercurially, like the brownish lizard we saw laying eggs on a patch of bare ground. Coming back to the same place a few hours later, we found it on the branch of a small overhanging tree; its skin was now dappled to fit the leaves spotted with sunlight. There were also moths to be found by daylight that mimicked wasps, so as to discourage predators. There were bats that pollinated plants by night, and I heard of a nectar-eating mouse that pollinated a flowering shrub. No relationship seemed impossible, and, for that matter, no size, after I saw a caterpillar of a nocturnal moth that must have been at least six inches long, looking like a stubby cigar. There were also walking sticks of an astonishing size, as well as giant grasshoppers, ants, and cockroaches in various areas. Stout cicadas in the forest canopy sounded like greatly speeded castanets, and they would die down and start up again, with the long rhythms of breath. Endless transmutations seemed commonplace alongside rivers that ran like paths among the stars, smoke from volcanos that joined the exhalation of clouds, hummingbirds that splintered the light from the sun.

Fifty kinds of hummingbirds have been found in Costa Rica, and some of the names given them reflect the glittering beauty of those vibrant, tiny beings, such as the scintillant, the violet sabrewing, the fiery-throated, the long-billed starthroat, and the purple-throated mountain gem, which I saw hovering next to the pink and white flowers of a shrub at a high elevation. Some tropical birds have such splendor in their plumage as to seem beyond need in any rational sense, although a quetzal, or a scarlet macaw, only displays the latent fire that their world sustains. Out in an open hillside one day I saw a long-tailed silky flycatcher as it perched on the very tip-top of a tree in the wind. Its feathers were of an elegant shade of gray, with light yellow markings. Trim and perfect it was, as soft as flowers. Then there were the butterflies, more than on all the continent of Africa in this tiny nation, of a dazzling variety of pattern and color I never knew existed, fast-flitting, "vadegating" flyers I chased with my camera and hardly ever caught. I also remember a silvery beetle in the hills that was like a ship at sea under the light of the moon. These are the forms of a supreme creativity, and any country that still has the means and the will to identify itself through them may still survive despoliation by forces beyond its control.

My fellow hikers and I were sitting on the crumbly lower slopes of Rincon de la Vieja. Jets of steam came out of small depressions and holes in the area, and their gases smelled strongly of sulphur. Yellow crystals rimmed holes where a liquid volcanic mud was boiling and bubbling. The ground was colored iron red and gray, pink, ochre, and yellow, and there was something about this thin surface of the planet's fiery womb that was curiously mesmerizing. We lingered there, sitting between the heat of the rock, rather than by the colder stream that ran nearby, as if we sensed where our deeper affinities lay.

Flying in by light plane to the national park at Corcovado on the Pacific coast, we passed over wrinkled and folded mountain slopes, brown as well as green in the dry season, here and there smoking with fires, the round clumps of spinach-green trees looking like part of an architectural model. Through intermittent cloud layers and scanty showers we finally saw the white brush-strokes of waves along the shore. The little plane landed in a grassy clearing, a narrow strip of bumpy ground, with high trees roped by vines on either side, while overhead, elegantly cut and plumaged swallow-tailed kites made tight turns and easy sweeps through the heated air.

When I first walked the trails at Corcovado, the rain forest seemed like a great, self-perpetuating wheel of light and growth. In spite of intermittent bird calls, the barking of monkeys, the sudden crashing of leaves where something moved, or gusts of wind through the clearings, it was full of an underlying calm. Its plants and animals seemed to attend on each other with an abiding patience . . . I think of those lizards with throbbing throats, in their perpetual suspension.

I heard of the jaguar, whose muscular body flowed with the grace of living water as it chased and killed an agouti or peccary in the forest. I watched orange-brown spider monkeys as they traveled through the leafy, open spaces between them with an easy, reckless freedom. When gaping human intruders stood below them they would shake the branches so as to knock down debris and try to drive them away. The bird calls from one part of the forest to another seemed to signal the stations of diversity.

Stealth and attack were waiting in that multiple containment. I saw several giant damselflies, whose gauzy wings, several inches across, looked like water surfaces dancing in the light; they were almost invisible except for a light blue or sunlight-yellow spot at the tip of their wings. This insect breeds in species of bromeliad that collect small pools of water, and it robs spiders of the food they collect in their webs, zipping in quickly and lightly to snatch it and carry it away. I have never seen such brilliant dexterity.

I stood cautiously aside as columns of army ants set forth their bivouac in a hollow tree on one of their periodic raiding expeditions, like "armies of unalterable law," devouring other insects, such as crickets and katydids, along their line of march. Many thousands of them streamed ahead, and the prey they drove before them, often escaping to the side, attracted birds to dart around and snap them up.

Then there were the ants that occupy acacia trees, in a sort of protective intimacy. The pioneer females cut out holes in the green thorns of the tree, hollow them out, and then lay their eggs, which hatch out into workers. Colonies feed on nutrient bodies in the leaves. They will attack any predator that tries to climb their tree, and they will even kill off competitive seedlings at its base that might take away its light. It has been found that in Nicaragua acacia ants will prune off the tips of the tree so that the crown grows into a kind of thorny hedge, a protection against predatory birds.

I am a watcher at a distance, filled with awe, trying to add to my understanding of these marvels, through information and knowledgeable guides. It is a matter of digging below the surface of our curiosity, and we can never dig deep enough. What does purpose mean that seems so demonstrable in these ants with their minuscule brains? Am I only to put down their behavior to nerve ends and chemical pheromones and let it go at that? How can we apply comparative values of intelligence to them if we are prejudiced in our own favor to start with? As for me, I think I live half in and out of dreams. We do not own intelligence; it is an attribute of the planet, together with all the fine degrees of perception and awareness in living things, so close at hand in the rain forest, that supreme architecture of life in space. The psychic receiver in us, the biological inheritor, is ready for each scent, sound, and motion within the trees. We have been here before. The life that is nourished and consumed at the same time, that grows its extravagant forms in all their means of escape and magnetic attraction, is still our basic sustenance. It is our inescapable origins that deserve a sacred name.

Out beyond the forest edge at Corcovado was the warm Pacific, with a dazzling sun by day firing a long, gray beach, where sea turtles moved slowly up at night to lay their eggs, often to have them dug out by local people, or predators such as dogs, pigs, or coatimundis. What little ones do hatch are preyed upon by ghost crabs, gulls, and frigate birds as they run the gauntlet to open water, where they are threatened by sharks and predatory fish.

At night the dazzling jewels of the Southern Cross climbed their vaulted ladders, and the planets shone like glow worms, or bio-luminescent organisms in the sea; while in the forests the animals listened, and the plants stirred in the great silence sanctioned by plenitude.

This procreant ceremony with its guide in the stars will not fail in its supreme timing because of the human race and its mindless destruction. We are its dependents. Night and the sun bring us to justice. One very hot day in the tropical dry forest at Santa Rosa, where the trail ran through a sparse growth of shrubs and trees and was hard to find again if you left it for any distance, an elderly woman in another group I was with wandered off and was lost. It took three hours to find her, now almost overcome by heat pros-tration. It just so happened that the old "norte Americano" had pinned a sign on her back since she was slow, which read: "Don't follow me." In the ambiguity of fate, that might have been inter-preted as good advice. She survived, in part because of common sense and her failure to panic, but this was a hint of the end of the line, as far as you go, although nothing really knows how far it goes. What is death, after all? I only know it through having lived. If I feared it, it was only because I was afraid in life. Under that tropical sun death seemed almost casual. What a common thing it is to lose your way and fall prey to that burning sun which pro-vides all limits, joining a desert we have never seen. This living, this dying, shared with every other form of existence, including fellow parasites and predators, some, like the insects, only living for a few hours, is not our making or determination. Duration is nothing, association everything.

Natural Architecture

Poems

The Gull

The wild white gull comes screaming, billowed and tossed
In the sacred air, over the shore and inland
On the storm. How far and soaring fast it flings
The springing magic of the earth, feathers
Aflame in the cruciform of blood and sky,
And tendons taut with excellence! How high
And blest it wheels in tribute through the wind,
To turn past beauty's shaping to the sea!

The Herring-Run

By day and night, out of the law of leaden tides,
Migration and death through the inland gauntlet, where the gulls,

Like vultures hunting high air of dying, circle and scream.

The pale blind fish, in millions, move from the ocean walls—
Salt gulfs and dark devouring—to fight the sun,
In the shallow waters crystal to a hunter's eye.

On the stream bed flowing, their sinuous shadows on the sand,
They waver backward with the weeds; processional
In tide and stars, pulsed forward by the drums of time.

Soft in the currents, spineless as the water's flow;
And then they leap! Taut daring at the wires, the high
And highest trial; their wounds; their white resplendent scales!

The male and female, power and spawn, rocket through rage
Of rocks, black storms and flailing torrents on their flesh.
To meet the silent lakes, perfection's morning womb.

They die shining. The splash of moons and golden lust
Of rivers loads the nets, as they protest and praise,
In the last quick leaps and running of their great desire.

The Wood Frog

I came across my cousin
sunning itself, and I presumed
on kinship with a touch. Like leaves,
joined in their camouflage to fox
and squirrel, an autumn russet,
it was a pulse of earth on earth;
the white neck fluttering, black eyes

steeper than lake water, black waters.
Then it let me pick it up
and put it down again—
so still and self-sufficient,
so far from me,
I gave up all presumption.

Music by the Waters

Out of the marbled underwaters,
artifacts of surf, comes the shining
of bubble and frog-green weed; the salivated
quartz egg; purple dye of greater storms
in minor shells; all things touched by tides;
patterns of water not of water;
castoffs, like speckled eyes from deeper sight,
tones on the mind. I picked them and they sing.

Comb Jelly

But for the eight, interior rays,
this might be a dislocated eye,
the vitreous humor, horrifying
on the sand. It is nine tenths water,
the sea's ally, and it devours
larvae like a pulsing flower,
a delicate, diaphanous engineering
with magic in its appetite.
One more of Hunger's masterpieces
to make us swallow what we see.

Natural Architecture

Moulded to the owl is what the owls spits out,
As dry cocoons of mice—gray fur, fine bones,
Eleven tiny skulls with yellow teeth—
Death fitted to digestion.
                              If steel and stones
Are what we love, let's swallow them, then gulp
Benignly like the owl, and send them forth
As buildings, shapes, desires, moans and groans,
But made of us. Leavings should not be waste.
Or else, how should we bless what we receive?

from

The Bird of Light

(1991)

Migrants in Winter

*D*AY ONE IS ANY DAY IN THE YEAR. LEAVES ARE born this minute; winter or summer, flowers never die. The fish circle on within the greater circles of the sea, and the birds in their migrations translate affinities from one hemisphere to another. This is the law of coexistent life which carries with it vast expenditure and sacrifice and is all we our-selves depend on for continuance. It is that day in which I, neither optimistic nor pessimistic about human prospects, look out over land and sea for more enduring guides, those who have practiced earth's art for periods of time which may be calculated by the human mind but are really incalculable in their changes. This has led me to see what we put down as mere birds as carriers of light and wisdom.

I have now had a love affair with terns for many years, even though these tirelessly flying, excitable, vulnerable birds have sel-dom come very close to me, having more often spun out of sight. That they keep returning to their nesting territories on home shores has become a source of restoration for me. These ancient travelers tie all shores together. Like other migrants, they will always be at a distance from me, but that only keeps me reaching after them. It is the essence of love in our experience that it keeps us half in turmoil, rejecting and rejected, torn away, rejoined again. All things move ahead in accordance with a passion endowed with immortal principles, like the earth itself.

I will never wholly know the terns because of the facts and information I am able to collect about them. I follow after them because the quality of their being is still wild, still unconquerable, out of the ocean of being that created them.

A few miles from where I live on Cape Cod, there is a raised island, or dune promontory, locally called Gray's Beach, where a colony of common and roseate terns have been nesting for many years. It lies out on the far rim of an extensive salt marsh, and is made up of sandy hummocks and hollows, shelving off into salt water from a narrow beach that merges with eroding banks of peat and a scanty growth of spartina grass. It is not literally an island except during periods of storm tides, when it is surrounded and at times invaded, by water, but for the terns it is an island of nurture between their arrival in May and their departure in August.

Now, in early winter, the salt marsh and Gray's Beach are bare and silent but for the wind and the distant roaring of the surf off outer bars. The dead stalks of the beach grass that keep the low dunes from blowing and breaking out are straw yellow, with a ragged look at the butt like old cornstalks. When I last walked out there in September, many terns were beating back and forth over offshore waters, diving for fish, but they had left their nesting areas behind them. It was then that I picked up the light and delicate skull of a tern with very large eye cavities and dully polished like a white pebble, with a faintly oily sheen. That suggested nightly visits from a great-horned owl. Repeated and consistent raids by that formidable predator, which will tear an adult tern's head off, can result in the complete desertion of a colony. At the very least, since the owl keeps the terns off their nests, night after night, a large number of eggs will fail to hatch out and chicks will die.

I also found a fragile cup, all that was left of a broken egg shell, a symbol of where life begins, the shell of the womb, the shape of the globe itself. Gray's Beach is close enough to mainland predators so as not to provide the best conditions for the terns, who prefer offshore islands less exposed to owls and marauding mammals. The better sites have been lost to them, principally because of an overwhelming population of gulls, the result of the vast supply of waste food we have opened up to them in the twentieth century. Still, Gray's Beach once sheltered a tern colony of several thousand pairs, which kept up its number for some years before it started to decline.

Tidal marshes are sheltered by offshore sandbars and barrier beaches, and their growth takes advantage of the embayments along the shoreline. The winds blow freely across their open ranges, and their tough, salt-resistant grasses seem to hold the year in place. Natural channels and manmade ditches take the tidewaters through all levels of a marsh, rising up and flooding over, then falling and withdrawing, a daily, nightly, permanent rhythm to which all its life is responsive.

A great blue heron, that almost spectral image of a prehistoric past, rises majestically out of the marsh, on big, bowed, misty gray-blue wings, then settles down some distance further on, disappearing into the confines of a ditch. A winter that freezes over creeks, ponds, and marshes for too long a time may be deadly for a heron. It may starve to death, although in an environment tempered by the heat-retaining capacity of the ocean, it may survive.

During a mild winter, some shorebirds may linger through December. On land, robins, an occasional thrush, and a few songbirds may find enough to feed on throughout the winter. On relatively warm and sunny winter days, some insects will appear before you in the air. The subtleties, the fine points of contact, between these lives and the surrounding world largely escape us who merely claim it as our exclusive territory. What do I know of the earth that its prior inhabitants are not already aware of?

We have to wait until late April or early May for the terns to start coming in from such far distant shores as Trinidad, Surinam, and Brazil, but life continually moves in coastal waters, and some inshore migration is still alive. Over the exposed flats at low tide, flocks of gray and white sanderlings, with many brown dunlins intermixed, are deftly probing the surface for tiny crustaceans or mollusks. I have seen flocks of a thousand or more in December and early January. A dog races in their direction, and a big flock instantaneously divides in two, each part skimming low, wheeling away, and settling down out of reach. At other times, they rise up, dip, turn, and swing like a casting of silver facets into the air, or dancing flowers, alternating the dark shading of their backs and the white of their bellies. When they flip over on their sides, reflecting the sunlight, it is as if they were deliberately courting it.

Such dazzling unanimity is as much a puzzle to those who try to unravel it as are the currents of a running brook. These birds are apparently without leadership, though they move as one, and at the same time the flock is made up of individuals who are acutely aware of their neighbors, and the spacing they need to fly with them. Their grace and precision derives from impulses over which human life has no control. Yet if this complex art eludes us, it is as spontaneous as the sight we receive it with. Is it not possible to follow the light through the medium of a bird? Without them, the days would go by without definition.

The sunrise, saffron and red, bleeds along the horizon above the trees, topped with small black clouds like a band of stylized waves. The day moves on, and a cold, brilliant northern light is cast over coastal waters winnowed and skewed around by the wind. As the morning sun begins to warm a thin coating of ice left by the high tide along the banks of the salt marsh, little white flakes suddenly snap off and fly up like so many flags. On the marsh level the grasses are matted down, like the coarse hairs of a dead deer I once came across in the dunes, while the cold wind whistles over them. A crow flies by, and then a Canada goose, a lone bugler looking for its companions.

Winter backs and fills with its polar opposites of light and dark. Periodic storms lock us in and inhibit most travel, but winter is a traveler in itself, moving on and out like the ocean waves that follow the future, on the forward edge of light. We hide from its reality, in the name, not entirely unjustified, of security. Winter is part death, part glory.

Arctic signs keep melting and reappearing, like the snow that gathers on the trees and in patches over the dunes. On a day between storms, sky and water work together over the open Atlantic on majestic variations in form. There are snowy caves in the dark cloud curtains over the sea, and low-lying cloud mountains ringing the horizon. Great dark wands reach into a gray sky where a few herring gulls are circling like hawks on fall migration over a mountain ridge. Bad weather, with high winds and sleet, is predicted after nightfall, but the tables of the sea are now flat and calm, and over them the waterfowl collaborate in waiting for the earth's next move. Hundreds of eider ducks raft off the cliffed shores; red-breasted mergansers cast over the surface like feathered lances; and Canada geese ride high on the waters like stately vessels. The great transformations of the winter sea and sky consign the world we ourselves construct to a makeshift status.

Throughout the month of December, people reported dead humpback whales floating offshore, and some were carried in by wind and tides. They died of causes so far undetermined, although it is thought that they may have been poisoned by mackerel which had ingested a toxic red algae. On December 13, the body of one of those playful, singing giants landed close to a nearby beach off Cape Cod Bay. The body was at first blown up out of all proportion by the gases of decay, since it must have been dead for some days. Then it collapsed after one side was cut away to make samples of flesh for analysis. It was the eleventh humpback to be reported, plus two minke whales.

Following a fierce storm, with temperatures well below freezing, light snow and a high wind that blew for twenty-four hours, the world was still dark along the shore. The black, grooved hide of the whale, which was thirty-seven feet long, sagged on its thick bed of rime ice. After struggling to reach it through the frozen mush, a few quiet onlookers stood around the body, paying their respects, and after a short time departed.

I measured the width of the flukes at twelve feet. A white flipper, a third of the whale's length, extended stiffly from its side, and the internal organs where the body had been cut away bore some resemblance to our own, enormously enlarged. They were a revelation of earth colors, in shades of red, gray, and a drab green, a dark interior now exposed to a dark day and an atmosphere of mourning. I sensed an unspoken question among us, common to the age, which has to do with how much injury our world is responsible for. We are continually faced with the vast disparity between man's power to destroy and his inability to control or foresee the consequences. What might be happening out there in deeper waters to further reduce the sum of life? If we leave the whales behind us, do we risk the loss of all we know within us of the ocean's power and stability?

Small flocks of dunlins and sanderlings are still active along the shore, running forward on twinkling legs, picking up their food out of the exposed sand and mud flats at low tide. Wild, fast-moving storms blow in with sleet and snow and then clear off and away, and the little birds keep reappearing. I find their tracks, like skeletons of leaves, etched in the wet sand of the beach. So long as their food supply is not covered over by ice, some will have enough to feed on.

Sanderlings have an extraordinary range. They are scattered across the planet, from North to South America, across the Atlantic to Britain, over the Mediterranean and Caspian seas to Burma, Indonesia, and Australia and, as the *Audubon Encyclopedia of Birds* ends the account, "etc.," a cosmopolitan, nearly universal migrant. They are very hardy little birds, pearly everlastings, like the flowers of that name. Dead shorebirds are seldom found; they get lost to wind and wave. They are like flecks of foam, ephemeral, though in that life and death context, omnipotent. Yet in recent years, the sanderling population has plummeted for reasons that are not entirely clear.

A few days and nights of below-freezing January weather, and ice begins to pack up along the shore until its broken white masses extend far out over the salt waters of the bay, brilliant in the sunlight. The sanderlings, with their food supply covered up, have disappeared from the local beaches. Since 400 miles a day is no problem for them, they might have flown to better feeding grounds far to the south of us, or found an ice-free shore on some other part of the Cape. It only takes a few days of sun and moderating temperatures to disperse the ice far and wide over the horizon, and a few small flocks reappear to feed over the now exposed flats. Sea ducks also move into the reopened waters. A great black-back gull picks away at the floating body of a young eider, shot by a random gunner, and has a hard time getting through its dense coat of down and feathers. Many gulls find food in lines of seaweed dislodged from offshore beds by ice and storm waves, to be washed in by the tides. Crab legs and bits of their shells litter the beach. Gulls are always waiting to seize their opportunities.

The little gray and white sanderlings keep reappearing at mid to low tide. If mud and sand are so frozen that the invertebrates they feed on are no longer accessible, these shorebirds can leave as quickly as they need to, on a "hard weather migration." Both local and long-distance migrants move to the high Arctic in the spring, just ahead of a frozen world and sometimes dangerously with it, when there is little food. Sanderlings that migrate to the southern continent after their young are fledged will fly all the way to the southern coast of Argentina, a journey of some 8,000 miles. The well-publicized flight of another shorebird, the red knot, takes it 10,000 miles from the Arctic Circle to the tip of Tierra del Fuego. Some individuals may complete the trip in as little as thirteen days, though most take longer than that. In overcoming distance, these migrants rival the Arctic tern, which travels between the Arctic and the Antarctic each year, a round trip of up to 24,000 miles; but their performance is even more spectacular, since the tern travels at a far more leisurely pace, taking months to make the journey and feeding over the surface as it goes.

Brian Harrington of the Manomet Bird Observatory reported a ruddy turnstone that flew 2,750 miles from Alaska to an island in the Pacific in only four days. Subsequently, a semi-palmated sandpiper, shot on its arrival in Guyana, on the north coast of South America, was found through the band on its leg to have been released at Plymouth Beach, Massachusetts, on August 12, 1985. It was picked up on the 16th, having flown 2,800 miles within those four days, to become the current champion, although this is not unusual. Shorebirds have been known to fly at heights of 10,000–20,000 feet on migration, and their speed has been timed at 40–50 miles an hour.

The truth is that no matter how fascinated we may be by the idea of record-breaking flights, they are not exceptional, but routine. It is not the individual shorebird, but the species that is capable of flying out from New England, nonstop across the waters of the North Atlantic, to reach the coast of South America. To accomplish this requires a massive consumption of energy. Individuals must have enough bodily reserves of fat so that they do not run out of energy during migration and perish.

The major feeding or staging areas, where many thousands of shorebirds congregate to fatten up during their migrations, are now few in number along the Atlantic seaboard, but they are vital to their future. Alternate sites have been lost to them, or further threatened by shorefront development and the destruction of wetlands. The toxic wastes, the herbicides and pesticides that continually wash out from the land and seep into remaining wetlands have unknown effects on their reproduction. Like other races, sanderlings have their "boom and bust" years, but it is estimated that their population has recently declined by 80 percent. This might in part be the result of chemical seepage in the river mouths and estuaries of Chile and Peru, where large numbers spend the winter.

Between the end of April and June, hordes of horseshoe crabs will lay their eggs on the shores of Delaware Bay, pulled in from deeper waters by moon tides which have been their signal for millions of years. In mid-May, between the 15th and the 20th, with a synchronized behavior that seems nothing short of miraculous if we were not aware of the beautifully timed and life-giving advents of the planet, thousands of red knots arrive to feed on this bounty.

The narrow strip of beach, extending for twenty miles along the shore, looks as if it were strewn with the litter and wreckage of combat. Thin-pointed spikes stick up out of the sand. Olive drab helmets lie out everywhere, many of them turned over, others half buried. Some are wedged between pilings that hold up the weathered beach cottages that stand over the beach. Through the murky brown waters just inshore, you can see these antediluvian animals, whose primitive eyes can only see changes between light and dark, as they wait to come in and mate. The males begin to arrive toward the latter part of April, and the females follow. Surges of egg laying along the coastline usually occur about two hours before high tide, and are intensified by a full moon. These primordially slow creatures, if they are unable to get back to water on the ebb tide, bury into the sand and wait for high tide. Many pairs of males and females are still attached to each other. Horseshoe crabs lay eggs by the billion, by the ton, a productivity that does not in itself account for their survival. They have evolved relatively unchanged for 350 million years because of their adaptation to the consistently stable nature of the shallow seas on the rim of the continent.

Laughing gulls, many of them local nesters in the marshes behind the beach, are everywhere, wildly crying in a cacophonic chorus. They jostle each other, standing on the backs of the horseshoe crabs, and continually peck in the sand for eggs. Clouds of trim red knots, medium-sized shorebirds with robin-red breasts and silvery gray wings, come skimming in off the water, to land with a typically alert carriage on the beach. There they feed insatiably on the eggs, each egg being about the size of small black caviar. A considerable proportion of the knots have reached this haven of plenty, nonstop from Brazil, a distance of 8,000 miles. They have several thousand more miles to go in order to reach Victoria Island, their nesting grounds in the high Arctic. To fatten up for this migration, it is estimated that they will have to eat one egg every five seconds for fourteen hours a day, doubling their weight in two to three weeks' time.

At the least disturbance, the red knots spin off by the thousands over the water, then return to the beach, with that swinging unanimity common to shorebirds. When they finally reach Victoria Island, they nest secretly in the tundra, widely dispersed, often miles from each other. Without this feast of eggs, strategically located, the knots would have a difficult time surviving. The fact that petrochemical companies are located nearby gives the ornithologists a major cause for worry. One major spill could mean disaster for crabs and shorebirds.

An international effort is now under way to conserve and protect such staging areas, critical for some fifteen species of shorebirds on their migrations, and none too soon. The term "gluttony," sometimes applied to this temporary but intense period of feeding required to sustain birds on migration, is probably a misnomer. Gluttony might better describe industrial society. We consume a large part of the world's resources on such a scale as to become indifferent to what sustains us. Short-term profit threatens long-term starvation, not only of land and life, but of our own perception. A society unaware of its dependence on the rest of life has little to stop its almost unconscious greed but crisis. We now fall back on a world conscience which is in the throes of being born.

That sanderlings, sandpipers, or red knots, those little bundles of fat, muscle, and feathers, could accomplish such conquests of distance is awe-inspiring, although it is no less true of the ruby-throated hummingbird. Aside from explanations to do with its high metabolism and its breast muscles, can we really account for the fire in that tiny, atmospheric fish of a bird? This past autumn, I watched them feeding on the nectar of jewelweed along a shore in Nova Scotia, before they disappeared on their southward migration. They are jewels in themselves, carrying invisible engines of futurity. Regardless of how we rate them in terms of their significance, the universe fashions the smallest of living things with such craft as to meet its exalted and relentless standards.

Still, these birds are on a tightrope of survival. Their migrations are highly dangerous and often subject to severe cyclonic disturbances, driving them off course. Predators rob them on their territories of eggs and young. Food at the right time is critical;

otherwise they are drained of their energy. They belong to one of the more fragile but enduring balances in nature, but their tenacity in following the earth's directions from pole to pole is a triumph in itself. There is a terrible discipline and urgency to these migrations, not unfamiliar to the history of human travel. Yet we do a great deal to shield ourselves from the kind of direct exposure experienced by the birds.

Blue sky and water days brighten the latter part of January, in between covering clouds, cold rain, and snow. A flock of about 150 sanderlings, with only a few dunlins, surprises me where I walk along the rim of the tide, landing only a few yards away, close enough for a quiet greeting. They hurry along, with that bright, crowd quickness of theirs. Then the whole flock lifts up and skims swiftly away, with a low crying that sounds like fine wires twanging in the wind. They are forever ahead of us. We only follow shorebirds to the shoreline.

Ritual

*T*HE MONTH OF MAY STREAMS FORWARD, IN ALL
its sequences of light. The air warms up, while southerly
winds still battle with the north. In this transmigratory
period, it still seems miraculous to me not that these seabirds can
find their way, but that they possess such a sureness of place,
from one pole to the other. It is a magic of fitness, of appropriate
measure on a global scale, which they carry in their minds.

In terms of their behavior, terns are so spontaneous as to be in-
separable from the present. At the same time, they exist in an
eternal present insofar as they follow the dictates of the sun and
the earth's travels around it. In a highly seasonal part of the world,
we divide the year into spring, summer, autumn, and winter, but
ultimately only one season dictates the infinitely varied terms of
life to all creation. The clouds are only temporarily described by
our classification of them into cirrus, nimbus, stratus, cumulus,
and their variations. They take their forms from continuous motion, and those beings who follow that motion in themselves can
never be on a lower scale than ourselves, who see fit to determine

all stages of it in terms of material possession and the human mind. As played out in the birds, the planetary rhythms have a supremacy which cannot be violated or reduced. The terns arrive on their territories, as they will leave them, obeying certain time-honored rituals, which amount to a high form of courtesy which we might do well to respect.

The terns are in a state of great urgency as they gather offshore and begin to move in, aggravated in their need to pair up and nest. In the vicinity of the nesting site at Gray's Beach, a female is making constant, chittering cries as she waits on a sandbar for attention. A male hovers over a tidepool nearby, then twists in the air and makes a slanting dive into the surface to pick up a minnow, which he brings to her. The fish is accepted and swallowed, but she goes on begging, and he tries it twice again while I watch, to finally break off and leave her there, perhaps to be more satisfied by him, or another possible mate, later on. These early indecisions are common enough in courtship, but they might contain some underlying doubt as to whether or not the birds have come to the right place.

Gulls circle and romp together in the springtime air, while others are scattered over the tidal flats, musically calling. A man and his girl friend go idling and bumping each other down the beach, swaying like trees in a wind. I walk out over the complex map of the tidelands, across their ripples and watery lanes and shallow pools. It is a silvery landscape and the sky is sending down light showers like so much sea spray.

Water spurts up from a hole made by a clam. As the tide begins to move in, wavelets bob and duck around me, gradually covering and wreathing the sands. Through my field glasses, I see a pair of common terns strutting around each other, heads and necks stretched up, tails cocked, wings lowered and held out partly on their sides.

Further out over the sands is a pair of roseate terns, recognizable through their black bills, their longer tails, and feathers of a more uniformly light gray than the commons. They get their name from a pinkish flush on their breasts, not always visible except when the light strikes them at the right angle. The stance of these birds when courting is extremely elegant. Their tails project behind them like spars on a sailing vessel. Their velvety gray wings spread out like a cloak, the hem nearly touching the ground, and their shining black heads and beaks point cleanly toward the sky, in a pose that is highly strict and formalized.

On both sides of the Atlantic, the population of roseates has seriously declined. In America, they have been classified as an endangered species. The common terns, more aggressive and adaptable, have managed to hold their own for the time being, but not without help from individuals and institutions protecting their nesting sites. Roseates are more vulnerable to the twentieth century's worldwide disturbances, and are disappearing . . . a bird of classic style that ought to be as precious to us as the Parthenon has been to the Greeks. But we let the great architecture of life slip away from us and what we no longer see before us we are unable, or unwilling, to compare with the lesser standards by which we value the earth.

Many of the birds engaging in courtship behavior before they settle in to nest may have been premated, which is to say, paired up during the previous season. Either they have spent the winter together, or they have recognized each other on arriving in the vicinity of the site. Even though premated pairs will start in to court and nest without much delay, just as many seem to join the majority in days of ground and aerial display. This is a process through which pairs are finally "bonded," and the whole colony established. It is difficult at first to tell the difference between males and females, until pairs start to copulate before nesting. In these early days, three, four, or five birds displaying together is quite common, which makes distinguishing between the sexes even harder.

(I do not know of any ready shortcut to identifying males and females. Years ago, the warden of a colony of Sandwich and common terns in Great Britain told me that he could tell the difference by their voices. Since he had been listening to them all his life, as had his father before him, I had no reason to doubt him.

He also contended that he could tell male from female by the way the black cap ended at the nape of the neck; it comes to more of a point in the male, and is a little squared off or blunted in the female. So far, at least, this last distinction has not worked for me, since the shape of the black feathers on their nests seems to depend on the way they happen to be holding their heads, up or down.)

J. M. Cullen, in her thesis on the Arctic terns,* describes an action she calls tilting in the mating display of the Arctics; the behavior of the commons is almost identical. These and other species have fully developed black caps during the breeding season, but their fall molt leaves them with a streaked or grayish patch on their heads, and a whitish forehead. The conclusion is that the black cap has a definite function during mating. In displaying before a potential mate, a bird will tilt its head so that the cap is hidden, or partly turned away from its partner. To show it directly seems to have an intimidating effect. If a female walks around a male in a "bent" position, with her beak pointed toward the ground—as opposed to an "erect" display with head and neck pointed upward—the male on his inside circle makes an effort to keep his cap turned away from her, because if she catches sight of it, she might move away.

Since males are probably made nervous, or put off, by the display of the cap as well, and since they are more aggressive than females in defense of territory, the display may have some significance as a threat, but is probably used more in avoidance and appeasement than as a direct challenge. If a male pecks at a female, or rushes toward her, she will tilt her cap to avoid further trouble, and males startled or frightened by something during a mating display, or while making their way through a neighbor's territory, will do the same.

Step by step, from the first hesitant approaches to the territory, to early nesting behavior, followed by established nests, egg laying, and the raising of chicks, the season is followed out with

*"A Study of the Behavior of the Arctic Tern (*Sterna macrura*)," thesis deposited at the Bodleian Library, Oxford, 1956.

formality and underlying discipline. After the terns have begun to settle in, the sands are covered with little chain patterns made by their feet where they have strutted around each other, while a high and wide chasing, fluttering up, circling, and gliding goes on overhead, at times loose, easy, and pliable, and at others very fast. All this effort leads up to a means whereby a colony can occupy old nests, or establish new ones over a given space, with order and understood boundaries. (On some islands, pairs of terns have been seen coming back to their exact same nesting sites over a period of many years.) In general, a male attempts to lead a female down to a proposed site, often with several males chasing after him, especially if he is carrying a fish. The sorting out takes days on end; it amounts to a continual trying out, a continual falling short, or erosion, of the efforts of males and females to form their "pair bonds."

Males may even put a great deal of effort into trying to attract birds that may not be the right sex in the first place, such as a male who seems to be behaving momentarily like a female, or a female that is already mated. Sex recognition often takes time. The combination of attack and escape that is part of all their efforts to mate is also a factor in temporarily holding them back from the serious business of nesting. They are edgy. They engage in maneuvers which are broken off, time and again. But sooner or later, a female becomes satisfied that her suitor has chosen the right space of chosen ground to nest in.

(Much of the time spent in finding an appropriate mate probably has an element of critical judgment in it, so far as the female is concerned. She needs a mate who is going to bring in plenty of fish and choose a good nesting hollow in the first place, and that implies discrimination.)

Scraping out little hollows in the sand represents an early stage in courtship ritual, but it is a practice that serves to strengthen emotional ties. (Emotion plays a very strong part in the life of these birds.) After a male and female greet each other, posturing, the male may walk over to a preexisting hollow which he has chosen, then lower his breast while scratching out backward in the sand. If the female is interested enough, she may go over and stand by him, or even replace her suitor to enlarge the scrape on her own. Such scrapes are often called false by the ornithologists because they do not lead to a final nest.

In a similar way, the presentation of fish on the ground is another ceremonial act that strengthens their feelings toward each other. A male parading with a fish before a prospective mate does a sort of goose step, breast forward, in a very conscious way. It is an athlete or a soldier strutting his stuff, displaying his medals or his victorious presence before the girls. She begs for this precious gift, bent down in a submissive posture, while making eager, chittering cries like a chick being fed by its parent. At times she takes the fish, swallows it, and then flies away without any obvious sign of gratitude. Or a tension between them results in a tug-of-war. She snatches at the fish, and he holds on so that they are left with two halves.

In another version of this behavior, the female grabs at the fish and the male flies away with it, as if displeased. They share contradictory feelings at this stage of the game. She has a compulsion to lay eggs, and he to start in on the nest. This results in slight acts of aggression. The inner testing that marks their attempts to pair up implies that the male may be just as frightened as the female, or enough afraid of her so as not to surrender the fish.

As I watch them, distant as they are from my own sense of reality, I sense something of my own ambivalence. Seasons of hesitation, nerves sprung in the wind, characterize us both. On a deeper level, all this avian maneuvering with its wayward rhythms follows an uncompromising need that brings energy into our own affairs and fear to our hearts.

As the days go by, the activity becomes more intense. At least a few terns are displaying whenever I walk out over the marsh to watch them, at a viewing distance. One of a pair might be on the ground with wings cloaked and tail cocked, while the other circles over it. Three will land simultaneously. With necks craned in the same direction and wings held out, they look like uniformed soldiers on dress parade. Swift chases are going on in the air, involving three, or as many as five or six at a time. They are constantly engaged in flying up from the sandy hollows and hummocks, leading away, breaking off, settling down again, and day by day, the general clamor increases.

In their wild, formal, and repeated exercises, they also inter-change with the sandy land they came to. Their rituals are rhyth-mically allied with the growing grasses now shaking and whipping in the wind, and with the waters trickling back and forth over the tidal flats, shivering, parting, coming together again under silken clouds.

Courtship flights follow the two main types of ground display, combining elements of both. A male with beak pointed down-ward, as in the bent display, tries to lead a female who adopts the erect posture, or a less extreme equivalent of it, with head and neck extended and tilted upward. They fly past each other, each one alternately falling behind and overtaking the other so that it looks as if they were swinging in the air.

When a male carries a fish on these flights, as a superior form of attraction, it often starts with three or more birds engaging in much evasive action, eventually evolving into two. The remaining pair then fly off together, interchanging positions as they go. The bird in front may swing downward and to the side, while the other flies over and past it. Then the procedure is reversed as the bird now in the lead moves back and downward. There is a lovely, tilting balance to their flight. The male sounds a clear "Keera," while the female may cry "Kip-kip" or "Tik-tik," and then his call may change to a rasping "Koh-koh-keearrh."

So the sorting out in the colony goes on and on, and I hear many other cries as the birds go through their nearly incessant flying up and landing again, many stridently challenging, connec-tive cries. Isn't this urgent practice, for days on end, what we are continually required to do, at times veering off wildly in the wrong direction?

The tension in these flights, the resolution of conflict in these rituals, is in the spring itself, where the ruffed grouse drums and the gulls bow to each other. No life lacks ceremony.

The tension of opposites lies behind the perfection of form and all appearances. So a leaf stirs in the wind and lifts like a bird; the insect is the image of the leaf it inhabits; the shiny seed of a red maple has a cracked back like a winged beetle. Unlikeness seeks out likeness everywhere. Throughout these relationships, unendingly renewed, are the elements of evasion and affinity, touch and recoil. The hunger generated in the worlds of life, the fish to rise and be met by a predatory bird, the fish to suspend or procreate in the tension of the waters, is back of all memory and behavior.

The more I see of courtship flights, the more they compare with human games. The natural ease of great ball players is in them, of champion skaters, or ballet dancers. At the same time, I doubt whether there is much that can equal their high flight and its glide to earth. This culminating flight involves the circling upward of a pair to a high altitude, with one bird leading the other. At some point, one of them folds its wings slightly and starts to glide easily toward the ground, while the other follows. The two of them bank back and forth from one side to the other, swaying and side-slipping together as if their whole life had been a training for such an act.

The roseates, a cut in elegance above the commons, have a beautifully reaching look to their bodies as they glide together. When a pair flies slowly over the territory, their wings, stroking with an effortless assurance that accompanies the steady flow of a wave, appear to lean and hang on the air. Pairs of both species will circle high over a colony, but the roseates often fly out in a great circling fetch over the sea. I have watched a pair of roseates rising so high in the brilliantly blue sky that I have almost lost sight of them, but their impeccable snowy feathers shone in the light of the sun, while their catamaran-like tails showed as white filaments. (Their tails are longer and more flexible than the commons, floating and bouncing on the wind.) Their skill is dazzling. In a strong wind, they look as if they were flying backward as they ascend, but they are in perfect control. With both commons and roseates, a very fast chasing and circling upward will often end in a wide zigzagging glide down.

Roseates arrive on the nesting grounds later than the commons, although their spring migration is probably faster, since they are superior flyers. While common terns move up the coastline, relatively close to shore, roseates fly higher and farther out over the ocean. By early to mid-June, after most of the commons are incubating eggs, or brooding chicks, some roseates will still be engaged in courtship flights. Nothing exceeds their slip-streaming across the sky, incomparably lithe and limber. At times they skate through the sky as if shot from a sling, and at others they sail like kites on a high wind, or knife through the air like mackerel in undulant waters. They remind me then of William Blake's "arrows of desire."

Both species make spectacular glides. After a passage of synchronized swinging, they appear to start tumbling, or revolving high in the air. This is apparently due to a form of gliding in which they turn as they fall, tilting one wing above the other on a vertical instead of horizontal plane. Whereas common terns may start a downward glide from five or six hundred feet, and Roseates from still higher, Sandwich Terns will circle up to several thousand feet. I have been told that from that great height, a pair will drop at a speed of sixty to seventy miles an hour, the pressure on their outer primary feathers making a papery, drumming sound. They plunge down toward the ternery at an angle of about sixty degrees until they are within three to four hundred feet of the ground, then sheer upward, to circle and land in an easy, finished way together. The whole arc of this masterful performance may take in as much as two miles. What a surpassing way to express the feelings of opposite sexes freed of their restraint!

A friend of mine once said to me as I was rhapsodizing about this dance of the birds: "How does that relate to me? Tell us about *ourselves.*" Hadn't I suggested parallels enough? I realize that very few of us, even when we are in love, have the ability to launch into paired maneuvers a thousand feet in the air. But I suspect that what stopped him from making the connection was the idea of "nature," which he had long since left to the scientists and the sentimentalists.

Courtship in animals follows certain stereotyped patterns that go back so far in the vast flow of evolution that we can only guess as to their origins. In that sense alone there is no use oversimplifying these rituals in our favor. Accustomed to pigeons billing and cooing in the city, people are inclined to think of birds as helplessly repetitive, incapable of reflecting on their own actions. Year after year, I have heard it said of the alewives, they just come back and do the same thing. Yet these fish, on their annual journey, are once again engaged in a revolutionary mission. To put down the birds in their sexual flights and courtship rituals is to underrate the profundity of the rhythm of the year. It also passes over their closeness to earth environments whose every mood may be a matter of life and death.

In the existence of a tern, love as we know it may be only an incident, which if at all relevant, seems to a high degree made up of aggravation. Yet in a short season, they carry out the paramount needs of love, and we ought not to be so niggardly or self-limiting as to deny it to them. The same, imperative inner demands send us ahead on our own migrations. Subconscious motivation is a common property of life. We are unable to escape our origins.

The inner conflict between nesting pairs and its resolution comes out of an earth engagement as mysterious as anything we will ever know. The term "pair bond" seems excessively limited by comparison.

Wild chases, accompanied by a great deal of clamor, increase as more birds come in and the colony establishes itself. The friction between attraction and intimidation fires their energies. At times, the element of hostility which is a part of their flights gives way to a fight, usually short-lived. A pair may start off easily enough but then drop to the ground with angry, gargling cries, in a flurry of beating wings. Or two birds, wings rapidly stroking, will rise from the territory, partly turning around each other and moving backward at the same time. The one rises above the other, and they will keep alternating in this way, each trying to be the one on top. It is an action that has some of the characteristics of a fight between two males on the ground, but often turns into a paired

flight that looks like courtship. These "flutter-ups" are mainly associated with nesting territory, and play some part in the recognition
by individual birds of their separate claims—which leads to the
idea that they are engaged in by males.

A vigorous fight starts up between two male roseates on the
ground. They peck violently at each other, wings beating, but
quickly break off. It might be said that the fight has served to define a mutual tolerance, an understanding that can be translated
into a few inches of territory.

Roseates, as compared with the commons, which like more
open ground, choose fairly thick vegetation to nest in, often making small, tunnellike openings at the edge of a heavy growth of
grass. In some areas, they also nest under boulders or in rock burrows where they are narrowly confined, and where mating rituals
have to be performed in a highly stylized manner. The male goes
in first, followed by the female. She starts by facing him, then pivots around, posturing, while he lowers his head, calling "Uh-uh-
uh-uh." Then the female goes back out, while he engages in some
scraping motions. Terns know where their boundaries are, though
they may be invisible to us, especially out in the open, but rock
walls enforce proximity, and the ritual has to be precisely carried
out, or the pair will fight.

On open ground, a pair of roseates weave around each other in
tight little circles, like matadors with their capes, while bowing and
craning their glossy black heads, tail feathers held up behind their
silvery backs, wings bowed out at their sides. There is something
stiff and military about it. This is a ritual which is perfectly tuned
to the rhythms of space and cannot be transgressed. Its formality
does not allow the slightest deviation, being no more tyrannical,
no less pure than those ice crystals I see forming on the water's
surface as winter comes. We invent our instruments, each one an
improvement on the last in our efforts to surpass the bonds of
nature, but life's perfected instruments are bound to laws beyond
our ability to see.

A male common tern flies in with a fish and offers it to his
prospective mate, having tried it before without success. At last,

the right signal has been received. She takes the fish and eats it, and he is stimulated to copulate with her. He circles her, four or five times over, while she turns, only slightly, after which he mounts her, standing high on her back for a minute, then quickly lowering to copulate. Then he postures briefly and they both fly off.

During the action another bird stands nearby, posturing in a sort of half-hearted way, as if it entertained the notion of joining them. For terns, three is not always a crowd. I have heard of a case in which an unmated male joined a pair that was already engaged in incubating eggs and was allowed to help. It sounds as if the married couple just got accustomed to having him around and gave him a key to the home, but there is a less whimsical explanation for it. Among various kinds of breeding birds there are unmated individuals, not sexually engaged with the nesting parents, who may help with incubating eggs, or even the feeding and rearing of the young. Such helpers are often younger birds who are in a sense shut out. They have difficulty in colonies where space is zealously guarded and occupied. As independents, they are not able to find a place to breed or obtain a mate.

Efforts at copulation do not always succeed right away. A male may mount a female and stand on her back for minutes at a time, teetering a little in an absent-minded way before he climbs off, with nothing accomplished. Repeated efforts are often made, but with consummation, egg laying soon follows.

In another part of the colony, a bird slightly enlarges a scrape in the sand, digging out backward while his mate stands aside. Then he stands back while she moves into the nest, plucking lightly at some grass. Finally both posture, circling each other, and then stand together on the nest facing into the wind, with an air of proud attachment.

The Speech of Terns

FOR MOST PEOPLE, ANIMALS SPEAK WITH A RUDI-
mentary voice. When you hear pigeons cooing in the city
park, you are certainly inclined, as I once was, to think of
them as little more than dumb birds, with nothing to say. This was
before I learned that their senses had more capabilities than I
knew how to express. Behind the outer details that we pass by
each day lies a vast range of perception and communication.

It is easy enough to think a distinctive species like a bird, with
one recognizable call, must lack individuals. This has been dis-
proved by a great many observers. That birds are individuals is
now accepted by any student of their behavior. During the nesting
season, certainly, when terns can be watched and listened to, they
show marked differences in traits. One bird will be unusually mil-
itant, another more passive. Some adults are better parents than
others, and will go on feeding their young for longer periods of
time. Many are simply incompetent. They wander off and stop
feeding the half-grown juveniles before they are able to fend for
themselves. This is a society with considerable differences in skill

and temperament. In their own fashion, they display almost as many vagaries as we do.

I seldom know how to interpret their constant interchanges, which can be just as quiet and subtle as they are loud. The motivation behind what terns are expressing to each other, in tones of varying intensity, is not easily grasped. This unique race has a vocal ability which might have some passing resemblance to a jarring musical instrument. Yet in terms of the basic urgencies of life, the call rings true. At the very least, with a complicated social structure, and a complex relationship to the changing facets of their surrounding world, the terns are not ones to give us examples in easy, animal simplicity. And just as water, land and air are constantly changing around them, interpretations of their behavior can never be expected to be final. There is an electric speech between any life and its environment which goes unheard.

I have often felt an element of offhandedness, or absent-mindedness, in their behavior, as if they were waiting on each other's signals before they acted. Now and then a tern seems to land almost forgetfully with a fish. It looks around and then flies away with it again. Or one bird will approach another and then break off contact, as if lacking the stimulus to follow through with whatever action it has started to perform. "One often gets the impression," wrote Niko Tinbergen in The Herring Gull's World, "that birds call when they are strongly motivated by an internal urge, and yet cannot satisfy that urge by proclaiming the activities to which it drives them." Calls are outlets for impulses and emotions which often require the right signals to set them off, so terns can appear to be highly ambivalent.

It is not so much that terns are always indecisive, but that they spend much time, as Tinbergen also put it, "in half-hearted, incomplete movements, before any unambiguous, overt act is performed." They have a limited set of these "urges," such as the need to copulate, to brood the eggs and young, to change over at the nest, or to forage for food, and these require the right situation. Like us, they often find it difficult to switch too quickly from one activity to another. If the bird is only half-hearted about its inner motivation, it will not carry through, but the stronger the feeling, the more direct the action.

To the human outsider, tern society may seem to have its contradictions, though that is preferable to thinking that nothing is going on of any significance. "Group adherence" on the territory has very little to do with "love." Antagonism, or something that resembles a case of aggressive jitters, seems permanent. So, if there is no love between them, how do they cooperate? During the nesting season, the outward evidence of cooperation is between pairs and when they flock together to mob intruders. Otherwise, their relationships look very edgy indeed. On the other hand, they are, at the very least, preoccupied with each other. Being highly territorial birds, terns nest in places which are as deeply mapped in them as their timing to the season. They are magnetically drawn to their nesting sites, though they can desert them in the face of disaster, and move to alternate ones if there is time. A common order is created out of underlying tension and that spontaneity which is so characteristic of them. Anger, distress, fear, and alarm are basic emotions they all share and signal to one another. Each cry or compulsive act can radiate out to others in the immediate vicinity, or spring the whole colony into action.

Terns communicate with high, harsh, sea-reflecting voices. Their tonal range is considerable. They may scream with excitement or descend into low, throaty comments at the nest. Their calls, as distinct from those of male songbirds on their territories whose singing can be long, complex, and elaborate, are short and emphatic. Gulls are said to have some ten distinct, recognizable calls. It is possible that the highly vocal and expressive terns may have more, though the variety of intonations behind the call escapes us for the most part.

In crows, on the other hand, some 300 separate calls have been found. The raven too, which Konrad Lorenz mentioned as the only bird he knew that could use a human word for conscious purposes, is a bird of such varied eloquence, so full of whim, sardonic and knowing behavior, that it filled the world of myth with stories about it. Crows and ravens have large brains in proportion to their body weight, which may explain their intelligence. Of course, this is a profound source of gratification to us whose brains are proportionately still larger, whether or not our use of them yields intelligent results. Where we lag behind the birds is probably in a superior quality of awareness, a responsive relationship to this sentient earth which we have been shamefully neglecting.

In the process of making ourselves the measure of things, we do not widen out the world so much as confine it. If man is the mirror, then all animals are defined through his sight, and that greater space in which they participate with such intricate style becomes subordinated to our exclusive use of it. I am suspicious of our comparisons of mental ability. What do we really know of mind in the first place? The mind and voice of the tern belong to a sphere we have hardly begun to respect. They know space who speak its magic.

Through their calls, terns convey information to each other, at times almost diffidently, and at others with considerable feeling. There is no mistaking the rapid, staccato cry they use when attacking an intruder, especially when it is yourself. It culminates with a wild shriek of "ahk!" "ahrk!" or "karr!" and at this pitch of excitement, they loose their droppings on your head.

Some of the calls of a common tern sound both strident and silvery, others harsh and deep. Still others seem to be little more than casual, absent-minded note takings, which may verge abruptly into high-pitched exclamations. It is always difficult to rely on written symbols for describing bird calls. It was pointed out to me, some years ago, that the "keearh" or "keeurh" call by which the common tern is known can also be heard as a nasal "ayhurr-ahn-ahn-ahn."

The most elaborate calls are made by birds advertising for their mates. A male cries out with a "keera!" or "keeyer!" to the female. Later on, during the early period of house hunting or establishing a nest, terns call "korkorkor" while posturing before making a scrape in the sand. Adults carrying in food proclaim it with a "keeyer," or "kitikeeyer." A bird flying by with a fish may utter a noncommittal "ketuh-ketuh," whereas one being furiously chased by others intent on robbing it will give a hysterical "kekearr!" of distress. The alarm call is a short "chik," or "chip"; with roseates this is "chivy" or "chewik." An abrupt "k-kaah" may accompany a brief flurry with another bird passing in flight.

They often sound as if they were making announcements about presentations, departures and arrivals, things to fly away from, things to be attacked. They may have a separate alarm call for a hawk flying overhead, for a man approaching with a dog, or a dog without a man. They seem to say, "I have something" (such as a fish), or "Move over," "Keep away" or "Give," all fundamental statements. Other than their distinct, recognizable calls, their cries vary a great deal depending on the circumstance. Human language is obviously much more versatile and complex than all this similar vocalizing. Yet what may sound very limited to us hides a wealth of gesture and response which is no less complex in its nature. If terns do not seem to employ conscious meaning with much elaboration, they still mean like mad, as those of us who listen are fully aware. Theirs is a language which is intensely felt, and joins a universal realm of symbolic communication which goes deeper than thought.

Ceremony and domesticity often go together. In that, at least we can recognize ourselves. We need rhythm, design, and common ritual in our lives, whether in sports, the dance, or at the family table. Common terns during nest relief seem to "talk" to each other. The female begs rapidly at first, with a "ki-ki-ki-ki," after which her mate may bring her a fish. They will both utter a low "keeyer." The male addresses her with that rapid "korr-korr-korr," which changes into a croupy "kuh-kuh-kuh-kuh." The sounds he makes are hoarse and watery, as if coming from somewhere down in a pipe, and change to a remarkable degree. A bird leaving its replacement behind at the nest may make a slight "tik-tik" as it plucks at some grass—a nervous relief from tension, and then a louder "tik-tik-tik-tik" as it flies away.

Although we classify birds as being among the higher vertebrates, we are still very wary of crediting them with mental and emotional capabilities which are anything like ours. But without some insight into our own emotions and states of mind, it would not be possible to understand their behavior at all.

Birds do not dwell on the mysteries. Ideas are foreign to them. But when I hear that sharp-edged tern voice again, striking across the sea-skimming air like a bell, I have no reason to think that I am superior to them. They lift my senses and my state of being into the company of the elect. What kind of an environment is it which we are only able to judge on our own terms?

Can birds be acquiring information through senses we know nothing about? It is clear enough that in some not too limited ways, they see more of the world than we do. If the quality of the marine environment is in their speech and searching lives, then it lies behind their perception. I watch them from a shore that looks out on a sea of awareness, wave after wave passing over infinite stretches of time with such majestic order as to elude the calculating mind.

from

A Beginner's Faith in Things Unseen

(1995)

Stranded

*J*HAD HEARD ABOUT THE BLACKFISH, ALSO CALLED pilot whales or potheads, from the time I moved to Cape Cod, but until recently I had never seen a live one. I did once come across some skeletons lined up along a local beach. The whales had apparently been part of a pod composed of family groups, because there were a number of young ones among them. According to local reports, the whales had died on this shore in the 1930s and been uncovered years later by storm waves.

Storms often bring revelations of hidden history in this sandy, malleable land. They periodically bury the evidence and then unearth it again. Not long ago, during a winter walk along the Great Beach, which faces the open Atlantic, I saw what looked like a giant sea turtle ahead of me, a dark brown, rounded back. It turned out to be the half-buried section of a hull from a wrecked sailing vessel, battered but well crafted, with wooden pegs holding the planks together. Since the use of iron instead of wood for larger ships came in during the latter part of the nineteenth century, I supposed that this was a lighter, smaller craft, perhaps a hundred years old. The surviving portion of the boat was about fifteen feet long. Four days later, after a storm that kept the wind booming all night while heavy waves smashed onto the beach, displacing and relocating huge volumes of sand, the wreck had completely disappeared, tossed back into the nineteenth century.

A few miles from where I saw this remnant, archaeologists were excavating an Indian site at the head of the beach, working intensively against the possibility that another storm might wash away all their work. In the eroding banks of peat above the shore, they had uncovered large trees that might be several thousand years old. On the evidence of an archaic spear point, they think that ten thousand years ago the bank was in a sheltered area five miles behind the present shoreline. So the world ocean beyond carves the land away and spreads its waters over whole continents, with supreme disregard of the way we measure time and history.

Under its shifting sands, the Great Beach hides the wrecks of a hundred ships or more, the debris of civilization. Where the beach slopes off into the Atlantic in fog, driving rain, sleet, sunlight, and showers, it becomes a broad highway of transformations, of tricks and illusions. Mysterious creations seem to rise before your eyes and disappear. The green, primordial surf pounds down the shore, carrying intermittent sounds of dying ships, falling houses, and crashing rocks along the clatter of its stones. Then it subsides, to repeat its histories. Nothing can claim it but creation.

The blackfish are relatively small—only twenty feet long—as compared to the big whales like finbacks and humpbacks, which are up to sixty or sixty-five feet in length. But they weigh some eighteen hundred pounds, two hundred pounds short of a ton. They once provided an extra source of income for generations of shore fishermen living in the towns along the inner circle of Cape Cod Bay. The whales were valued not for their meat but for their head oil, which was refined and used to lubricate light machinery, clocks, and watches. It fetched sixty-five dollars a gallon, good money in those days. The oil came from a lump the size of a watermelon in the whales' heads, which gave the animals the name of potheads. In the 1850s, according to Henry Kittredge's book *Cape Cod*, Captain Daniel Rich cut his mark on the sides of seventy-five blackfish stranded on the beach between Wellfleet and Truro and made one thousand dollars out of them.

When the spouts or rounded backs of the blackfish appeared offshore, townspeople would rush down to the shore and launch their dories or other small boats. They would surround the whales, yelling and beating on the water with their oars. The quarry panicked, headed in, and beached themselves. The "shore whalers," as they were called, then got to work with knives and lances, killing the poor beasts with great vigor. They usually shared the profits on an equal basis, possibly because there were not many lawyers and insurance people around in those days to complicate the business.

This method of whaling was convenient for those who did not want to hunt whales over deep water, and the whales aroused great excitement in the towns where they landed. "Drift whales" were thought to be a blessing sent through the grace of God, and in one instance grateful parishioners of the church in Eastham used part of the whaling proceeds to pay the minister's salary.

Those of us who rarely see blackfish and who certainly have never seen half a town engaged in cutting them up would not enjoy watching the process. Phil Schwind, a native of the Cape who died in the spring of 1992 at the age of eighty-five, has described a scene from the 1940s in his book *Cape Cod Fisherman*:

> Then the murder started. I know of no other word that would fit. Those great beasts, their thin, external skin as black and shiny as patent leather, beat the sand with their tails; they sighed and cried like monstrous babies. Their gasping was pathetic to hear as the tide ran out and left them helplessly high and dry, but what fisherman stops to listen when there is money to be made? Armed with a

razor-sharp lance on the end of a ten-foot hickory pole, Cal came up behind the flipper of the nearest blackfish and beat the creature three or four times over the head. When I protested, Cal explained, "You have to warn them you're here. I've lanced fish I didn't warn first and had them jump clear off the sand. Somebody could get hurt that way."

Cal drove the lance into the side of the creature, again and again, trying to make a bigger and bigger hole. Blood poured out in torrents, "gushed" is a more exact word. It splattered us and dyed the beach a bright red. One and then another he killed, working down the beach through the whole school.

It was dark before we finished lancing; my job was to hold a flashlight so Cal could see. Sometimes the fish were so close together we had to climb on one while it was still alive to lance another. Behind us blackfish in their death throes were heaving and moaning with blood-choked sighs. Their great tails lashed the sand, making a sound like a whole herd of horses galloping across hard ground.

Little more of the blackfish was used than the forty- to fifty-pound chunks in their heads, although their thick coats of blubber contained tons of oil, and their bodies contained tons of good meat. After the cutting was over, the remains were buried in the sand above the tideline before the stench became unbearable. Waste has been an almost built-in part of the economic thinking in this country.

Edward Howe Forbush, in his *Birds of Massachusetts*, published in 1920, describes a trip he took in 1876 to the St. John River region of the Florida wilderness, where there were multitudes of shorebirds along the coasts and lagoons. Arriving at Lake George, he saw "vast dense flocks" of wild ducks, a mile or more in length. Eagles, hawks, and owls were common, as were wild turkeys. This original abundance was irresistible:

Practically all tourists were armed with rifles, shotguns, revolvers, or all three. These armed men lined the rails of the steamboats and shot ad libitum at alligators, waterfowl or anything that made an attractive target. There were practically no restrictions on shooting, although the steamers never stopped to gather in the game, but left it to lie where it fell.

Frank Dobie, who wrote extensively about the traditions, animals, and folklore of Texas, said that the treatment of wildlife by the pioneers was "beyond belief." Even after the fates of the passenger pigeon and the buffalo were well known, people considered everything wild that came before their eyes fair game.

In his book *Karankaway Country*, Frank Dobie's friend Roy Bedichek, the Texas naturalist, describes an annual event of the late nineteenth century, in which so-called sportsmen would gather together as if on a fairground to shoot all the prairie chickens within range. These birds were males during their spring courtship rituals. First prize went to the gunner who shot the most birds, judged by the height of his pile of corpses. After the festivities were over all the piles were left to rot on the ground.

The relentless gambling with the resources of a continent continued until conservation laws were enacted, but our wasteful habits have continued. The early killing has left a residue of indifference to animals that is shared to a large extent by millions of Americans.

The blackfish, more often called pilot whales these days so as not to confuse them with fish, a race to which they do not belong, feed on squid in deep water along the edge of the continental shelf. During the summer and early autumn, the squid move closer inshore to feed, and the whales follow them. It was estimated that in the waters off Newfoundland during the late 1950s some forty-seven thousand pilot whales were taken. The original population is thought to have been no more than sixty thousand.

The tendency of these animals to herd closely together in family groups made it easier to drive them inshore. But what makes them strand voluntarily, if that is the right way to describe it? Theories have been advanced about parasitic infections of the inner ear, or inattention to what kind of bottom the whales might find themselves in, especially during frenzied feeding. It is possible that the whales become confused during migration when they swim out of deep water into Cape Cod Bay. The Cape is like a hook, starting from its stem on the mainland and curving around to its northern tip at Provincetown. The waters of the bay are relatively shallow, no more than eighty feet in depth. A sandy reef or bar near the mouth might confuse the whales if they swam inside it, and could not find their way out, or a storm might come up to further disturb their sense of direction. They might then swim in toward gradually shallowing waters and become even more disoriented as their geomagnetic sense was scrambled. It is also theorized that beaches with flat profiles disturb the whales' ability to echo-locate. Whatever the explanation, after countless generations the pilots seem to have been unable to hand down the knowledge that a trap like Cape Cod must be avoided.

Each school has at least one leader, and if the leader panics, giving calls of distress, the rest follow. Phil Schwind, who is of the opinion that the leader is not necessarily a male, says these animals could be herded like sheep. People used to drive around them with their boats, which by the 1940s were equipped with motors. Their method was to wait until the moment when the tide started to turn back and then cut off one of the animals, which might be of either sex, and wait for the rest to follow. (After the forties, the once-precious head oil was superseded in the marketplace by refined petroleum and no longer had any value.)

The blackfish will not be separated, even under extreme conditions. They have a powerful sense of unity, and they are highly sensitive to each other's movements, needs, and inclinations. Such highly social animals communicate through a complex repertoire of underwater calls. Apparently each individual has a distinctive whistle. Pilot whales belong to the family of dolphins, so you might suppose them to have similar ways of communicating, although their social structure is much more tightly knit and familial than that of other species in the group. Dolphins trade information through a variety of clicks, whistles, and other strange sounds. A group of dolphins makes decisions as to when to move out to sea from near the coast, or when to go fishing at night. According to Kenneth Norris in his book *Dolphin Days*, about the spinner dolphins of the Pacific:

> Each school member can detect the emotional level and alertness of the others, just as the wolf can tell by the pitch and tension in another's call where it is in the chase. Under the greatest excitement, tension on its vocal cords may cause its voice to break just as our own voices break in heightened circumstances.

Norris supposes an

> emotional glue that gives richness and nuance to a metaphoric communication system. Just as our spirits rise when we are listening to a symphony and its tempo increases, . . . so might something like emotion be transmitted throughout a school. . . . We routinely talk about future events when we say something simple like, "Let's go to the store." But the dolphin school, it seems, must match event and action while it acts out an emotionally based metaphor of what is going on.

What their refined use of signals means at any given moment remains to be understood and can only be found out, if at all, through patient, untiring research and a painstaking accumulation of data. Dr. Norris indicates that isolated signals may be symbolic, a given sound indicating a given circumstance. That, he says, is about halfway to being a word.

In a society so estranged from animals as ours, we often fail to credit them with any form of language. If we do, it comes under the heading of communication rather than speech. And yet the great silence we have imposed on the rest of life contains innumerable forms of expression. Where does our own language come from but this unfathomed store that characterizes innumerable species?

We are now more than halfway removed from what the unwritten word meant to our ancestors, who believed in the original, primal word behind all manifestations of the spirit. You sang because you were answered. The answers came from life around you. Prayers, chants, and songs were also responses to the elements, to the wind, the sun and stars, the Great Mystery behind them. Life on earth springs from a collateral magic that we rarely consult. We avoid the unknown as if we were afraid that contact would lower our sense of self-esteem.

Now I come to my first meeting with live pilot whales. It was on September 30, 1991. I had driven down to the parking lot at the head of the local beach in East Dennis where I often walk, especially at low tide, but I was stopped by a policeman. He told me that seventeen whales were stranded on the beach. So I left the car farther back in town and walked to the beach the long way around, through the thickets and dunes behind it. When I reached the beach, I saw a line of onlookers who were cordoned off on the sands just above the waterline. In their midst was a small, young whale lying dead on the sand. Others, still alive, had been removed and taken to the nearby channel of Sesuit Harbor to recuperate. In the shallow inshore waters were five knots of rescuers, or would-be rescuers, each holding on with quiet but obviously weary determination to a large, shiny black whale. The backs of the pilot whales were exposed, and the rescuers kept pouring water over them to keep them from drying out. In one case, a huge eighteen-hundred-pound animal was being carried onto the beach on a front-end loader by a number of people who had managed to get a stretcher under it. A line of people in deeper water farther out was trying to prevent another whale from moving in. The silent insistence in the animals was stunning to watch.

The rescuers were showing the strain. "I'm tired," one woman was heard to say. "It's more frustrating than discouraging. You try to help these animals but you don't know what to do. I wish we could learn the language of pilot whales."

In a later conversation, Phil Schwind, with memories of older and rougher realities, said to me that he felt sorry for those poor volunteers standing in cold water up to their waists for hours on end, desperately trying to hold back the whales, as if they could stop nature.

What nature is, we seldom seem to know. It is hard for us as "thinking animals" to understand behavior like that of the stranding whales, and we are too ready to confuse it with mass psychology. Yet in the great seas where these animals live, cohesion is a strategy for survival. When something happens to one animal, all the rest are in danger and respond.

The whales at East Dennis had been part of a larger group that had stranded four days before in Truro, farther down shore of the Cape, where an effort had been made to save them from themselves. Later on, some of the survivors of the East Dennis stranding moved to Yarmouth. It was highly discouraging to the rescue teams, who had congratulated themselves on managing to persuade a whale to stay off the beach and swim away, to have it strand somewhere else. Other whales would simply wait offshore until the tide lowered and then strand themselves again.

During this period of stranding, five young whales, first three and then two more, were thought to be in good enough condition to be moved to the New England Aquarium. After a period of rest and careful feeding, they were successfully released at sea and their movements tracked in the months that followed. Science benefits from these efforts. The whales are an important source of information, a good, long-term investment in knowledge. Methods improve. Institutions are encouraged to tackle larger species of whales in the future, to add even more knowledge and hope. These very laudable efforts are also part of our need as a society to impose our will and to succeed in solving problems that face us. This need brings strong emotions with it—tears for hope, and tears for failure. But in the final analysis, we do not know why pilot whales strand, or what we could possibly do to prevent it.

There was something about that scene on the beach, with its ardent, tired people and the silent black whales bent on moving in to the terrible shore that affected me profoundly. As I was starting to leave, a buried memory welled up inside me, a waking dream. I remembered a feeling of being alone, of being detached, pulled away from all familiar surroundings and support. It had come to me a long time ago, when I was a boy, and I vaguely associated it with the dark weight of the city where we lived. Perhaps it was the immense drawing power of the ocean at my feet that helped bring this dreamlike memory out into the open. It was a very real feeling of removal and dislocation, but I do not equate it with fear, or dread anticipation of what was to come next. I had simply been pulled away from all familiarity and faced with some inexorable darkness of cavernous dimensions. But in some way, the memory brought me closer to those deep-sea animals than I could have imagined possible.

As I walked away down the beach, I passed a flock of sandpipers standing and scuttling along the wet sands at the edge of the beach. A blue light was cast around them from the water and the sky. Beyond them the ever present gulls watched the horizon, and a few crows scavenged for food over the tidelands. The sanderlings flew up spontaneously and sped off to land farther down the shore.

Ringing the coasts of the world, the birds are one measure of its tidal complexities. Each kind seems to stand out as an embodiment of light, commanded by the unknown depths of creation. They are on earth's inspired and urgent business, carrying its many worlds of being far into a future that requires of each of them a certain perfection.

Birds, fish, whales, and human beings live on the edge of oblivion, which often snatches them out of the air or the depths of the sea. During their varying spans of life they are all creation's people, each singularly endowed to follow out the life of the planet. Without this great company we would hang in a void. A chance meeting with a dying whale, a flock of sanderlings, or a passing bird testing the atmosphere may be a revelation, however fleeting, of the underlying powers that lead us on and define our being. We come closest to nature, in its beginnings and endings, its Alphas and Omegas, in the darkest corners of our dreams.

On a recent visit to the city, I learned that pilot whales are known to dive down to at least eighteen hundred feet below the surface of the ocean. I was repeating this to my wife as we were traveling downtown in a bus. I heard a schoolboy sitting opposite us ask, "Do they really dive that deep?" When I answered, "I believe so," he turned his head and lapsed into a reverie, where we left him as we climbed down from the bus.

A Faire Bay

*I*n about 1939 or 1940, I was riding on a train between New York City and Washington, D.C., idly looking out the window at the passing landscape full of industrial plants and then scattered houses and open fields. I heard the man in the seat behind me lamenting all the open spaces that were going to waste, as if they were missing parts of a jigsaw puzzle that should be entirely built by human effort. As one who had been brought up with open fields, and also because we were traveling through one of the most densely populated corridors in the nation, I felt very much annoyed. Later on, the thought came to me that my fellow traveler was simply an American idealist. His ideal was Progress, expressed in terms of smoking factories and busy towns from coast to coast. He believed in a right to expand, embracing the notions that fueled Daniel Webster's earlier speeches in the heady days of "westward the course of empire."

Although the "great open spaces" set the American dream on fire, progress was slow enough at first to accommodate land and nature. But it was our intention that the lands should accommodate us in all that we wanted from them. Still land and nature held their own, no longer wilderness but still full of space that was only partially settled, enough to cultivate local understanding.

Following World War I and a surge in population, Progress turned into

Growth, which began to take on the characteristics of an avalanche. It was now a world of megalithic trade, one that looked back at settled, landed places with nostalgia, but one in which substitute illusions were manufactured every hour of the day. The reality was a homelessness that spread across the globe.

Ahead of our train was the Chesapeake, one of the major bays of the world, a great natural engine of exchanging waters and land. To early settlers it seemed inexhaustible in its natural riches, a place to live in for a thousand years. The great rivers whose waters ran into it and then out to the sea were handy arteries of commerce. The inner, native world of such a bay was one of rich and complex interchange. Its produce grew from the confluence of major rivers and a warm, temperate climate, and its local as well as migrant fish and birds shared in oceanic tides.

Industrial development and the growth of cities began to poison the arteries with human waste and chemicals. Grasses died, fish populations dwindled, the Chesapeake began to shrink. General possessions and universal property rights were overriding the freedom of the waters. The land was governed by absentee owners, who may have never seen or touched it. With the abandonment of natural law, the people began to lose their grasp of essential detail. They began to lose track of where their food came from. The human world was subjected to an unending stream of information which had little substance and ignored the land. The energies which might have been channeled into an exchange with the natural universe and all its societies was being spent on trying to control human disorders. Communication and Utility are overriding goals in our world, but nothing truly useful is ever accomplished without love.

So it is that the people who really know the Chesapeake, working night and day to "Save the Bay," are fully aware of its own original place in themselves. We cannot fly away from the great centers the earth has provided. They are permanently embodied in the land's first inheritors, fish, birds, crabs, oysters, grass, and trees, which can speak to us of what lasts and is not ephemeral, in greater exchanges of a universe of motion.

Unbridled growth is constantly running up against the limits of resources, and is at the point of no return. We are engaged in an experiment, if it can be called that, of disengagement from an earth to which we owe our own creation. Yet we can never be completely dematerialized from where we live. Refuse our attachment, and invite estrangement, even from ourselves. Those people whose homes and places of origin have been buried by an earthquake or lie under a major flood often insist on returning to where their houses or shelter once stood. Position and inner proportion are still as much alive in us as are the stations of the sun. This is a visceral as well as spiritual lodging. When violated, it can result in the unleashing of passionate violence and war. We can know where we ought to be without those illusions of omnipotence and self-sufficiency that beset us. We cannot expropriate the ancient depths of nature in ourselves. We were never above the land, or superior to it, any more than we are superior to the rest of nature. We are its dependents.

"Pull down thy vanity," said the poet to himself, as he landed in jail.

"A Faire Bay" was written for "Music of the Spheres," a group under the direction of flutist Katherine Hay and Frances Thompson McKay. It was read to music composed by Frances McKay entitled "Rites of Passage," and played at St. Mark's Episcopal Church in Washington, D.C., in the fall of 1987.

It is, said Captain John Smith, ". . . a faire Bay
compassed but for the mouth with fruitful and
delightsome land. Within is a country that may have
the prerogative over the most pleasant places of Europe,
Asia, Africa or America, for large and pleasant navigable
rivers. Heaven and earth never agreed better to frame a
place for man's habitation."

Out of the waters of the Chesapeake came a wilderness
store of food—oysters, crabs, and clams, unending schools
of fish; and in the glistening marshes where waterfowl fed
on smartweed, wild celery and widgeongrass, sea lettuce
and eel grass, were river otter, muskrat, beaver and mink.
Gentle, shallow waters along a shoreline of four thousand
miles seemed to invite the world in to share its riches.
And the Susquehanna and its great estuary flowed with
a primal energy founded in the vast, still unknown
continent behind them.

It was a tidal world in motion, never the same, as
we ourselves have been in motion ever since we found it,
taking all we could to satisfy our needs. But can we take

so much that we become strangers to the Bay? Will the
fishing ruin the fishermen, and the harvest of the rivers
die? Can we subdue and conquer these great waters
beyond their capacity to receive us?

Where the Chesapeake lies under the mists of dawn,
or opened out to sunlight-shattered waters, its surface
falls and rises, inhaling, exhaling, like the lungs of the
living world.

The Bay is a state of being, a great heart pulsing
with the tides, exchanging sea and river water in
its veins.

Twice a day the sea mounds in and rolls its free length up
the Bay. Twice a day great water masses mix and change,
as river waters run toward the sea.

In this body is the earth's desire. The fishes and the
plankton suspended in its depth respond to beauties of
transformation, everlasting change. Storms pass over them
and they abide.

Now the thunder rolls, and pounds the great *tympanum*
of the Bay. Low and heavy it rolls and rumbles.
Lightning swells and flashes over the long, low shores,
and flying sheets of rain fall in out of violent darkness
with a wind whose spirit strips the trees.

So the Chesapeake has felt the hurricanes
across its giant back, in their wild screaming—
boats scattered and sunk, trees uprooted,
islands washed away . . .
in that fury the outer seas unleash,
born of the world ocean and its invincible demands,
moving in with judgments past undoing.

The mighty Susquehanna, empowered by a hurricane,
rising on the flood,
once drove the sea back
farther than living memory;
but the sea returns for its unending
conflict and collusion with the river.

The storm is over. The clouds clear off
toward that everlasting blue
which is the testament of vision,
the breeding ground of hopes and dreams;
and everything on earth prays to the sun.

"Life is a pure flame, and we live by the invisible sun
within us."

　　　　　　　　　　　　　　　　—Sir Thomas Browne

Every cove, inlet and marsh, each creek and river has its
own distinction, known to every life that seeks it out.
Here is the wildness we rejected, the food we still
demand, the oysters and the clams, the crabs and fish that
were also the food of the people who lived with this land,
in intimate dependency, thousands of years before we
came, and gave their now legendary names to the rivers of
the Chesapeake: Wicomico, Rappahanock, Choptank,
Potomac, Poconoke.

"We always had plenty; our children never cried
from hunger, neither were our people in want. . . .
The rapids of the River furnished us with an abundance
of excellent fish, and the land being very fertile,
never failed to produce good crops of corn, beans,
pumpkins, and squashes. . . . Here our village
stood for more than a hundred years, during all of which
time we were the undisputed possessors of this
region. . . . Our village was healthy and there was no

place in the country possessing such advantages, nor
hunting grounds better than those we had in possession.
If a prophet had come to our village in those days and
told us that the things were to take place which have
since come to pass, none of our people would have
believed him."*

River water streaming and coiling in its abundance,
backtracking, pausing, running to the sea—
Out on the great Bay the passion of rip tides pulling
at the boats, rifting human balance and releasing it—
This energy and fury, and innate calm,
the bold dignity of waters running their own free way,
while the life within them
holds under the distant magnets of earth and sky.
Do we not belong here? Can we return?

White fog settles in over the shining grasses,
and tired boats, tethered to pilings,
lie on their own shadows.
Tidewaters gulp, and unseen fishes splash.
There is a whisper in the wind
over a deeper silence, where we might remember
being born.

Oh Chesapeake, how can we forget your marshes with
their tidal swirling in our ears, and their inclusion of the
multitudinous facets of light? These are sacred channels,
keeping the tidal rise and fall of birth and death in an
eternal balance.

When showers pass and clouds blow by, the
"Johnny Crane," holding its yellow spear in readiness,
reflects sky blue upon its wings.

* Ma-ka-tai-me-she-kia-kiak, or Black Hawk, Chief of the Sioux and the Fox. From
Touch the Earth, compiled by T. C. McLuhan.

While in a warm hour the frogs are croaking with the
voice of water, a slim egret, with pure white wings and
body like a shell, lifts from tall grasses with a snoring cry.

In September, the young menhaden flip and turn their
silver bodies in the shallow river winding through the
marsh. How beautiful the fishes, every tribe with its
precious distinction, white perch, yellow perch, shad
and alewives, the slim young catfish and the striped bass.
They have tracings on their skin of water's varying light,
delicate and unequaled markings. Fishes lift the human
spirit out of isolation.

To fill and lay waste the marshlands, to deliver them
unto degradation, is to lose our own protection.
They shelter origins, and the earth requires them.

Out beyond the channeled grasses, across the spreading
waters, the winds are chasing an immortal distance.

The colonists came in from everywhere, around the
compass, around the clock, settling into these generous
shores; and they shot the deer, treed coons, stewed
squirrels or snapping turtles for dinner, trapped beaver
and muskrat, fished the rivers and raised corn and
tobacco. They warred with nature and enjoyed its fruits.
Canoes, punts and piraguas, bateaux and barges, flats,
pinnaces and shallops plied the rivers. Out over the Bay,
skipjack, ketch and yawl, sloop and schooner, grew in
number so as to rival whitecaps on the waves. They raced
their thoroughbreds and quarterhorses; they hated and
they loved; they argued, quarreled and sometimes moved
away. The watermen dredged for oysters, tonged for
clams, and the soft-shell crab was a regional triumph.
Home-cured ham, pork and pone, turnips and salad

greens, hog jowls and black-eyed peas grew from this abundant land. And in the evening, when the golden sunlight of autumn flushed salt meadows and a hundred thousand wings wheeled in the air and began to settle in, their appetites were whetted by the splendor of the geese.

America was settled by a world from overseas that cut down what it found, and then moved on. Fire and ax destroyed the primal trees. Tobacco robbed the soil of its fertility, and the exhausted fields were abandoned to the wind and rain.

Erosion sent the topsoil down the Susquehanna, the Rappahanock, the Potomac and the James. For every mile, each year, hundreds of tons of sediment went into the Bay, and the Chesapeake began to age before its time.

Far out, the sanderlings skim across the headlands and the beaches, and wheel above the criss-crossed, tumbling green waters, as the spokes of the sun's wheel strike through running clouds.

A yellowlegs, turning on itself, yanking through the shallows, whips out its piercing whistle, and the gulls with their shivering, silvery screams and laughter, cry out for water's magical locations.

Backed by the continent, fed by its rivers, entered by the majesty of the sea, the Bay still speaks a language of capacity, of endless patience, but it will never endure a race that only knows how to spend earth's substance on a world of waste and greed.

Water is birth and mystery,
water in our hearts and minds,

the engines of love and deliberation.
Water is our guide,
however far we turn away.

America meant "improvement." Rivers were channeled,
dammed, bridged over, made useful for navigation.
We did not want them to stand in our way, with their
own rules. We did not like them to run free, leaving us at
the mercy of their floods and periods of low water,
refusing us passage. We improved them, and left them
behind. We loaded their timeless journeys with the deadly
passage of our wastes.

"The rivers of Virginia are the God-given sewers
of the State."
Thus spoke the nineteenth century.
Long live convenience.
God save Virginia.

The germinative rivers, the bringers of life, began to
carry more black oil and poisons to the Bay. The silver
alewives and the shad, mounting the rivers in their
spawning fire, were blocked by dams and started to
disappear. The famous sturgeon was nowhere to be
found. Marsh plants began to die; underwater vegetation
died; numberless oysters never reached maturity. What
has happened to the rockfish, the great striped bass that
spawns in the prolific waters of the Chesapeake, the pride
of all the states that border on the sea? Why is its
progeny being cheated of existence?

The eye of the Chesapeake is clouded over. While the
rivers send their foul discharge into its heart and lungs,
our own senses fail. Water is light and vision. Without its
clarity we soon go blind.

What lies under these pulsing, ribbony waves? Billions of
gallons of industrial waste, a desolation of herbicides and
pesticides, sulphates and nitrates, chlorine, gas and oil.
What lies there but a wasting of the heart?

Only man can destroy the Bay; only man can destroy
himself.

We are the victims of our own ignorance and love of
power. We do not know the limits of these waters, until
we pass them; and we never gave ourselves the time.

Native Americans declared: "A frog does not drink up the
pond in which it lives."

That suggests a frog's intelligence may be on a higher
level than our own. But there is time, within the earth,
for recognition.

Still and always, the seabird lifts to the impenetrable
light that dances on the tides—
And the eyes of schooling fishes stare ahead into the
waterways of the future.

These are true inheritors, children of amplitude, as it
was in the beginning. They live at home with mystery,
the great design of life, in which all species are kindred.
We cannot live outside them and survive.

Until we learn to recognize these waters in ourselves, they
will age, sicken and die. Violence will be returned for
violence, dying for dying. The rivers will turn against us;
the Chesapeake will have its vengeance; the continent will
call us aliens, strangers to its spirit. When the great

network of living veins and arteries begins to shrivel and dry, the spirit of the people dies. The seas within us die.

America is not the product of industry but of shared existence.

To give up on the Chesapeake is to give up on ourselves. Listen to it. Watch its cosmic, universal eye. Rediscover sanity. Return. Come home again. Come home.

Fire in the Plants

*I*N THIS TRANSIENT EXISTENCE, YOU NEVER KNOW whether the person you just met might be the one to whom you have said good-bye. One morning when I was a boy in New Hampshire, my father and I stopped by to have a brief chat with Mr. Rowe, an elderly man who lived up the road from our place. As we talked with him he was leaning over the pasture fence in front of his house, which stood at the foot of Sunset Hill. The very next morning we heard that he had died. For some reason, that meeting made a profound impression on me. Old man Rowe did not have much to say, "keeping to himself," as did others in the neighborhood, but later on, I felt as if I had been present at a significant crossroads in local history. That meeting still hangs in my mind like the imperishable falling of golden leaves.

Our home territory, which was being discovered and inhabited by summer people, was the woods and shore of a major lake that was traversed by steamboat for the sightseers and yet was still defined more by its ancient rocks and forest trees than by any conquering "improvement." The house was built on a rocky slope above the lake, and my boyhood was punctuated with the sound of dynamite, as the interminable boulders were blown up for the sake of lawns and gardens. In spite of local scattered farms and fields, the forests still commanded the landscape, and reached like waves over the mountains and out of sight.

We lived in a cultivated clearing, while clearing out on a major scale was occupying much of the rest of America. I was brought up in an atmosphere of order and civility which many people in contemporary society might find highly cramping to the modern style of uninhibited expression. I have long felt that my parents' generation was haunted by the dark weight of World War I, and by the possibility of another one, gathering before them. I confess that there were times when post-Victorian restraint aroused feelings of rebellion in me, and I was tempted to think that I might break away and hop aboard a freight train heading west. My temerity was never tested. I was kept from the open road by the advent of World War II, when I was drafted into the army.

My grandfather had bought his land in New Hampshire from local farmers in the last decade of the nineteenth century, at a time when many farms were being abandoned. The Lake Sunapee area was not a resort on anything like the scale of Bar Harbor, or Newport, Rhode Island. There was one large hotel, and lodging houses only a few miles away. My grandparents' house, enlarged as the years went by, occupied what was essentially a clearing on a hill leading down to the lake. Before he was married, my father had a log cabin on the place where he used to stay during off seasons, hiking and fishing. Some years after inheriting the main house, with the aid of skilled Italian masons who had settled in the area, he started construction of a rock garden that extended down the rocky slope below the house. It was a Herculean task, this "gardening in granite," as he called it, but watching the plants over the years, on his return from work as an archaeologist in New York and Mexico, was a great source of pleasure to him.

My father loved gardens, no less than did my mother, whose main interest was in roses and flower beds. As a result of her childhood experience at the old family farm in Ipswich, where "the great pasture" was meant for livestock rather than trees, New Hampshire's wild trees and the untended parts of its landscape were not altogether to her liking. It was the resistant part of the land she found hard to tolerate. My parents' attitudes represented two different, if not irreconcilable, views toward a stubborn land that still retained much of the character of a wilderness.

Mother had some decided ideas about flower beds, roses in particular. To her, I think, roses were a symbol of civilization, lifting their lovely heads above the unruly disorder of the outside world. She would tolerate no intruders in the rose beds. Mice, as well as the moles that made humpbacked trails across the lawn, were unacceptable. Weeds were torn out on arrival, as were forest seedlings, which were everywhere. My mother's efforts to cultivate roses were annually frustrated by the realities of New Hampshire. At least half of them were "winter killed" and had to be replaced, a fact that did not stop my mother for a moment.

She had a deep-seated antipathy for snakes, which had biblical authority behind it, and her attitude toward other intruders such as the insects that attacked us or invaded the flowers was unflinching. With a natural perversity of my own, I once introduced a garter snake into the house, to educate her, I suppose, and her response was almost terrifying. Mother had a strong vein of the "practical" in her, which she applied to all unnecessary flights of the imagination. I told her that I believed in flying saucers, and one year I actually saw one spinning in the sky, or so I thought. Wasting no time in rescuing me from my delusions, she phoned the weather bureau, which identified the object as one of their high-flying instruments. It was never easy to detect the chinks in her armor, although like the rest of us she had unspoken fears she did not find it easy to admit. Wilderness was a concept she was unable to understand, but she took courage from inherited ideas of order and behavior, as did my father. Even so, in a country with a relatively small population by comparison with today, and a wealth of space, they never overpowered the natural world around them, but accommodated it. A wilder space, visible and invisible, governed our lives. That, I know, was the reason why a greener condition in a lawn free of weeds did not interest me half as much as a deeper, still undiscovered meaning in the trees, where I might hear an owl, or walk through drifting snow.

After having to move away from our house in New Hampshire, dislodged by circumstance and the plunging moods of my times, I still returned on many occasions to pursue a silent dialogue with the trees. I hear in them a condition that parallels my own. In their successional stages of growth, pines, maples, beech, and canoe birches seem to embody a shared time created out of a permanence that defies us. There is a hemlock that I have faced since my year one. It stands on the lake side of a cottage we used to stay in during the seasons of spring, autumn, and winter. I hardly noticed the tree as a boy, but it is still there, as if it had patiently waited for me while I was absent for so many years. Its tall, straight reddish-brown trunk looks smooth and youthful, now that I am entering old age. Since hemlocks grow to be four hundred years old or more, it may be still there, growing ahead of me several centuries from now. That tree is a signal for me of imperishable growth. Cut them all down and we would live in a land untenanted by any certainty. Those great trees, growing ahead of and behind me, are my protectors, with their branches gently dipping in the wind, shedding sunlight and snow. They are generators and providers. Why should we refuse their priceless heritage?

The northern trees are travelers, responding to the great age and space of the continent. "Our own native flora," wrote Edgar Anderson in *Plants, Man and Life*, contrasting it with the European, "was bred for our violent American climate. It goes into winter condition with a bang. The leaves wither rapidly, they drop off in a short time, frost or no frost. In their hurry many of them leave enough chemicals behind to give us brilliant fall color. Virtually all the autumnal green which one sees in the eastern and central United States is European."

The hurricane of 1938 left indescribable wreckage behind it, uprooting trees, knocking down wide swathes of white pines by the lake and in exposed clearings. In the woodlands, the evidence can still be seen of rotting trees now becoming part of the leaf mould.

But the trees grew back undefeated, competing for space, in a co-existent, tight race for air, soil, and sunlight. Beech, birch, ash, maple, and hemlock have claimed former territories and moved into new ones. I marvel at their vitality and insistence. In their silence, receiving, standing, rather than escaping as we do, creating their own shadows, rebuilding the character of the land, they tell us where we are. They are subject to long or short cycles of blight and disease. Individual trees are uprooted by strong winds. An isolated pine is hit by lightning and bears the scar. Some trees, as if in a desperate struggle to claim their own space, tend to displace or kill each other off.

I have seen a mountainside covered with dead balsam fir, killed off by rime and ice driven into the trees' tissues by winter storms. The seedlings come in thick again to take their chances within the extremities. The endurance and hardihood of those trees is worth more than a moment's reflection. Born of a magnificent, varied, and violent continent, they follow its lead without fail. The more we destroy them, the more rootless we become. Whenever I find myself in the presence of an old white pine, stirring and creaking like a schooner on the high seas, I honor it for bringing back the grand dimensions of earth history.

My sister and I were constantly criticized by our father for the improper use of words. He himself was not an author, as his father had been, but an archaeologist. Nevertheless, he inherited an older tradition of proper usage. "Bad grammar" was frowned upon in those days. We did our best to improve, I suppose, without having much sense of verbal construction, but how to say things correctly seemed to me to be less important than what was being left out. What's within a name? Words often tricked me with double allusions, and names too seemed to hide a wealth of meaning. It took a more advanced education for me to see why plants had to have Latin names in an intellectual sense, but in the meantime they seemed to have lost their lives to names. I knew garden species by what they were called, as well as by their look and their scent, but that knowledge tended to limit me to plants that were considered acceptable. What were those wretched weeds that were sent packing as soon as they appeared? Nothing, as I learned later, but a whole universe of plant life. I was not aware for a long time that the red trillium, the local name for which was "Stinking Benjamin," which grew in wet places in the spring and had a bad smell, attracted carrion flies, but that may be the reason I was never told about it. It was pretty to look at, but "unattractive" to smell. My private quarrel with the civilizers was that they claimed too much and let in too little. My liberators were always being disguised by the names they were given. Surely, flowering plants, I began to think, were more, said more, than a recital of their component parts.

One evening, in later years, when an amateur pursuit of natural history had led me out into wider and wilder fields than horticulture offered me, I spent an hour or more watching a flower fold up in response to the setting sun. It seemed at the time a miraculous revelation. Where had I been not to realize that flowering plants were working partners of the sun? Why had no one ever suggested such a thing before?

When I felt it was important to me to know what a salt marsh was composed of, I began to learn its distinctions. Every species there was expressing itself in terms of the tidal, rhythmic character of its surroundings. The colors of the salt-tolerant grasses changed with the seasons, from wide patches of blue-green or yellowish-green that looked like the shadows made by traveling clouds, to fall colors of tawny gold. Very early in spring when the new shoots were starting to appear on the surface of the marsh, I looked down at where the spike grass and blank grass grew on the marsh edges. I could see that, at this stage, individual stems and leaves were starting up in clear distinction from each other. There was no undifferentiated emergence in this process of growth. The grasses were forming a scaffolding of intricate design. It is through such minor observations that we begin to take the measure of ourselves.

A society interested only in quick results has little time to spend on the rhythmic responses in a salt marsh or a wood that might be its salvation. At times I think that all the plants, birds, fish, and every other living organism are waiting for our departure so that they can resume timeless engagement with the earth. Since I learned that plant seeds can live in a state of suspended animation for extraordinary lengths of time, I have felt that they must be responding to their inner pulsing of the earth itself. Buried seeds may live in a state of dormancy for widely varying periods, germinating most often when the soil is disturbed and they come to the surface. Experiments have shown that many common agricultural seeds can remain dormant and viable for decades. Seeds of an arctic lupin found in the burrows of lemmings in Canada's Yukon territory were still viable after an estimated ten thousand years. It is thought that they had been buried and insulated in a frozen state by a landslide. It is as if seeds can internalize time in themselves, as part of a strategy of dispersal. Some species that specialize in colonizing open ground can, in effect, wait in a dormant state until the ground is disturbed, with the result that they are more widely dispersed.

Much has been made of nonverbal communication, or "body language," in humans and other animals. It would never occur to most of us that plants "say" anything at all, except in terms of what we read into them, or try to use them for. Yet in their responses to this wonderfully rhythmic and varying earth they are the most expressive of all the forms of life.

The New Hampshire of my youth led me, following Emily Dickinson, to amplitude and awe. The long stone walls never quite ended in a sad and unfinished history, but opened out, like the great American land itself, to endless possibilities. The presence of original space, and not its alteration at human hands, encouraged me, as the years went by, in looking for all the significant detail from which I had been distracted by my times. It was not identification for its own sake that moved me ahead but the alliances it revealed. I began to see the worlds of life as centered in a mystery of light. The distinctive worlds, of birds, fish, mammals, insects, and plants, were never as fixed as our naming tended to make them, but shared in the rhythmic patterns and cadences of the earth and sea. Particulars became of the greatest importance to me, because they led me not only to an understanding of diversity, but also to a brilliance in creation. All the environments I ever visited were not only distinct in themselves but shaded off into the unseen and the unfinished. Human isolation from the rest of life on a scale the modern world has made possible is inadmissible in the rest of nature.

Perhaps because I was used to looking at plants in terms of our manipulation of them, the life of plants once seemed passive to me. I did not credit them with an independent existence. It did not occur to me at first that what is rooted in the earth must share in its powers of integration and expression.

A little further climbing, which always characterized New Hampshire in my mind, led me up its granite slopes with their plates of mica shining in the summer sun. There I learned to recognize some of the tundra species of plants that hug the cracks and crevices for their sparse nutriment and shelter. Hundreds of thousands of pitiless arctic winters describe this adaptation. They exist not by virtue of their ability to avoid exposure but to embody it. They deserve the name of endurance as much as any early arctic explorer stranded on the ice floes of the Canadian north. There is a power in their fragility. They are residents of the most extreme environments on earth, and all climates in between. A single leaf is a map in outline of their universal travels.

There is a bog not far from where we lived in New Hampshire which is surrounded by hardwoods and evergreens. Only during the past one hundred years its plants have been filling in what was once a pond. In living memory, people have been seen rowing a boat across it. I have gone there a number of times out of fascination for this process of colonization and closing in. In its rhythmic response, though carried out over a longer period of time, it seems like the beat, the systole and diastole, of the human heart. This bog is limited in extent. Because it is highly acidic and low in nutrients, it supports only a limited number of species. Some birds feed on its fringes and a varying amount of insects occupy it in season. It is here that the carnivorous pitcher plant survives, employing some ingenious devices to attract and consume the food it requires.

The leaves of the pitcher plant are goblet- or trumpet-shaped. The flowers are red, borne on single stems, and are cross-pollinated by a fly, whose larvae feed on insects that are trapped by the plant and also ingested by it. These insects, attracted by the plant, or accidentally landing on it, are caught by fine, sticky hairs that line the underside of the leaves. At the bottom they are drowned by rainwater that has collected there.

One fine autumn day I peered into one of the leaves and saw the fine, downward pointing hairs, and the red, almost animal-like veins that ran through their green material. The sunlight turned the leaf into a semi-transparent vase. At its base a small pool of rainwater had collected and there were the drowned bodies of insects floating on the surface. I also glimpsed some glistening larval eggs down there, which were apparently able to survive the coming of frosty weather.

Stealth and deceit are employed by this remarkable plant, to drown the innocent and save the elect. There is no fear or love in it, at least as far as we know them, seizing us unawares. Death is fitted to digestion, and reproduction is carried on the wings of a fly. But in its containment of the grand design, nothing beats it for economy. It leads, by extension, from hell to paradise.

I think I have the silent chemistry in me of the lands in which I grew up. At any season a cool wind often passes across my face. I hear the sound of water, salt or fresh, booming in the distance, or trickling nearby. The brown color of the soil is reflected in the coats of the animals that live there, such as the woodchuck or the deer mouse. Under the leaf litter and between the roots of the trees is a teeming world of ants, centipedes, millipedes, sowbugs, and other nearly invisible creatures thriving in the moist and protected soil. The roots are my own assurance of gravity and holding on. My inner clock circles with the trees as far as the skies that wheel above our house. And I count on all-pervading greenness to fix the sun. I hold my hand with its own veins and arteries up to the sunlight, and see in it the image of a leaf.

I am something of a stranger to the desert. My trips there have only been of short duration. I was not encircled by trees or bodies of water in that arid land, but taken far out to a range of radiant light and color. And there the plants are expressing, in often spectacular form, their open engagement with the sun. It is as if they consumed the light and at the same time had any number of devices to protect them.

A beginner in the desert, I am not only thinking of how to avoid direct exposure to a sun I am not accustomed to. I also wonder what is called out in the human spirit by such openness. One is shunted from glaring light to the other polar extremity of nightfall dropping like a vast dispensation of mystery for which we have no adequate words. There is great antiquity here, which flies in the face of the modern world's desertion of it. The vast distances of the past have their true integrity and meaning out there. It is fortunate that there are native people who have an unbroken connection with it in their minds. I was told of a Papago in recent years who was looking at a petroglyph on a cliff face in Arizona, and said, "See, my ancestors, still dancing for rainbows."

The giant saguaro cactus, which can grow up to fifty feet in height and weigh twelve tons, has a life span of two hundred years. It has the capacity to store a great amount of water in its spongy tissues. Within four to six hours of a heavy rainfall, it shows a measurable increase in circumference, swelling up like a great bellows. At the same time it sends out thousands of inches of root hairs into the desert soil. Heedless development has destroyed great numbers of these desert giants. Their peril calls to mind the greed that threatens to decimate the African elephants and their magnificent heritage.

Several years ago, I went with Gary Nabhan, botanist and author, on a three-day trip starting from Organ Pipe Cactus National Monument in Arizona. We drove west on the Mexican side of the border through desert country that was like a vast wild garden, as a result of unusually heavy spring rains. Some of the flowering shrubs stood out like great lanterns, attracting scintillating hummingbirds with their blossoms. I learned that the flowers of the desert primrose change color from pink to white, a decoloration that serves as a signal to various kinds of insects that the plant has stopped pollinating, and need not be visited. Other plants I was introduced to were able, through fuzzy, spiny, or thorny surfaces, to reduce solar input, the extreme intensity of the desert light. I saw in a blue Papago lily a color which was as deep and arresting as any grotto in the Mediterranean. Plants hold onto what is typical of them in any given environment, but they also embody any number of varying characteristics. I was starting, in myself, to move in response to a vast range of expression, and I pitied us for all our reductions and evasions in the interests of human domination. Should we not be highly offended at being cut off by a poverty of thought from all the living resources that are open to our hearts and souls?

Gary and I reached the northernmost corner of the Gulf of California, where a beach bordered far-reaching tidelands. Its silty sands were deposited by the once mighty Colorado. I saw a number of shorebirds there, western sandpipers, kittiwakes, bristle-thighed curlews, and a few black brant, a western race of those small geese I love to watch off Massachusetts. The birds are those who carry the sense of the globe's geography, and I go back to them to locate myself on migratory routes we seldom follow. To hear the musical calls of the gulls along another shore is to realize that each distinctive song or call is part of the fluctuating environment from which it rises.

After a meal and beer at a Mexican village just behind the beach, and a few more welcome lessons in desert plants, we headed for a high dune on which we spent the night. The night was beautifully clear and deep, with a sky full of trellised and trailing stars. Each star seemed to me to have its corresponding light in a desert flower.

I woke up to a pale blue sky, and as I looked out across the desert to the east, a brilliant eye appeared over a line of low hills. It was soon followed by the red-orange, yellow, flaming turbulence of the dawn, and it seemed as if all the desert flowers, like fires in themselves, were responding in any number of graduated ways. As the light of a new day flooded over land and sea, I thought of all the awakening and responding of all the lives I could not see. The watchers of the night took to the shadows, as the plants received the sunlight. I could hear a rooster crowing. Then a beat-up old pickup truck with a broken muffler roared out on the main road to the village.

So, out of uncountable years, endless opportunities are opened up again in another rising of the sun, and they belong not to a single species like the human race, but to the universe of life. We are all upgraded by the light, so strictly interpreted by the desert plants. It is in this great poverty shared by every living thing without exception that we are discovered, not as the identifiers only, but as the identified.

from

In the Company of Light

(1998)

The Way to the Salt Marsh

*F*ROM OUR HOUSE ON DRY HILL, A NAME ONCE given it by natives who knew its character, it is about two miles to the beach on Cape Cod Bay. I am now obliged to walk, except when driven, having lost my driver's license because of poor eyesight. This might be thought of as a serious handicap, if not a tragedy, by the army of drivers who fly past us every day, but walking puts me on the right level with all I have been missing in our world. I have joined up for many field trips in various parts of the world, in order to make an educated guess about what I was looking at. But behind that, deeper than any name, category or explanation I have learned, there has always been an interior equation I have not quite reached. What lasts, in our self-made, invented society?

The oaks and the pitch pines have now grown back around us, some to a fair height, though stressed and stunted in many places by their heritage of exposure to salt-laden winds, fungus diseases and a hundred years or more of wood choppers. We can no longer see the water from the hill; but at some times of the year, the sea winds are almost constant. We are not so enclosed in stars and spruce as we are in Maine, but all the sky above the trees is encircled by a global light. During clear weather, the dawn over the eastern horizon is ushered in by a wide band of color changes from red and pink to saffron and gold, until the fiery, orange-red of the great eye itself lifts into the sky. As the day leaves us, the sunsets over the open shore are often spectacular, especially after a storm, and so the vast circle is round once again.

My son Charlie, his wife Joanne, and I were walking down the beach, toward the end of a wild and windy day, and at first we saw no gulls. The gulls are not only scavengers. They are long-distance watchers, scanning the shore for opportunities. They understand the tides, and move back and forth with them waiting to pick up what they leave. Further along the shore they line the banks of Stony Brook at its mouth, where the alewives move in from deep water and return.

On our walk, the wind was still very strong, and the offshore waters, rock-green in color, were in a state of torment. The wind was so loud that we could hardly hear our own voices, while the waves plunged and fell for miles along the sands; but it had begun to clear and a glorious sunset was waving its flags behind the racing clouds. Suddenly a number of gulls appeared, flying low over our heads, cruising slowly into the wind, and repeatedly calling. Perhaps they were only trying to keep in contact with each other, but in that setting, their response seemed profound enough. I have seen terns fly up from their nesting colonies, as the sun was going down over the sea, and then again at sunrise, in tribute to the light. Nothing so primal passes without ceremony.

The rest of life does not lose time by exceeding the speed limit. The era of slow travel, so goes the illusion, may have been set back into oblivion, never to be restored, like the so-called "good old days." But planetary complexity is kept in order by infinite patience, and periods of time which are long enough to insure stability. So at my time of life I have a great deal of lost patience to catch up with. What can tell me anything useful about where I live except those who are still in place, like a box turtle approaching

100 years of age without benefit of modern medicine, or a beautiful green snake once fairly common here, as slim as the grass. Grassroots insure a future in a way that the communications network ignores. All information can now be instantaneously transmitted . . . in one ear and out a million others.

As I walk down from Dry Hill, the dead, brown oak leaves, turned white by an early morning frost, are crunching under my feet. A horde of grackles with cries like rusty hinges have long since swept through these woodlands, feeding on acorns for a few days. Now a blue jay lands on a bare tree, and its pitched scream pierces the sky's vision through the branches. Why such a note of triumph, from this brassy and beautiful bird? It might be because the jay helped repopulate the continent with oak and beech trees after the last ice age, ten thousand years ago, dropping the seed as it explored new territory.

Last summer I picked up the unattached cup that held an acorn, but it was not empty. In its interior was one of those perfect and delicate constructions that preceded human ingenuity. This cup was crisscrossed by the fine threads of a spider web. At its base was a drop of water, in which a tiny larva was wiggling, and as I peered in more closely, I found a small spider lying in wait. The larva may have been one of the kind that find their way out of spent acorns. The spider was probably waiting for what small insects might fly or wander in. Spiders are highly proficient in the art of waiting. How important is a drop of rainwater or dew to their enterprise? As an amateur, I am always waiting for further insight or advice that may not be forthcoming.

During the late fall and early winter, I often hear the deep-throated hooting of a great horned owl coming out of the pitch pines. It reassures me that the landscape has not been so thinned down by our occupation as to lose one of its original inhabitants, with a voice of command.

The crows are seldom absent at any time of the year. They harass the owls. They are constantly in touch with each other. Their vocabulary seems ample for their needs, as they come together and disperse. I am sure they have a better sense of location than I do. Whenever one or more of them stops in some tree on my way, I fancy that they might be exchanging sardonic comments like: "Here comes another who does not know where he is going."

Late in the day, as darkness was coming on, toward the end of a season of migration, a troop of white-throats sped by me to land somewhere down a driveway lined by a stone wall, perhaps to spend the night. They came in with such assurance and almost military dispatch as to make me think they knew the place before they got there. Birds hold the foreknowledge of voice and place together in their memories.

I never see a white-throated sparrow without thinking of its song, an uplifting chant out of the spiraling evergreens of the northern forest. Their high, tremulous, whistling call rises out of the sun-draped ground. It may sound like "Oh, Canada, Canada, Canada" to our ears, but this bird sings of what is, and the right place to be, and for that I dearly love it.

In all of nature there can be nothing more expressive than silence. When I think of the gentle swallows that occupy the barn loft in Maine for much of the summer, while I work below, I think of how they steady my mind. Aside from an occasional shriek of alarm as I am coming in, or leaving, they are relatively quiet. What I hear are little bursts of liquid chatter between intervals of silence. The adult birds are intensely busy flying out to catch insects and returning to their young, which gives rise to what we might call comments, or low exclamations. But as the days move on, the overall tone, like the humming in a beehive, is what tempers my mood. It is not to be deciphered on the surface. It amounts to a subterranean recognition, a compliance with the season of nature. Our barn has become a "community center" for swallows over the years, a place to which many will return. It is said that the young return to the nest where they last heard their parent's voice. That seems to imply that all life is eternally domestic, no matter how much distance is put between the traveler and the nest. As for me, I know a company of swallows, and of terns, or "sea swallows," has always added more to my interior space than I knew existed before I entered their world.

One branch of the wide band of salt marshes that extends along the shore of Cape Cod Bay is only a mile from where we live. In order to reach it, I have to cross a highway, which I regard with some suspicion. When the coast is clear, I hurry over to the other side where there is an inlet to safety. At this point there is a very small house, now an antique store, but once a liquor store where our friends and neighbors used to go to fulfill their need for spirits. It was owned by Blanch and Lloyd (pronounced "Lo-ed") Coggeshall. Her father was a cook aboard a lightship off the coast.

A road once crossed over the marsh at that point to reach the small town of East Dennis, which spreads over the headlands behind the shore. This road, only a few hundred yards long, was abandoned by town authorities in the 1960s. The entrance to it has been almost closed in by thickets on both sides. Walking in over this narrow lane, I once met a cottontail which streaked across in front of me, reminding me of my own feelings when faced with a speedway.

The old road is breaking up, restored to the status of a trail. Thick bunches of switch grass, blond and sparkling in the winter light, with their graceful, curving grass blades, are marching down the center, having thrust their way through the asphalt. These plants grow again where it was their right to grow, on the upper slopes of a salt marsh. That which is appropriate is "ecology," and is determined in the living cell.

The road was built over the marsh, and a channel was cut at one point for the tidewater to run under it. The original culvert is still there, taking the rising and receding waters from one side to the other. Late in the season, I have seen schools of alewives still racing in as they often do, trying to reach the far ends of any inland waterway. A marsh sparrow flies in low to the tall reeds that line the path and drops down to lose itself on the ground between their stalks, scurrying away like a dark mouse. In mid-January I found the intact, uneaten body of a small striped bass, possibly dropped there by a gull. That led me to think that young, medium-size bass might be wintering in the marsh ditches and channels instead of migrating offshore.

I seldom meet people on my walks during the "off seasons" before the summer crowds arrive. When I do, individuals stand out against the open expanses of the marshes in all their singularity, like a passing marsh hawk, or a great blue heron. Every word they utter, and the feelings they express, no matter what the content, seem memorable. A salt marsh sanctions space and a rooted integrity. Those who pride themselves on cramming a thousand years into a minute cannot be aware of its unending reliability.

Because of their salt-tolerant grasses, the tidal marshes are the one self-sustaining landform along the northeast coast. Millions of acres of marshland and inland wetlands have been dredged, filled, and disposed of. This has been justified on the grounds that we, and our advanced machines, can reclaim marshlands and even recreate them where there were none before. Even lakes, bays, and rivers can be turned into buildable land. So we could drain away the life blood of the continent. This staggering lack of connectedness in our minds now leads to millions tumbling out of the cities and moving on to devour the plains and the forests beyond them.

The wide, flat, and silent expanse of the open marsh lies out before us in its serenity. It is covered in wintertime with thick, coarse, brown grasses like the heavy coats of a prehistoric animal. The long sound of the surf comes in under a light fog that hides white dunes. A marsh lies in the arms of the sea.

The marsh is one of the most receptive environments on earth. It is always open to the sky and all the winds and weather that flow in and recede like the tides in endlessly recurring motion. In its own, self-generating body it accommodates innumerable forms of life all responding to that common sea. The centuries pass, and its patience deepens. Even in winter when it looks dark, brindled in color like a day that is as dark as evening, it never sleeps.

All the passing winters vary in their temper. Last year the ditches looked snow-blind, covered with ice, for many weeks. This year they have been relatively free of it. As spring begins to come on, the minnows dart in the ditches, and at the right time, the fiddler crabs emerge from their burrows. The surface waters dance like a colt frisking in a meadow. The new light is an invitation to that dance and ritual that accompanies the freedom to be. And the male redwing lifts its epaulettes in a gesture of praise. We can thank the marsh for all its transformations, and above all, for its constancy.

Life in Space

CAPE COD IS IN MOTION, AND NOT FOR ANY OF THE reasons we can summon up, in our hurry to control planetary space. It moves because that is what the great sea ordained. The sea both adds to its sandy shores and takes them away, year after year, but over time it is being gradually reduced. Perhaps in another fifteen thousand years as a result of constant erosion, and a rising sea level, the Cape will be submerged, a great line of sandbars lying far offshore.

The shores on both sides of the Cape are annually worn down by storm waves. Some property owners, on the back side of the Cape facing the brunt of storms from the open Atlantic, have become alarmed enough by shifting beaches, lost sand, and undermined cottages, to call for action. They have advocated the construction of a huge seawall to barricade the shore against the power of the North Atlantic, even if it breaks the treasury.

Although we are not in synchronization with the land which so many of us no longer depend on, we are still subject to laws of motion and change which will survive us. I have walked over the salt marsh and through the town many times, and made many minor discoveries along the way, but it is the sea beyond which has always called me. I have often brought feelings of fragility with me, but I can count on its vast indifference to calm me. That which returns no immediate answers to my complaints encourages my aspirations.

Out over the sandy flats at low tide, I can see all history being carried away toward distant lands. I watch the wiggling trails of a periwinkle and think of how long it took for that small creature to get here from Europe. The empty shell of a clam brings all the voices of the sea to my ear. I have found thousands of dead shells lying out on the sands at the end of summer, for no more reason, I suspect, than the sea's almost unlimited capacity for regeneration.

"Diebacks" and overpopulation are measured by the great conditions of survival, which we are too limited to regulate. I have seen tiny, nearly invisible creatures of the plankton, twitching and turning in cosmos of their own, behind lighted glass. The flats are pitted with endless, small holes that indicate subterranean communities that change in content and form all the way around the globe. Although our own, manufactured traffic displaces us every day, it is the calmness, the enormous holding power and containment of the earth ocean that keeps us in check, no matter how far we fly away. We cannot conquer all of space and be citizens of it at the same time.

Millions of people now exclude nature and "nonhuman" life from their daily concerns as if it could be so easily dispensed with, as if old Mother Nature has been finally brought to her knees and is no longer capable of causing us more grief. When the fragment of a meteor from Mars, two billion years old, came to light, showing possible traces of life in its chemistry, those who announced it on TV said that no amount of time and money would be spared to prove it. We would no longer be alone in the universe. It has now been revealed through the Hubbell telescope that our own sun is only one of innumerable suns beyond us, stepping-stones toward the unknown. Many light-years past the Milky Way, suns and planets follow the universal light. We may not be alone or even, contrary to our hopes, unique. Yet we are always surrounded by the reception of light. How many eyes has the sea?

I think, as another winter moves out, of the flowers of late spring that cover our back meadow in Maine sloping down to tidewater. It will be covered by a broad, blazing banner of flowers, each with an "eye" at the center, facing the light. Wide swathes of yellow hawkweed are joined by Indian paintbrush. Here and there are pockets of white chickweed, like star clusters, and bunches of little bluets with an intensity of color that rivals the blue-eyed grass.

The meadow is alive with motion and receptiveness. Small brown, skipper butterflies swirl up together, and the azures, the sky-blue butterflies, fly up and pirouette like ballet dancers. (The azures I see earlier on the Cape, beginning in May, fly low over open ground nectaring on flowers of the *Arbutus*, at almost running speed. In a magical display during courtship they use their sky-reflecting wings as signals to each other.)

I sense electric affinities between the flowers and the ground from which they spring. The whole field flows with light, under cloud shadows and a gentle wind. I stand in the company of delicate powers. Natural history and ecology bring me close, but never close enough. As the season moves so does the field, from flowers to grass, from grass to snow. The flowers create their own space; they all face the light of the almighty sun, which is so close, and at the same time as incredibly distant as any other star. There is no end to this ritual.

Last year, a cold fog moved in out of a cold sea, soon after we arrived, and completely surrounded us. I walked out to the edge of the field, and there was a smell of fish. The night brings in new distinctions, as one tidal world succeeds another. When were we ever alone?

The untiring vitality that surrounds and invades us is surely not distinguished by human occupancy detached from all others. It is now acceptable to make a distinction between the nonhuman and the human, which effectively turns the human race into an extreme minority, and isolates the human spirit. How can we claim to be a higher order of life and dismiss all that sustains us at the same time? My admiration goes out on the tide to all forms of life that do not share my vanity.

The fog's fine screen drifts in during the early morning hours to vanish in blue air. The ceremony of the seasons passes on ahead of our short lives, changing every day. The wind and snow, fire and flood, thunder and dark rain, tell us, step by step, how it was we came to be.

Following World War II, we had dislodged whole populations from custom, place, and home, to the extent that they became almost unrecognizable. I was not sure of what I had come back to. The known world was full of closed subjects, and I began to meet No Entry signs wherever I went. The rights of possession had begun to march in. It was at this time that I read two books by Rachel Carson, *The Sea Around Us* and *The Edge of the Sea*. They had an exhilarating effect on me. How could I have missed out on the sea of life which began at our front door, and had always been waiting for me? Real space, I thought to myself, was not in human power to organize, circumscribe, and narrow down for its exclusive use; it belonged to every organism on the planet. Then the gates started to open for me, and I walked out to join the distance.

Inside the long rocky coastline of Maine are the wild gardens of the sea flourishing within the give and take of the tides that roll in from across the Atlantic. Pemmaquid Point, massive shoulders of bare rock uptilted from their original beds, thrust outward to the open sea. Long, broken off and rounded forms of schist lie out like great columns from some ancient temple. People who have dared to walk out to the edge on the farthest point of the land, have been surprised and swept away by unexpected waves on a rising tide. Gray rock and shining sea seem uncompromising in their austerity. But the rock, along its cracks, pools, and fissures, also protects a great variety of colorful forms of life, nourished by the clear, cold water of the pouring tides, all the way back to the "splash zone" closest to the land.

I perch on the edge of one of the long pools behind the last outer rock wall, careful not to slip and join the surf. Stones and boulders rattle under long strands of green and yellow weed. Coralline algae clings to the rock, with tufts of Irish moss, and other reddish brown seaweed. I can see a small green crab, a northern rock crab, a red starfish, and a green anemone. Great numbers of barnacles are cemented to the rock faces, sending out feathery "feet," small nets to gather in their food, the minute organisms in saltwater. All the long rocky shoreline has a substratum made of their empty shells. When the light of the sun moves over them, all these wonderful, swarming pools share in the benefits of its light, in a graduated procession back to the limits of the land.

Lunging seas drive me from my precarious seat. I have only learned a very few of the organisms in the tide pools. Many are invisible. I have a very long way to go, even with the aid of a *Guide to the Seashore*. Thousands of secret relationships hide in these tidal arms, held in mutual balance by an incomparable artistry that eludes me. I peer in and I seem to see more than recognizable forms. These tidal pools, with often grotesque creatures from a human perspective, may be hiding places for miracles. These extravagant gardens go back to the beginnings of life. They hang on a balance with immensity. I feel that vast holding and containment in my own unexplored and waiting interiors. As the great sea rises again in its rhythmic response to the moon, I am held for a brief period of time by the magic of all I can never own.

Out beyond both rocky and sandy shores are the outriders, the seabirds that have been cruising by for time out of mind. They measure the waters of the globe, while we put them down as slaves of their food supply and victims of their environment. At the same time, we tend to victimize all environments to serve our elusive and temporary ends. In spite of a growing concern about our destructive behavior, and an increasing number of conservationists, we still treat primal life as something to subdue and conquer, as if it occupied another planet. Still the future can never be in our hands if we refuse an equation with the rest of life. We are only self-limiting, and set ourselves apart, as if the human mind needed no associates. But science is unable to prove what happened at the big bang, and the big brain has yet to prove itself.

If you want to know the sea, look for its messengers. October is the month for gannets, migrating down from their nesting sites in Canada. On the tip of the Gaspé Peninsula, these magnificent birds nest along the high cliffs of Bonaventure Island, in great numbers. Wary of their formidable beaks, I once walked close enough to them as they sat on their nests to take their pictures. They were constantly rattling and groaning, and left their nests to hunt for food in the swelling seas below them, gliding off effortlessly with wingspread of six feet.

The northern gannet is a "plunge diver," and may be seen off the Atlantic coast during its fall migration. Gannets fly in wide sweeps over the surface of the sea, hunting for schools of fish. When they spot them, they turn, then drop on folded wings to strike the water like a spear, leaving a visible spray behind them.

After one major storm in October, when the wind battered the shore all night long, it began to abate, and I walked down to the beach in the afternoon. The waves were still plunging and heaving for miles along the sandy shore. At one point they had cut down the dunes and washed tons of sand off the beach, uncovering all the stones and boulders once buried by it.

Two young gannets, with black plumage, forced closer to the land by the storm suddenly swung in close to the beach, hardly a hundred yards offshore, and then turned, to glance and veer away, and race downwind, at great speed. These birds play a profoundly intimate role in the life of the sea, testing their powers against its own. They defeat my lazy mind.

That large sea duck, the common eider, also plays an integral part in the life of the coastal waters. The males, black and white, with a pale green wash on the back of their heads, and the females, a pine brown, migrate south from Maine and Canada, coming by the thousands during the late fall and winter to feed on mussel beds around the Cape and its islands. They are bred and born of the saltwater and the coastal islands. Whenever I see one I smell salt and weed, and feel the constant plunging and pull of the surf through rocky shores. Birds of great, stolid calm and dignity, the eiders reflect the stature of their surroundings.

There is a very large rock, just off Nauset Beach on the exposed outer shore. One day I saw a big flock of eiders on the waters nearby. They were moving slowly on the surface, perhaps waiting for a change in the tide, as the gulls do. They were facing in the direction of the rock, as the currents welled up around it. Suddenly the whole flock changed direction, streaming away from the rock, as if they were on a fulcrum of the swinging tides. Eiders ride the northern seas with an almost regal authority. They are, after all, at home in space.

Among the Pawnee, reverent watchers of the heavens, the stars were never disconnected from the Earth. Their cyclical movements were directly associated with the seasons. Part of their calendric year was divided between what they called the South Star and a small group of twinkling stars known as the Swimming Ducks. The Swimming Ducks appeared in the sky over Nebraska in February as the ice began to melt in the sloughs as the wild ducks swam out into open water. The Pawnee also observed a ceremony for the Evening Star, which appeared with the thunder, in early spring.

Higher math may be light years away from myth and the "primitive" observances of the changing seasons, but astronomy only reaches from where we stand.

As I mentioned before, William Butler Yeats wrote that man invented death. Man also invented the concept of time, using it in increasingly refined and meticulous ways, which led to a separation of powers between man and nature, until it was possible for a technological-industrial age to declare that Nature might only be of limited use, determined by ourselves. This might also have contributed to the idea of empty space, and the motivation to conquer it, which was our custom with unsettled land. Contrast our mathematically controlled universe with how our ancestors saw it. The constellations were rushing through space like great bulls, leaping antelopes, and deer. Eagles soared there, along with swimming ducks, and other symbols of fertility, as well as the crabs of the sea. And high in their midst was the great hunter Sagittarius, with his splendid bow and quiver of arrows that could slip through the reaches of space like silvery fishes. How we shook that enchanted universe off our backs like a dog dashing out of the water.

On a quiet day in February, the temperature was forty degrees. The waves were rippling in lightly out of a calm sea, and the flats were half-covered on an ebbtide. Suddenly, the horizon was broken by a long dark flight of shorebirds. They cruised along parallel to the beach shore, and then, with swift and simultaneous unity they landed to spread out over the sand, scurrying over the surface and pecking into it for food. It was a large flock of up to a thousand individuals, some of them gray and white sanderlings, but the majority were black and reddish brown dunlins. A dog ran out, splashing in shallow water, and they all flew up again, with an audible beating of their wings. They swung in the air like a great basket, as if thrown by a long, invisible arm. They turned with beautiful unanimity and landed again farther down the beach, to spread out, explore the beach for amphipods, or other crustaceans, which had come to the now sun-warmed surface of the sand from deeper down, where they survive in freezing weather.

These sea shorebirds are tough little "globe trotters," and would spend a few weeks more exploring the coastal sands before heading for their breeding territories in the High Arctic, all the way between James Bay, Canada, and Alaska. During the winter the dunlins feed on clams, worms, insect larvae and, amphipods, in intertidal areas down the Atlantic and Pacific coasts, as far as Mexico. Some of the Alaska birds spend the winter along the coasts of East Asia. Their breeding range from outside North

America extends to Iceland, Greenland, and Scandinavia. They are also seen in Great Britain, the region of the Baltic Sea, and in far eastern Russia. There are six known species; and so, they circle the globe.

The American population of these birds dates back to the late Pleistocene. The distance of their migrations, for so small a bird, are astonishing. In flight, their cruising speed has been estimated to be between 72 and 80 kilometers an hour, and in some circumstances, such as an attack by a predatory merlin, this may exceed 150 kilometers an hour.

To watch those shorebirds fly in to a bare, relatively empty beach, whose ribbed sands extended toward an unseen horizon, was like being visited by brilliant strangers from the moon. But in their reaching, they were an extension of myself, of ends I had not yet imagined. In their high awareness they seemed to touch us all in our neglect. I was not alone on the beach. The earth had once again rescued me from exile.

Then a few people joined me who had walked in and were watching the birds. One of them, who had once shingled the roof of our house some twenty-five years before, had come with his family. He was the grandson of D. H. Sears, who ran an ice cream parlor we used to patronize; it had the best ice cream on the Cape. His wife was originally from Newfoundland and had lived on the shores of Witless Bay, overlooking a seabird colony. There was also a woman of Scottish and Dutch descent who had not forgotten her origins, where the sea winds blew along the coasts of Europe.

As they were admiring the birds, I felt as if the beach had now become a place for first landings again. We were all immigrants who had come to a revitalized part of a local shore that extended around the world.

UNIVERSITY PRESS OF NEW ENGLAND publishes books under its own imprint and is the publisher for Brandeis University Press, Dartmouth College, Middlebury College Press, University of New Hampshire, Tufts University, and Wesleyan University Press.

ABOUT THE AUTHOR

John Hay is the author of *The Run, The Great Beach* (winner of the John Burroughs Award), and *The Immortal Wilderness*, among many other books on nature. He is past president of the Cape Cod Museum of Natural History and former professor of environmental studies at Dartmouth College.

ABOUT THE EDITOR

Christopher Merrill's books include *Watch Fire* (poetry), *The Forgotten Language: Contemporary Poets and Nature* (editor), and *The Old Bridge: The Third Balkan War and the Age of the Refugee* (nonfiction). He teaches at the College of the Holy Cross.

LIBRARY OF CONGRESS CATALOGING-IN-PUBLICATION DATA
Hay, John, 1915–
    The way to the salt marsh : a John Hay reader / edited and with an introduction by Christopher Merrill.
    p.   cm.
    ISBN 0–87451–864–4 (pbk : alk. paper)
    1. Natural history—New England.   2. Natural history.   3. Nature conservation.   I. Merrill, Christopher.   II. Title.
QH104.5.N4H38   1998
508.74—DC21   98–3921